"One of the paradoxes of our time is that as our knowledge of and power over the material world grow, the souls of so many people starve for meaning. The art of spiritual direction—the art of guiding and feeding the human hunger for God—has never been more urgently needed. In this book, the authors have written a superb guide to giving spiritual direction, and receiving it as well, worthy of the masters. I highly recommend it."

—ARCHBISHOP CHARLES J. CHAPUT, O.F.M. CAP.
Archbishop of Philadelphia

"The demand for sound spiritual directors far outpaces the supply, leaving so many who could be helped toward sanctity stumbling on the journey. Those who have the capacity to be solid directors through having received good formation in the art of prayer and holy Christian living often hesitate to take on guiding others because all they think they know is what they have received in direction themselves. That's why Fathers Acklin and Hicks have done the whole Church, present and future directors, and the directees they will guide an enormous service in fusing the Church's spiritual wisdom and their extensive experience into a superb, systematic primer. This work will help present directors improve how they exercise this art and give those who are being called and asked to serve as directors the confidence and competence to say fiat to this sacred responsibility."

—FR. ROGER J. LANDRY
National Chaplain, CatholicVoices USA, CatholicPreaching.com

"*Spiritual Direction: A Guide for Sharing the Father's Love* is a trustworthy guide not only for spiritual directors, but for all of us who seek the guidance of the Holy Spirit."

—ARCHABBOT DOUGLAS NOWICKI, OSB
St. Vincent Archabbey, Latrobe, PA

"In the tradition of the Church, FOCUS has long recognized the importance of solid spiritual direction for its missionaries. Fr. Tom and Fr. Boniface draw on that rich tradition to provide an accessible text on the many facets of spiritual direction. Those involved in, or considering, spiritual direction will be sure to mine many gems from this work."

—Curtis Martin
Founder of Fellowship of Catholic University Students (FOCUS)

"Locked away in the depths of our souls is the most intimate part of our being—a place which at times is known to God alone. Yet, if we desire to advance in our quest for God, the role of a gifted spiritual director is essential, and can be pivotal in opening up those depths to allow for greater healing and light. This is a most delicate and sacred art for which directors would do well to seek ongoing formation. St. Teresa of Ávila knew firsthand how much harm could be done by 'misguided guides'! Here is where our Fathers come to the rescue in outlining with great care how to guide souls willing to embark upon that 'itinerarium'— the journey of a soul to God. This book takes the reader on a thorough exploration of this topic, including guidance for both directees and directors on both the spiritual and the psychological plains. We are reminded of the preciousness of each soul and the love, patience, and prayerfulness that are necessary qualities for those entrusted with directing souls in their relationship with God. Their love for souls and lessons learned through experience come through clearly in these pages, along with hope for the marvels that can be wrought in souls by God's grace. May this book bear the fruit of great holiness for priests, religious, and laity who long to deepen in their own prayer life and are called to lead others on that same path."

—Mother Dolores Marie, PCPA
Our Lady of the Angels Monastery Hanceville, AL

"This book beautifully describes the relationship of the spiritual director with the spiritual directee, in light of the director being an instrument of the Father's mercy. Spiritual directors will be encouraged, enlightened, and formed by this book. Using Scripture, the writings and lives of the saints, and years of experience journeying with religious and laity, Father Tom and Father Boniface share a wealth of knowledge, experience, and practical examples to help form their fellow spiritual directors. The relationship between spiritual director and spiritual directee is one of vulnerability and trust. Father Tom and Father Boniface help their fellow spiritual directors to practically form relationships which best help the directee to open up vulnerable communication, not only with the director, but more importantly, with the Lord. Man and woman were made for union with God. The experience of this union was lost with the Fall of Adam and Eve, redeemed in the life, death, and Resurrection of Christ, and made possible again in heaven. The life of fallen man and woman is a journey to open our wounds to the Lord and to find healing. This book forms spiritual directors in how to journey with directees in their interior lives to find healing and union with the Lord."

—JEN SETTLE
Managing Director of the Theology of the Body Institute
and Consecrated Virgin

"Three cheers for this fine book on spiritual direction including much supportive psychology. The authors' numerous insightful examples will be a treasure trove for every spiritual director."

—PAUL C. VITZ, PHD
Professor, Divine Mercy University,
Professor Emeritus, New York University

"Spiritual directors will welcome *Spiritual Direction: A Guide for Sharing the Father's Love* as a long awaited friend that will accompany them in their ministry. Those being trained will find answers to questions they may never have thought to ask and a resource to turn to for years to come. Anyone involved in the ministry of Jesus, reconciling the broken to the heart of the Father, will receive wisdom and a reverence for the work of the Holy Spirit in the human heart. This book is a precious gift to the people of God!"

—Neal Lozano
Founder of Heart of the Father Ministries and author of
Unbound: A Practical Guide to Deliverance

Spiritual Direction

Spiritual Direction

A Guide for Sharing the Father's Love

Fr. Thomas Acklin, OSB &
Fr. Boniface Hicks, OSB

EMMAUS
ROAD
PUBLISHING

Steubenville, Ohio
www.EmmausRoad.org

Emmaus Road Publishing
1468 Parkview Circle
Steubenville, Ohio 43952

Library of Congress Cataloging-in-Publication Data
Names: Hicks, Boniface, author.
Title: Spiritual direction : a guide for sharing the Father's love / Fr.
  Boniface Hicks and Fr. Thomas Acklin.
Description: Steubenville : Emmaus Road Pub., 2017.
Identifiers: LCCN 2017024018 (print) | LCCN 2017030408 (ebook) | ISBN
  9781945125560 (ebook) | ISBN 9781945125683 (hardcover) | ISBN
  9781945125553 (pbk.)
Subjects: LCSH: Spiritual direction--Catholic Church. | Spiritual
  formation--Catholic Church.
Classification: LCC BX2350.7 (ebook) | LCC BX2350.7 .H53 2017 (print) | DDC
  253.5/3--dc23
LC record available at https://lccn.loc.gov/2017024018

Nihil Obstat:
The Reverend Monsignor Larry J. Kulick, JCL, VG
Censor Librorum

Imprimatur:
The Most Reverend Edward C. Malesic, JCL
Bishop of Greensburg
Date: February 23, 2017

The nihil obstat and imprimatur are official declarations that a book or pamphlet is free of doctrinal or moral error. No implication is contained therein that those who have granted the nihil obstat and imprimatur agree with the contents, opinions or statements expressed.

Cover image: *Landscape (Christ on the Road to Emmaus)*, ca. 1650-60, Roelant Roghman, The State Hermitage Museum, Saint Petersburg, Russia

Cover design and Layout by Margaret Ryland

Contents

Dedication

FOR FR. SILVAN ROUSE, CP, who was a faithful, loving spiritual father for countless men and women, including the authors of this book, and whose encouragement was the initial seed that led to this work. May he rest in peace and may all that he worked for come to fruition—especially more widespread contemplation. He labored in the spirit of St. Paul of the Cross so that every Christian may enjoy communion with the Crucified and learn to remain with Him in the sacred silence of faith and holy love, resting on the bosom of the Father.

Foreword

F R. THOMAS ACKLIN, OSB AND FR. BONIFACE HICKS, OSB have written a classic. This work will be seen as one of the best references for spiritual direction.

The lost (or forgotten) art of spiritual direction goes back to the first centuries of Christianity, to the Fathers of the Desert. We could also say this art goes back to Christ Himself. We all know this story: a woman invited herself into the house of Simon the Pharisee, and there, weeping at the feet of Jesus, she kissed and wiped them with her hair. What did she see in Jesus? From all that she heard about Him, and from what she saw, she felt she could finally rest her burdened soul in His presence. A good spiritual director allows us to rest our burdened souls and to find ourselves made new again by God's grace.

Unfortunately, we have lost or forgotten this art, and although spiritual direction has always been treasured by the Church, for some reason we have taken it for granted. Popes have lauded the important role of spiritual direction, but it seems that seminaries and houses of formation just assume that the art is learned "by osmosis," obtained magically with a theology degree, religious consecration, or by ordination. On the contrary, this art must be learned and cultivated. Fr. Tom and Fr. Boniface help to show us how.

The approach to spiritual direction found in these pages is unique and beautiful, especially the chapters on interiority and vulnerability. Reading this book has helped me to slow down a little and see myself once again as a spiritual father (of a diocese). I believe that priests and bishops who invest some time in reading this text will have a similar experience and find that the time spent in these pages renews them in their calling to be spiritual fathers. I also believe that those seeking to grow in their spiritual lives through spiritual direction, as well those committed to assisting them as spiritual directors, will greatly benefit from the wisdom and practical guidance in this work by Fr. Tom and Fr. Boniface.

I hope every seminary, theologate, and house of studies will offer a course in the art of receiving and giving spiritual direction. I also hope that everyone will see in this classic a helpful guide for the careful, sensitive, and traditional wisdom that is essential to the art. May a new springtime dawn for spiritual direction, and may the Church rediscover her ability, like Christ Himself, to "heal wounds and to warm the hearts of the faithful."[1]

BISHOP GREGORY MANSOUR
Maronite Bishop of the Eparchy of St. Maron (Brooklyn)

---

[1] Pope Francis, interview by Fr. Antonio Spadaro, SJ, "A Big Heart Open to God: An Interview with Pope Francis," *America,* September 30, 2013, http://www.america-magazine.org/faith/2013/09/30/big-heart-open-god-interview-Pope-Francis.

Acknowledgments

W E WOULD LIKE to acknowledge Archabbot Douglas and the monastic community of St. Vincent Archabbey, through whom our vocations as monks, priests, and spiritual directors have been fostered. We would also like to thank the St. Vincent Seminary faculty, staff, and students whose love and support have encouraged and sustained our ministry throughout the years. We are grateful to all those who took time to read drafts of this book and offer feedback, especially the Franciscan TOR Sisters; Neal Lozano; Christopher Lafitte; Paul Vitz; and the St. Vincent seminarians, especially Mike Faix. We extend a special thanks to Fr. Roger Landry for his helpful suggestions. We thank all of our own mentors and directees who have provided the human context in which we could listen together to the Holy Spirit and learn the paths of spiritual direction. We are also grateful to Scott Hahn and the editing staff at Emmaus Road for their willingness to share this work and for the layout, design, and excellent professional assistance in bringing this labor of love to publication!

Introduction:
A New Springtime for
Spiritual Direction

T HE CONDITION OF the human person, marriage and family, healthcare, and other major institutions has left many individuals badly wounded in the modern world. As a result, the need for spiritual direction—or the accompaniment of a spiritual guide—is becoming more prominent in our world where so many are suffering from so many wounds.

In an interview with Fr. Antonio Spadaro, Pope Francis described the responsibility of the Church to address this crisis:

> I see clearly that the thing the Church needs most today is the ability to heal wounds and to warm the hearts of the faithful; it needs nearness, proximity. I see the Church as a field hospital after battle. It is useless to ask a seriously injured person if he has high cholesterol and about the level of his blood sugars! You have to heal his wounds. Then we can talk about everything else. Heal the wounds, heal the wounds. . . . And you have to start from the ground up.[1]

---

[1] Pope Francis, "A Big Heart Open to God."

In the twentieth century, the psychological sciences developed an independent approach to handling these wounds. The approach of psychology, at first, became adversarial and at odds with the Church. Later there was an uncritical embrace of all things in the human sciences. Finally, after a century of study and development, the Church has developed a harmonious integration, steering away from a psychologism that would replace God, but also steering away from a solely spiritual approach that would neglect the insights into human nature discovered by the psychological sciences.

With this integrated approach in mind, we can also learn much from the advice of Pope Francis, who explains that "the ministers of the Gospel must be people who can warm the hearts of the people, who walk through the dark night with them, who know how to dialogue and to descend themselves into their people's night, into the darkness, but without getting lost."[2] That is precisely the kind of accompaniment one should experience with a spiritual director.

In addition to those who suffer from deep spiritual wounds, many people can benefit from the spiritual formation that is consolidated in spiritual direction, namely those who hear the call to care for others through priestly or lay ministry. Training for this ecclesial ministry already has intellectual and pastoral elements that require reading, study, and the guidance of experienced teachers. At the same time, intellectual knowledge is insufficient to truly form ministers of the Gospel of Jesus Christ. Knowledge needs to be integrated with each person's own history and relationship with God such that it truly forms his soul. This happens best in spiritual direction. The United States Conference of Catholic Bishops declared this in the Program for Priestly Formation under the heading of *spiritual formation*: "Since spiritual formation is the core that unifies the life of a priest, it stands at the heart of seminary life and is the center around which all other

---

[2] Ibid.

aspects are integrated."[3] In the vision presented by the Program for Priestly Formation, spiritual direction provides the dynamic force that brings together the personal spiritual formation of each seminarian. "The spiritual director should foster an integration of spiritual formation, human formation, and character development consistent with priestly formation."[4] This means that the spiritual director is the integrating factor! The same logic applies to religious and lay spiritual formation. Indeed, the Church has called spiritual direction an "efficacious means of formation so well tried and proven in the Church."[5]

Furthermore, Pope Benedict XVI strongly recommended spiritual direction for *everyone*:

> As she has always done, today the Church continues to recommend the practice of spiritual direction not only to those who desire to follow the Lord closely but to every Christian who wishes to live responsibly his or her Baptism, that is, new life in Christ.
>
> Everyone, in fact, especially those who have heeded the divine call to follow Christ closely, needs to be accompanied personally by a guide reliable in doctrine and expert in the things of God, this guide can help people to watch out for facile forms of subjectivism, making available their own knowledge and experience lived in the following of Jesus.[6]

---

[3] United States Conference of Catholic Bishops, *Program for Priestly Formation*, 5th ed. (Washington, DC: United States Conference of Catholic Bishops, 2005), http://www.usccb.org/upload/program-priestly-formation-fifth-edition.pdf, no. 115.

[4] Ibid., no. 129.

[5] Congregation for the Clergy, *Directory on the Ministry and Life of Priests: New Edition* (Vatican City: Libreria Editrice Vaticana, 2013), no. 73.

[6] Pope Benedict XVI, Address to the Community of the Pontifical Theological Faculty "Teresianum" of Rome, May 19, 2011, https://w2.vatican.va/content/benedict-xvi/en/speeches/2011/may/documents/hf_ben-xvi_spe_20110519_teresianum.html.

Spiritual Direction: A Guide for Sharing the Father's Love

In sum, this means that there are a great number of people, both the wounded in need of healing and those generous souls who are seeking to serve the Church, who would benefit greatly from spiritual direction. The sad reality, however, is that there are far too few men and women prepared to offer spiritual direction. We believe that the time is ripe for many men and women to embrace the ministry of spiritual direction to accompany the wounded, to assist the faithful in hearing the voice of God, and to model the love and mercy of God for the many who are seeking Him but do not know Him or have false images of Him.

Pope St. John XXIII recognized how a spiritual director can create a sea change in the Church through the formation of saints. "How many times a surprising renaissance of Christian life in a diocese will find its real explanation in the silent work of a holy spiritual director, who has known how to train generations of holy priests through his teachings and his example."[7] Dom Jean-Baptiste Chautard, in his classic work *The Soul of the Apostolate,* recognized that spiritual direction can be time consuming, but it is an incredibly fruitful investment of time for pastors. "Have you ever noticed what a great importance the writers of the lives of saints give to the spiritual directors of those whose biographies they compose?" He continued, "Do you not think that the Church would have many more saints if generous souls, especially priests and religious, received more serious direction?"[8] Likewise, Pope St. John Paul II called for a renewal of spiritual direction in his teaching on the formation of priests: "It is necessary to rediscover the great tradition of personal spiritual guidance which has always brought great and precious fruits to the Church's life."[9] In harmony with these

---

[7] Pope John XXIII, Address to Seminary Spiritual Directors, September 9, 1962, in *The Encyclicals and Other Messages of John XXIII,* ed. Francis X. Murphy and Ferrer Smith (Washington, DC: TPS Press, 1964), 129–135.

[8] Jean-Baptiste Chautard, *The Soul of the Apostolate* (Trappist, KY: Abbey of Gethsemani Press, 1943), 172.

[9] Pope St. John Paul II, Post-Synodal Apostolic Exhortation on the Formation of Priests in the Circumstances of the Present Day *Pastores Dabo Vobis* (March 25, 1992), no. 40, http://w2.vatican.va/content/john-paul-ii/en/apost_exhortations/documents/hf_jp-ii_exh_25031992_pastores-dabo-vobis.html.

sentiments, the Congregation for the Clergy issued a document with some instruction for confessors and spiritual directors saying, "In present circumstances, while there is an increasing demand for spiritual direction on the part of the faithful, there is, likewise, an increasing need to better prepare priests to give spiritual direction. Such training would enable them to afford spiritual counsel with greater diligence, discernment and spiritual accompaniment. Where the practice of spiritual direction is available it issues in personal and community renewal, vocations, missionary spirit, and the joy of hope."[10]

Pope Benedict XVI likewise recognized the need for spiritual directors and appropriate training for those who undertake the ministry of spiritual direction.

> "Spiritual direction" also contributes to forming consciences. Today there is a greater need than in the past for wise and holy "spiritual teachers": an important ecclesial service. This of course requires an inner vitality which must be implored as a gift from the Holy Spirit in intense and prolonged prayer and with a special training that must be acquired with care. . . . To be able to carry out this indispensable ministry, every priest must tend to his own spiritual life and take care to keep himself pastorally and theologically up to date.[11]

Pope Francis expressed similar thoughts both regarding the need for spiritual directors and in terms of the formation of spiritual directors. Specifically, he taught that men or women who

---

[10] Congregation for the Clergy, *The Priest, Minister of Divine Mercy: An Aid for Confessors and Spiritual Directors* (Vatican City: Libreria Editrice Vaticana, 2011), no. 66, http://www.clerus.org/clerus/dati/2011-08/08-13/sussidio_per_confessori_en.pdf.

[11] Pope Benedict XVI, Message to Cardinal James Pope Francis Stafford, Major Penitentiary, and the Participants at the XX Edition of the Course for the Internal Forum Organised by the Apostolic Penitentiary (March 12, 2009), https://w2.vatican.va/content/benedict-xvi/en/messages/pont-messages/2009/documents/hf_ben-xvi_mes_20090312_penitenzieria.html.

carry out spiritual direction must be wise, experienced in prayer, formed according to the wisdom of the tradition of spiritual direction, and also supported by insights from psychology.[12]

For Whom Is This Book Intended?

This book is primarily intended to support individuals who are being drawn into the ministry of spiritual direction. This includes priests who see the need to offer more spiritual direction as part of their priestly ministry. It also includes consecrated religious and lay faithful who find that people are coming to them for guidance. From ancient times, spiritual direction has been a ministry that is initiated by others. In other words, men and women did not set out to become spiritual directors, but others started seeking them out and they saw that as the manifestation of a call in their lives. We envision this book as a support and guide for one who finds himself in this situation.

This book can serve those who are not yet being sought out by would-be directees but could be in the future. For example, various people in the helping professions (nurses, hospital chaplains, hospice volunteers, teachers, coaches, etc.) are in a position to listen to and support individuals whom they are serving and with whom they develop one-on-one relationships. For a spiritually-minded person, this listening and support can start to take on the shape of spiritual direction. The same rationale applies to parents as to those in the helping professions. This book offers some principles and insights that can assist many people in more effectively accompanying others, especially in their spiritual lives.

This book can also be helpful for individuals who are striving to grow in their own spiritual lives. In it we consider how various aspects of the spiritual life emerge from and are fostered by a one-

---

[12] Pope Francis, Address to Consecrated Men and Women of the Diocese of Rome (May 16, 2015), https://w2.vatican.va/content/francesco/en/speeches/2015/may/documents/papa-francesco_20150516_religiosi-roma.html.

on-one relationship with a spiritual director. By reading about and reflecting on these aspects of the spiritual life, we believe it will help the recipients of spiritual direction and anyone who is seeking to grow closer to the Lord to better understand spiritual development and growth in the Holy Spirit.

Priests

The Catholic Church has strongly encouraged priests to be prepared to offer a ministry of spiritual direction. In the *Directory on the Ministry and Life of Priests*, she stated:

> Along with the sacrament of Reconciliation the priest will not fail to exercise the ministry of spiritual direction. The rediscovery and extension of this practice, also at times outside the administration of Penance, is of great benefit for the Church in these times. The generous and active attitude of priests in practicing it also constitutes an important occasion for identifying and sustaining vocations to the priesthood and to the various forms of consecrated life.[13]

The Church reiterated this call for priests to carry out the ministry of spiritual direction as a high priority in pastoral ministry in a document issued by the Congregation of the Clergy in 2011 on Confession and Spiritual Direction:

> It can be said that attention to the spiritual life of the faithful, guiding them on the way of contemplation and perfection, and assisting them in their vocational discernment, is a real pastoral priority: "From this point of view, the pastoral work of promoting vocations to the priesthood will also be able to find expression in a firm and encouraging invitation to spiritual direction.... Priests, for

---

[13] Congregation for the Clergy, *Directory on the Ministry and Life of Priests*, no. 73.

their part, should be the first to devote time and energies to this work of education and personal spiritual guidance: They will never regret having neglected or put in second place so many other things which are themselves good and useful, if this proved necessary for them to be faithful to their ministry as cooperators of the Spirit in enlightening and guiding those who have been called."[14]

Every priest involved in pastoral ministry carries out some form of spiritual direction on a regular basis in the confessional or in the regular pastoral care of the faithful. Some priests, however, may discern a call to a more extensive ministry of spiritual direction. Pope Benedict XVI encouraged all priests to be open to this call as he taught about St. Joseph Cafasso during the Year of the Priest:

May St. Joseph Cafasso's example serve as a reminder to all to hasten towards the perfection of Christian life, towards holiness. In particular, may this Saint remind priests of the importance of devoting time to the sacrament of Reconciliation and to spiritual direction, and to all the concern we should have for the most deprived.[15]

Women Religious and Lay Spiritual Directors

While spiritual direction is a natural part of priestly ministry, not only priests are called to give spiritual direction. In fact, historically, spiritual direction was a spontaneous movement among the Desert Fathers and Mothers (who were not ordained clergy) as individuals came to them seeking spiritual wisdom. "Spiritual direction is not an exclusive charism of the presbytery: it's a

---

[14] Congregation for the Clergy, *The Priest, Minister of Divine Mercy*, no. 71.
[15] Pope Benedict XVI, Audience of June 30, 2010, https://w2.vatican.va/content/benedict-xvi/en/audiences/2010/documents/hf_ben-xvi_aud_20100630.html.

charism of the laity! In early monasticism lay people were the great directors."[16]

Furthermore, not only men, but also women can serve as spiritual directors. Pope Francis expressed this as a significant, concrete expression of feminine participation in Church ministry:

> Give consecrated women this function [of spiritual direc-
> tion] that many believe is only for priests; and also give
> concreteness to the fact that a consecrated woman is
> both the face of Mother Church and of Mother Mary,
> and that is going forth in maternity, and maternity is not
> only having children! Maternity is accompanying growth;
> maternity is spending hours next to a sick person, a sick
> child, a sick brother; it is spending one's life in love, with
> that love of tenderness and maternity. On this path we will
> find even more the woman's role in the Church.[17]

In this book, for simplicity, when referring to individuals in general we speak of men, but with the understanding that these words are traditionally inclusive in the English language. We do not consider spiritual direction to be an exclusively male form of ministry, but recognize the important role that women can also play as spiritual directors.

The Approach of This Book

A number of books have been written about spiritual direction and each makes its own unique contribution. Because spiritual direction is an art rather than a science, there will never be a definitive, final word spoken about it. To the contrary, spiritual direction invites as many nuanced approaches as there are unique relationships. The approach to spiritual direction discussed in these pages

---

[16] Pope Francis, Address to Consecrated Men and Women of the Diocese of Rome.
[17] Ibid.

is guided by many years of prayer, study, and experience. Drawing from the Roman Catholic tradition, we present an approach that is found in Scripture and the writings and lives of the saints, which we can also validate through our own lived experience.

A unique aspect of this book is the inclusion of some reflection on the experience of spiritual direction. As a genuine relationship, spiritual direction affects not only the directee, but also the director. At various points, we reflect on the inner experience of the director along with the ways that the director can discern and guide the inner experience of the directee. We hope that the concrete examples, drawn from our experience, also help to reinforce the framework that is presented in these pages.

Basic Structure of a Spiritual Direction Meeting and Structure of This Book

The first part of this book follows the basic structure of a spiritual direction meeting. A one-on-one meeting for spiritual direction will generally consist of a brief beginning, a very substantial middle, and a brief end. Because spiritual direction is a human encounter in God's presence, not a liturgical ritual, it is not bound to a particular structure, but in general it includes those three movements.

The beginning of a meeting reflects the human, one-on-one quality of the encounter that is a definitive characteristic of spiritual direction. Of course, the one-on-one dynamic persists beyond the beginning and continues throughout the entire meeting. We discuss the unique dynamics of a one-on-one encounter in Chapter 1.

The middle portion of the spiritual direction meeting should be led by the directee. The director primarily listens, but also asks some questions or provides short responses for the sake of clarification and encouraging the directee. The goal of this middle portion is to help the directee go deeper into his interior life, open up areas of vulnerability, and see how God is working in his life. To understand how best to navigate this portion of the spiritual direction meeting, we will spend several chapters looking at the structure of the interior life (Chapter 2), the dynamics of vulnerability (Chapter 3), and the most effective approach to listening that will facilitate the directee's vulnerable sharing of his interior life (Chapter 4).

The last portion of a spiritual direction meeting generally focuses on shining a light on God's work in the directee's life, based on all that has been shared. After patient, prayerful, empathetic, and attentive listening, the spiritual director has access to the vulnerable interior of the directee. This access gives the spiritual director the opportunity to communicate God's merciful love to the directee in a deep and powerful way. The director represents God for the directee in a quasi-sacramental way and, building on the dynamics of human trust and vulnerability, has the opportunity to make God's presence and mercy explicit and felt for the directee. This indicates the power that the spiritual director can have, and should make clear how much responsibility and care must accompany that power in the spiritual direction relationship. This final portion of a spiritual direction meeting, communicating mercy, will be the focus of Chapter 5.

In the second part of this book we explore some other important considerations that arise in the practice of spiritual direction. The principal focus of spiritual direction is on the directee's relationship with God. Because of this, all spiritual direction must lead to the practice of prayer (Chapter 6). While the spiritual life for every person is unique, the general patterns and thresholds of prayer are discussed in Chapter 7. Psychological insights are presented throughout our approach as a necessary help for understanding the human person as he shares himself in spiritual direction. While it is important to recognize that a spiritual director is not a psychologist, some further insights into our psychological makeup can assist the spiritual director in understanding the directee and in helping him to invite God's healing into his mind and heart (Chapter 8). In the last chapter, we consider the spiritual director himself, examining what qualities are important for a spiritual director to have and what struggles or experiences he may confront through the course of spiritual direction. The spiritual director's proper preparation and ongoing spiritual and emotional health are the focus of Chapter 9. A spiritual director can find further inspiration and spiritual support in the lives of the saints and so we present some saints for spiritual directors in the Appendix.

By exploring the dynamics and dimensions of spiritual direction throughout the remainder of this book, we hope we can provide guidance for both director and directee in order to make their relationship more fruitful. At the same time, although spiritual direction is the primary and explicit focus of this book, we will also share much about the subtleties of a personal relationship with God and the dynamics of prayer. Because every one-on-one relationship can and should incorporate elements of one's relationship with God, we expect that the content of this book will also be helpful in the development of other one-on-one relationships. In particular, the insights should prove helpful for deepening relationships between close, intimate friends, between parents and children, between pastors and parishioners, and many others.

The Great Grace of a Spiritual Director

Our hope is that this work inspires more men and women to respond to the call to become spiritual directors and forms those who have taken up this ministry. In so doing, we dream with Pope St. John XXIII about the new generation of saints who might be formed under the guidance of spiritual direction, and who will be capable of bringing about a renaissance in a world that is suffering and growing old.

St. Faustina is an example of one saint who brought about a renaissance of mercy with the faithful help of her spiritual director. She lamented not having always had a spiritual director: "Oh, if only I had had a spiritual director from the beginning, then I would not have wasted so many of God's graces."[18] St. Faustina identified some of the benefits of having a spiritual director: "Oh, how great a grace it is to have a spiritual director! One makes more rapid progress in virtue, sees the will of God more clearly, fulfills it more faithfully, and follows a road that is sure and free of dangers. The director knows how to avoid the rocks against which the soul could be shattered. The Lord gave me this grace rather late, to be sure, but I rejoice in it greatly, seeing how God inclines His will to my director's wishes."[19] She also pled for more spiritual directors like her own: "O my Jesus, if only there were more spiritual directors of this kind, souls under such guidance would very quickly reach the summits of sanctity and would not waste such great graces! I give unceasing thanks to God for so great a grace; namely, that in His great goodness He has deigned to place these pillars of light along the path of my spiritual life. They light my way so that I do not go astray or become delayed in my journey toward close union with the Lord."[20]

May this work, and the ministry undertaken by all who read it, usher in a new springtime for spiritual direction and ensure that God's graces are not wasted.

---

[18] Maria Faustina Kowalska, *Diary: Divine Mercy in My Soul*, 3rd rev. ed. (Stockbridge, MA: Marian Press, 2000), no. 35.

[19] Ibid., no. 331.

[20] Ibid., no. 749.

PART 1

THE FUNDAMENTALS OF SPIRITUAL DIRECTION

1

One-On-One

I HAVE NEVER told this to anyone before." A spiritual director
will often hear this breathtaking admission from his spiritual
directees. Later on in their journey together, a spiritual director
cherishes those moments when his spiritual son or daughter states
reflectively, "Spiritual direction has changed my life." The one-
on-one dynamic of spiritual direction, with its focus on Christ,
facilitates self-discovery, an integration of faith, healing, and personal transformation. It is a powerful setting in which individuals
deepen their relationship with Christ and experience His healing
and merciful love.

"Now there are varieties of gifts, but the same Spirit" (1 Cor
12:4).[1] Spiritual direction is a participation in the work of the
Holy Spirit that allows directees to receive the gifts of the Holy
Spirit in a personal way. We know many truths about God in
a general way, for example, that God loves everyone, that God
forgives every sin, that God has infinite mercy, and that God has
died for us on the Cross to bring new and eternal life in the
Resurrection. Those truths are critically important and make up
the objective content of our Christian faith. The challenge is that
each person needs to know that those truths apply personally to
him. In fact, those truths are about a Person—three Persons, actu-

---

[1] All biblical references are from the Revised Standard Version, Second Catholic
Edition, unless otherwise noted.

ally—and those Persons want to have a personal relationship with each human being. The Holy Spirit personally reminds us of all that Jesus taught us (see Jn 14:26). He personalizes these universal truths so that each one of us can receive them, tailor-made, in our own particular circumstances on any particular day. The spiritual director, in concert with the Holy Spirit, plays a profound, quasi-sacramental role in personalizing these truths for a particular directee in particular circumstances.

The examples we will use in this book are based on real experiences but with details sufficiently changed to anonymize them. Here is an example showing some broad dynamics of grace at work in spiritual direction: There was a man who had left the practice of the faith and found himself back living with his parents when his career aspirations fell apart. He started struggling with depression and even with faith in God, questioning, "Is there a God? Is there a Church?" He was encouraged to seek out spiritual direction.

The spiritual director asked him if he prayed, and when he said, "Very little," the spiritual director asked him, "How do you think about God?" It became clear that his relationship with God was impersonal. He said prayers, but made no personal connection with any Member of the Trinity. In trying to talk about it, he realized that he did not know how to see God as a person. The spiritual director asked why it might be hard for him to think of God as a person or speak to Him as a person. He shared how he saw God as an issuer of demands and he did not want to interact with this demanding God as a person. After spending some time listening, clarifying, and reflecting back what the directee shared, during which he gave the directee a chance to put words to his experience, the spiritual director felt he had sufficient understanding to offer some insight.

The spiritual director proceeded to explain things that the man had surely heard before, but that he really heard now for the first time: namely how God is a Trinity, a relationship of three Persons in one God, and that it is particularly in Jesus that we see the Face of God. Jesus is the Face of God and the face of Jesus is mercy. Jesus shows us that God is personal and His nature is one of infinite, self-giving love.

The man was astounded, because he had never thought of, or tried to relate to, God as love. Neither had he tried to relate to the Father or Jesus as real Persons. He had never understood God in that way. He always saw God as demanding. In the context of spiritual direction, the man had the opportunity to explore his own beliefs, put them in order, and share them. Furthermore, he had the experience of being listened to and understood, which opened up his heart to trust and gave him a capacity to receive truth. The spiritual director modeled God's personal love for the directee. In that context, the truth given by the spiritual director found a home in his mind and heart and was able to shed a new light on his understanding. Both director and directee were impressed with how the Holy Spirit was at work in their encounter. Everything fell into place. And so the journey *began.* This new light gave the man a new energy and hopefulness that helped his depression and despair to lift. He found he had a new enthusiasm for his journey with God and he began to talk more about his developing relationship with God and with others.

The spiritual director is not a guru who pulls magic phrases out of a hat, but simply a mediator and intercessor whose loving attention helps God to be more tangibly present. God has the power to work without mediation, but He has made it clear that He wants to work through us. Even when God intervened directly with St. Paul, for example, he then sent him to Ananias for a mediated assistance (Acts 9:10–19), and then to the Apostles (Gal 1:18; 2:1–10). In our example, this man could not take in some truths of faith on his own, but he was able to take them in through the mediation of a spiritual director. He was able, within a personal relationship with the spiritual director, to recognize that he could have a real relationship to God, and this helped deepen his relationships with others as well. Sometimes we simply cannot put it all together, and it takes another person who can listen to our story and also listen to the Holy Spirit to spot the gaps and help to connect the dots for us. God is delighted when His children are able to assist each other in coming to know Him and love Him and He assists us in this through the power of the Holy Spirit.

Original Solitude

> The Lord God formed the man out of the dust of the ground and blew into his nostrils the breath of life, and the man became a living being. The Lord God planted a garden in Eden, in the east, and placed there the man whom he had formed. . . . The Lord God then took the man and settled him in the garden of Eden, to cultivate and care for it. The Lord God gave the man this order: You are free to eat from any of the trees of the garden except the tree of knowledge of good and evil. From that tree you shall not eat; when you eat from it you shall die. (Gen 2:7–8, 15–17)[2]

This passage in the Book of Genesis highlights several things that are important for us. We see how, from the beginning, God relates with and takes care of man personally, one-on-one. He prepares a paradise for him and gives him a mission and the wondrous opportunity to unite his will to the divine will by carrying out a commandment. This union of wills is the classic definition of friendship (*idem velle, idem nolle*).[3] The one-on-one relationship between God and man takes place in creation, engaging man's body, with his senses and his whole being. This one-on-one relationship leads him to an awareness of himself: a self-consciousness, a deeper understanding of himself.

Pope St. John Paul II described this as man's "original solitude" saying, "When we analyze the text of Genesis, we are in some way witnesses of how man, with the first act of self-consciousness, 'distinguishes himself' before God-Yahweh from the whole world

---

[2] New American Bible, Revised Edition (hereafter: NABRE).

[3] "Wanting the same things, rejecting the same things."

of living beings (*animalia*), how he consequently reveals himself to himself and at the same time affirms himself in the visible world as a 'person.'"[4] Man's interaction with God is different from his interaction with the whole world of animals. He can talk to God and listen to Him. He can walk with God and receive a command from Him. He has the possibility of self-determination in his relationship with God. His one-on-one interaction with God helps him to know himself. Later we see how his one-on-one interaction with woman helps him to know himself as well, but personal relationship with God is primary to who man is and is more fundamental to his humanity than any human relationship. Indeed, the relationship of man with God is what makes any other relationship possible.

The Fundamental Relationship

The Book of Genesis reveals that man's fundamental relationship is with God. Before he is in a relationship with other human beings, and even with creation, man is in a relationship with God. This is the ground of all his other relationships. In this relationship, God cares for man. He forms him with His own hands, makes him in His own image and likeness and, in an extremely intimate gesture, breathes into his nostrils the spirit of life. We see the marks of intimacy in this description of creation. God takes personal care in forming each man, beginning with the first man.

God created a garden, a paradise, where man had "original happiness" (in the words of St. John Paul II). The subsequent verbs likewise carry the tenderness of that one-on-one interaction: God "placed" man in the garden and "settled" him there. He took care of all that man would need, giving him food and work and the opportunity for self-determination by giving him a command.

---

[4] Pope St. John Paul II, Audience of October 10, 1979, no. 6 in *Man and Woman He Created Them: A Theology of the Body*, ed. Michael Waldstein (Boston, MA: Pauline Books & Media, 2006), 160.

This foundational relationship described by the Book of Genesis is fundamental for everyone. More intense than our human development in our mother's womb and our connection with that woman who bore us is our one-on-one relationship with God who personally "knit [us] together in [our] mother's womb" in the first moment of our existence (Ps 139:13). In fact, we can also add that He conceived us in His mind, even before He formed us in the womb, for He knows and loves each one of us eternally.

Every individual is in relationship with God in the deepest part of his being, and when any human being stops and looks inside himself he can come to recognize that he has always been in relationship with God. Man has been discovering God in silence since the beginning of time. Unaided by Judeo-Christian revelation, there are many impersonal ways that have been used to describe man's relationship with God. For example, God has been described as a life force moving through creation in Taoism or as the summation of all being with which one can unite one's consciousness through the absorption of nirvana in Buddhism. This is not what God reveals to us in Christ, however. The Christian revelation presents something far more bold, personal, and intimate.

The Word Became Flesh and Dwelt Among Us

In the Incarnation, in Jesus Christ, our one-on-one relationship with God takes on a radical shift. The personal connection, previously only dimly perceived, now takes on a face and a name and a voice. God becomes radically present, visible, and tangible, and He is even moved from within by His own human heart. Our one-on-one encounter with Him takes the form of a face-to-face encounter and even a heart-to-heart encounter. This encounter changes everything and it defines what it means to be Christian. "Being Christian is not the result of an ethical choice or a lofty idea," Pope Benedict XVI wrote, "but the encounter with an event, a person, which gives life a new horizon and a decisive direction."[5] Part of the "new horizon" Pope Benedict involves the transformation of all of our relationships. our one-on-one relationship with God is at the core of o... being, when that relationship develops, every other relationship develops as well. When the foundational relationship is redeemed, it becomes a wellspring of redemption that can and should flow to every other area of our lives as well.

Conversely, all our relationships can touch on and color our relationship with God. Jim, a veteran of recent Middle Eastern wars, saw many terrible things that traumatized him. He had seen fellow soldiers blown up in front of him and he had interpreted that as God's unfaithfulness. He had a hard time believing that God ever keeps His promises. One would naturally suspect that Jim's inability to trust in God was due to these traumatic war experiences. But after talking about these at great length, the spiritual director suspected that this distrust was rooted in something deeper and asked Jim to share a bit about his personal history.

In response, Jim shared about his relationship with his mother. He shared that his father had left when Jim was very young and as a result Jim's mother had never trusted her son. This made it hard for Jim to trust himself. Furthermore, Jim's mother herself never kept her promises or followed through and Jim could not trust her. It seemed obvious to the spiritual director that Jim's war trauma was significant, but that it had even more power because it was compounded by the deeper insecurity that came from Jim's relationship with his mother. When Jim realized that his distrust in God and distrust in himself—his skepticism that anyone would ever keep their promises—was rooted in his relationship with his mother, it opened up the flood gates. It helped him free up his view of God from his view of his mother and opened his heart to a lot of healing. He went on to get married and have children. He grew closer to God through the Scriptures, and though he had

---

[5] Pope Benedict XVI, Encyclical Letter on Christian Love *Deus Caritas est* (December 25, 2005), no. 1, http://w2.vatican.va/content/benedict-xvi/en/encyclicals/documents/hf_ben-xvi_enc_20051225_deus-caritas-est.html.

many ongoing questions, he now was able to trust the answers. He was able to trust himself and others enough to take some significant and necessary risks to develop a different career, support his family, and move on in life.

In Jesus Christ, God takes on our fallen humanity—all our sin, our wounds, and our brokenness—and by bringing it to the Father through the Cross, He redeems it. Our humanity is redeemed by becoming part of the one-on-one embrace of the Father and the Son. This opens up new possibilities of intimacy in all our relationships. Redemption of our human relationships becomes possible in the redeeming love of the Father. Forgiveness can pour forth from our hearts when we experience the forgiveness of the Father. Deep relational wounds can be healed through the deeper relationship we have with God, who is Himself a perfect, interpersonal Relationship of Love: Father, Son, and Holy Spirit.

Jesus not only took on our fallen nature and carried it all the way to death on a cross in a perfect attitude of trusting surrender to the Father, He also carried it beyond the abyss of death into an eternal, heavenly embrace of love in the Resurrection. Furthermore, in the Resurrection, when Jesus remains with us in His glorified body, He keeps all the most intimate parts of our humanity. He is flesh, not a ghost, with wounds in His hands and His heart that are wide open for us. He is invincible, but He does not become invulnerable. He keeps His pierced human heart and His pierced human hands and feet.

The intimacy that is possible with God because of the Incarnation, in an encounter with Him in His glorified body, becomes most powerfully manifest in the sacraments, particularly in the Blessed Sacrament, the Eucharist. In the deepest human intimacy, like that experienced by a married couple, the union of bodies that brings forth new life and the deeper union of the couple still is only a fraction of what is possible with God. God brings about the total union of bodies by becoming food that we can consume completely. God gives Himself completely to us, fruitfully, faithfully, definitively, and uniquely in a way that every other human love strives for but never fully achieves. God, in the Incarnation and in its fruit given fully in the Easter mysteries, is made fully available and vulnerable to us in the Eucharist. This is the consummation of every longing for love that we have. In the sacraments we have the union of heaven and earth communicated to us one-on-one.

Even our death is transformed by this one-on-one relationship with God in Christ. Through the death and resurrection of Christ, our death no longer becomes an interruption or termination of our one-on-one relationship, but our relationship with Christ continues even through the passage of death. Jesus is the only one who can make this journey with us and by His entering into death, He has removed the isolation that is inherent to our dying. He is the only one who can accompany us throughout every moment of life and can even accompany us in the moment of death.[6] Furthermore, He has made death an even greater intensification of our one-on-one relationship with Him, for in death we shall see Him as He is. This blessed vision will transform us and consummate our capacity for a one-on-one relationship with Him: "we shall be like him, for we shall see him as he is" (1 Jn 3:2). Furthermore, every other relationship will be affected by this one-on-one beatific vision. By becoming like Him, it will increase our capacity for union and the prayer of Jesus will be fulfilled, "that they may all be one" (Jn 17:21).

The Dynamic of One-On-One Relationships

From the Book of Genesis to the Gospel of John to the Book of Revelation, we read how God enters into one-on-one relationships. Namely, He gives Himself. When God created the heavens and the earth, the seas and all that is in them, He gave of Himself. We discover the patterns, the fingerprints of God, throughout

---

[6] See Pope Benedict XVI, Encyclical Letter on Christian Hope *Spe salvi* (November 30, 2007), no. 6, http://w2.vatican.va/content/benedict-xvi/en/encyclicals/documents/hf_ben-xvi_enc_20071130_spe-salvi.html.

all of creation.[7] When God gave Eve to Adam, He gave Adam a human being made in His own image and likeness. Namely, He gave of Himself. In fact, He even fashioned the creation of Eve such that Adam had to give of *himself*: he gave a rib, which, as St. John Paul II explained, symbolized his very life.[8] God gave Himself in the immortality of the Tree of Life, in the command to work, and in the opportunity for free, self-determination in the command never to eat from one of the trees. Even after man fell, through disobedience, God responded to the original sin by coming, Himself, to the garden to draw man out from his hiding place. As salvation history unfolded, God gave Himself by speaking to Abram and to Moses and by forming covenants with them. He gave Himself in His abiding presence with the Israelites in the wilderness and by speaking through the prophets. In His presence in the temple and even in the authority entrusted to His judges and kings, the dynamic of God's relationships with man is always self-gift.

God demonstrated this dynamic most boldly and profoundly in His self-gift in the Incarnation of the Son, conceived by the Holy Spirit and born of the Virgin Mary. Even as man, His only way of interacting was through self-gift, even unto death on a cross. Now in His glorified body, He continues to give Himself, as our food, in the Holy Eucharist. Nothing could be farther from the truth than the idea of God as a watchmaker who does not get involved with or stay involved with His creation. God is always intimately involved, constantly making a radical self-gift in all of creation and in every personal relationship with every human being. Our response to that gift is another story, however.

When, through sin, man resists the self-gift of God, God does not cease giving Himself. The divine dynamic of one-on-

---

7 Pope Benedict XVI, Post-Synodal Apostolic Exhortation on the Word of God in the Life and Mission of the Church *Verbum Domini* (September 30, 2010), no. 8: http://w2.vatican.va/content/benedict-xvi/en/apost_exhortations/documents/hf_ben-xvi_exh_20100930_verbum-domini.html.

8 Pope St. John Paul II, "The Meaning of Original Unity" in *Theology of the Body*, 160. See also footnote 15 on the same page for further explanation.

one relationships is never-ending, unconditional self-gift. At the same time, sin introduces suffering into that dynamic. Man suffers because it contradicts his being, made in the image and likeness of God, to resist God's self-giving love. God also suffers, because, although He is impassible, He is not "incompassible."[9] In Jesus Christ, this is revealed most vividly: God suffers in our human flesh. The dynamic of sin, as resistance to God's love and failure to trust, introduces suffering into the one-on-one relationship between God and each person. At the same time, that suffering becomes a pathway of redemption and transformation as God's passionate love is manifested in the vulnerability of human flesh. In the flesh of Christ, God takes on all of man's suffering and, through trusting obedience, brings it into the eternal, loving embrace of the Father.

In this we have the pattern intended for one-on-one relationships. They are meant to deepen infinitely through self-giving love. Self-giving love is manifested in human ways through time, actions, gifts, and even in heroic moments through giving of one's own body by donating an organ, by donating a whole life in martyrdom or, more commonly, by donating half of one's DNA, in marital union, to create a new human life. All of these are instances of the "grain of wheat" that falls to the ground and dies and so bears much fruit (Jn 12:24). The fulfillment of our human life comes from living out our one-on-one relationship with God, modeling every relationship on the divine dynamic of self-giving love. When we live in God in this way, our humanity shares in His divine life.

One-On-One at the Human Level

In the first chapters of Genesis, we see how fundamental our one-on-one relationship with God is. We begin our existence alone with God. At the same time, that relationship is intended to grow

---

[9] *"Impassibilis est Deus, sed non incompassibilis"* in St. Bernard, *Cantica Canticorum*, 26, n. 5: PL 183, 906.

out into other human relationships. God summarizes it in saying, "it is not good that the man should be alone" (Gen 2:18). According to the logic expressed in the Second Vatican Council's *Gaudium et Spes,* man "cannot fully find himself except through a sincere gift of himself."[10] Adam, at first, had no one with whom he could live out the divine dynamic of relationships: total, self-giving love. Said another way, Adam had no one to live for and no one to die for. The intimacy we have with God is meant to be lived out through one-on-one relationships with our fellow man.

Furthermore, the dynamic of all our human relationships is supposed to be patterned on our relationship with God. The fundamental principles governing that first human relationship between Adam and Eve were derived directly from their relationship with God. They were made in God's image and likeness, their relationship developed within the context of God's creation, and their freedom to love was formed under the guidance of God's commandments—to be fruitful and multiply, to cultivate the earth and subdue it, and never to eat from one of the trees.

In fact, Jesus revealed that the one-on-one relationship with God necessarily depends on how we live out our one-on-one relationships with other human beings. After restating the great commandment, to love the Lord our God with all our heart and mind and soul and strength, he placed another commandment next to it: "You shall love your neighbor as yourself" (Mt 22:39). Although both of those commandments are in the law, by placing them together and adding, "and a second is like it," Jesus taught us how essential our human relationships are to living out the commandment to love God above all things. He reemphasized the point in expressing the new commandment, "This is my commandment, that you love one another as I have loved you" (Jn 15:12). He even made this the criterion for the final judgment: "As you did it to one of the least of these my brethren, you did it to me" (Mt 25:40).

---

[10] Second Vatican Council, Pastoral Constitution on the Church in the Modern World *Gaudium et spes* (December 7, 1965), no. 24.

Preaching and Group Settings

There are other settings in which an individual's one-on-one relationship with God can be nourished and universal truths can be personally embraced. One setting that is central to the life of the Church is liturgical preaching in particular and various kinds of spiritual conferences in general. Regarding liturgical preaching, Pope Francis described eloquently the way that the deacon, priest, or bishop personalizes the Gospel for the congregation, working in harmony with the Holy Spirit. He recognized that God is already speaking with us, but He also intends for that communication to become audible at times and He works through the liturgical homily in this regard: "The homily takes up once more the dialogue which the Lord has already established with his people."[11] Pope Francis described the homily as "heart-to-heart communication which . . . possesses a quasi-sacramental character: 'Faith comes from what is heard, and what is heard comes by the preaching of Christ' (Rom 10:17)."[12]

A good spiritual director has some significant advantages which can make him a good speaker or a good homilist because he is in touch with the dialogue between God and His people and because he has developed a sensitivity for the heart-to-heart communication that God wants to have with each one of us. In another sense, the dynamics of public speaking are very different from the dynamics of spiritual direction. Public speaking requires a certain ability to project oneself to many people at once. The courage and confidence required to speak to a large gathering of people, as well as the stamina and detachment of not receiving feedback or seeing results, make demands on the speaker that are not as burdensome in spiritual direction. At the same time, the personalization, tenderness, mercy, and love that can be commu-

---

[11] Pope Francis, Apostolic Exhortation on the Proclamation of the Gospel in Today's World *Evangelii gaudium* (November 24, 2013), no. 137, https://w2.vatican.va/content/francesco/en/apost_exhortations/documents/papa-francesco_esortazione-ap_20131124_evangelii-gaudium.html.
[12] Ibid.

nicated through the one-on-one relationship of spiritual direction can have a much deeper impact on the recipient than that which is ordinarily received in the general context of a conference talk or liturgical homily.

Another setting that can be very helpful for healing and deepening one's personal relationship with God is a group setting. Share groups, group therapy, Bible studies, and other peer sharing contexts can help to personalize the Gospel as we hear testimonies from others in similar circumstances. The way that one mother receives the love of Jesus can be a great encouragement for another mother to receive His love in a similar way. The struggles of one man with an addiction can provide insight that can help another man with the same addiction to understand his own struggle and believe in God's presence and love for him. Twelve-step programs have provided an incredible service to men and women searching for healing and growth in their one-on-one relationship with God. There are even programs of group spiritual direction which can be very supportive and effective, particularly for some individuals. In certain cases, group spiritual direction can be effective when the spiritual director does not have time to meet frequently enough with people individually, or it can serve to reinforce individual spiritual direction that is being received concurrently.

These settings are not substitutes for spiritual direction, but mutually support it. A person in spiritual direction may be even more open to hearing the voice of Jesus through a homily at Mass or through a personal sharing in a group ministry context. Likewise, the content of homilies or the impact of personal sharing become good points for reflection in the context of spiritual direction.

Sacramental Confession and Psychological Counseling

Another one-on-one ministry related to spiritual direction is sacramental Confession. In sacramental Confession there is an optional opportunity for counsel. If a penitent goes regularly to the same

priest for Confession, that counsel can offer a deeper insight and
a regular confessor can provide a ministry very similar to spiritual
direction. Likewise, the manifestation of the conscience in confessing sin is an important dimension of the self-giving intimacy
that marks the ministry of spiritual direction. The difference is
that the manifestation of the heart in spiritual direction includes
more than sin. Also, the time allotted for spiritual direction is
often much lengthier than confession. As already mentioned,
spiritual direction can certainly be offered by Christians who are
not priests, as was the case originally with the Desert Fathers.

Counseling is another ministry similar to spiritual direction
in that there is a one-on-one relationship that delves into the
interior of the patient. One distinction, however, is that, unlike in
counseling, there is not always a problem or a disorder that is being
addressed in spiritual direction. Another distinction is that counseling focuses primarily on the human and psychological and less
so on the spiritual. For this reason, a counselor need not necessarily work in a Christian worldview and may still be very effective
in helping his patients. Spiritual direction is always focused on the
directee's one-on-one relationship with our Triune God.

Spiritual Direction: Sharing Our Relationship with God, One-On-One

There is an implicit expectation that in the first human relationship between Adam and Eve, the personal relationship with God
would be explicitly shared. The Scriptures recount that Adam, not
Eve, received the commandments to cultivate the earth, to eat of
any of the trees, and never to eat from one of the trees. Implicitly
we can presume that those commandments were also binding for
Eve and that it was Adam's responsibility to share the revelations
from his one-on-one relationship with God with his wife. It was
the first faith sharing.

Our one-on-one relationship with God grows when it is
shared. One way for this to happen is through faith sharing. This

is required of all Christians in the command to evangelize: "Go therefore and make disciples of all nations" (Mt 28:19). This relationship is shared through our actions as indicated in the oft-quoted words attributed to St. Francis, "Preach the Gospel always, and if necessary, use words." Another privileged setting for sharing our one-on-one relationship with God is in spiritual direction.

Spiritual direction is a one-on-one relationship between a director and a directee in which the directee's relationship with God is the fundamental reference point. Every person's one-on-one relationship with God is the most fundamental relationship in his life, but it must develop and grow. Every relationship affects our relationship with God, but the special relationship of spiritual direction can play an irreplaceable role in developing the directee's one-on-one relationship with God because it deals most directly with that relationship. Spiritual direction can touch on everything in the directee's life, but the primary focus is on his relationship with God. The spiritual director helps the directee to see God's role in everything else. The Congregation for the Clergy summarized it nicely: "Spiritual direction is not simply a doctrinal consultation. Rather it concerns our relationship and intimate configuration with Christ."[13]

Spiritual direction is an opportunity to open one's heart totally to another person, sharing the most intimate memories and experiences, all the way to the foundation of one's being: the relationship with God. As St. Augustine expressed, God is more intimate to us than our innermost self.[14] As the directee makes the journey of trust and vulnerable self-revelation, the intimate, innermost depths of the soul begin to come into view. Through spiritual direction, a person can develop his one-on-one relationship with God and at the same time discover new depths in his own soul. He can also allow love to heal and transform those depths. As that transformation and healing take place, everything else in life is affected in a positive way, "that God may be everything to

---

[13] Congregation for the Clergy, *The Priest, Minister of Divine Mercy*, no. 69.
[14] See St. Augustine, *Confessions*, bk. III, chap. 6, no. 11.

every one" (1 Cor 15:28). There is no need for spiritual direction in heaven, because in heaven everything is unveiled and we know God and everyone fully, even as we are fully known by Him (see 1 Cor 13:12). If the dynamic of spiritual direction is lived out well, however, it can become a taste of heaven as the depths of the soul are opened up and the self-giving love of God becomes more immediately visible and tangible.

The power of spiritual direction is so significant that Pope St. John XXIII said to seminary spiritual directors:

> The future of the Church, it might be said, rests greatly in your hands. It is true that the training of seminarians requires harmonious cooperation and effort on the part of all the faculty members of the seminary, under the wise and kind direction of the rector. But the most important role is yours, for your action is carried on in the inner depths of consciences, where deep convictions take root and where the real transformation of the young man called to the priesthood takes place. The breath of the Spirit of the Lord initiates and sets a crown on this [transformation]. But in the ordinary course of events, it will be hard for the young man to know how to follow His inspirations without the expert guidance of the spiritual director.[15]

Notice the Pope's emphasis on where the work of spiritual direction takes place, "in the inner depths of consciences, where deep convictions take root and where the real transformation . . . takes place." Pope St. John XXIII referred to that place within which our one-on-one relationship with God develops. This is the place that is opened up in spiritual direction and where so many formative things take place in our souls.

St. Faustina similarly experienced this with her spiritual director, Bl. Michael Sopocko, who saw the depths of her soul where God shared His secrets with her:

---

[15]   Pope St. John XXIII, Address to Seminary Spiritual Directors.

This priest is surely guided by the Spirit of God; he has penetrated the secrets of my soul, the deepest secrets which were between me and God, about which I had not yet spoken to him, because I had not understood them myself, and which the Lord had not clearly ordered me to tell him. The secret is this: God demands that there be a Congregation which will proclaim the mercy of God to the world and, by its prayers, obtain it for the world. When the priest asked me if I had not had any such inspirations, I replied that I had not had any clear orders; but at that instant a light penetrated my soul, and I understood that the Lord was speaking through him.[16]

It is for this reason that St. Faustina heard Jesus say later that she should reveal everything to her spiritual director (with "boundless sincerity") and that he would have a special grace to know and understand her soul:

And now I am going to tell you something that is most important for you: boundless sincerity with your spiritual director. . . . From the moment when I gave you this priest as spiritual director, I endowed him with new light so that he might easily know and understand your soul.[17]

---

[16] St. Faustina, *Diary*, no. 436.
[17] Ibid., no. 1561.

2

Interiority

S IMPLY SAID, interiority is about what is happening inside of us,
namely, how we assimilate and process our whole lives. Interiority involves our thoughts and our feelings, our motivations
and memories. Parts of our interior life are evident to an external
observer, but not all of it. Our interior is complex and sometimes contradictory. Our thoughts may conflict with our feelings,
for example. Likewise, we may behave almost like two different
people in different situations. As St. Paul testified: "I do not understand my own actions. For I do not do what I want, but I do the
very thing I hate" (Rom 7:15).

Let us consider an example that illustrates some of the healing
that can take place when a directee truly opens up his interior life
in spiritual direction, complete with contradictions and especially
with the parts of himself that he does not like or does not know
how to handle. The spiritual director's broader knowledge and
attentive listening to the Holy Spirit can help to bring insight,
healing, and peace to the directee.

A seminarian named Tom came to spiritual direction with a
lot of contempt toward himself. He felt that he was emotionally
weak and he despised that. He wanted to be stronger. His spiritual
director saw Tom's perceived emotional weakness as sensitivity
and asked him how sensitivity was handled when he was growing
up. Tom shared that sensitivity was not encouraged and sometimes
even trampled on when he was growing up. It was because of that

that Tom started to despise emotional weakness. In response to this, Tom's spiritual director began a long process of affirming sensitivity. He repeated many times, "You are a very sensitive person," and he repeated many times how beautiful that is, and how much God loves sensitivity.

Tom began to open up and trust his sensitivity more. Many sessions of spiritual direction ended in crying, even sobbing and trembling, during which Tom's spiritual director simply kept affirming his sensitivity and saying what a gift it is. He encouraged the tears and quietly loved Tom in the tears, giving him the safe space to express the feelings in his heart. Tom's spiritual director always kept in mind the importance of Tom's sensitivity and brought it up at different times. For example, when Tom spoke about certain hard experiences in the military, his spiritual director asked him, "How did you handle that, being as sensitive as you are?" Tom replied simply, "I didn't know how sensitive I was." In this way, over time, Tom began to recognize and accept his sensitivity more and more. As he did so, he also began to see how his sensitivity was a great gift. It made him capable of expressing deep love and concern for others.

As he began to accept his sensitivity, he was able to accept other things in his interior life as well. He was able to let go of self-accusation about events from earlier in his life, for example his girlfriend's suicide. He was able to face his own sins and accept forgiveness for them—those sins committed both earlier in life and in an ongoing way. He had struggled with sexual addiction, but some part of that was driven by unattended feelings. As he attended to the feelings and opened them up in spiritual direction, the addiction diminished significantly and he was able to redirect those energies to better things. He was able to feel and speak about things that he was very conflicted about, especially things that led to tears and shame. Through his trust to open up his interior life—his feelings and thoughts, fears, motives, and interpretations of reality—and the affirming response he received from his spiritual director, Tom became more familiar and at peace with the complexity of things that were happening inside of him. His hatred for vulnerability changed slowly into a deep appreciation for vulnerability. This also opened him up to discern a vocation to the priesthood and gave him the confidence he needed to move forward. He has learned to feel deeply and to love deeply and is an excellent priest, both prayerful and compassionate.

Delving into Interiority

In the beginning, in original solitude, God was with Adam alone. We continue to have this relationship with God, the relationship that is more fundamental than every other relationship; we describe it as deeper, or more interior. It is deeper within us than anyone else can reach. Truly it is even deeper than we, ourselves, can reach (*interior intimo meo*—"more interior than my innermost," as St. Augustine wrote[1]). It is a place within us where we touch Truth and it requires a radical honesty to access that level of interiority. When we reach the interiority where God dwells within us, we are getting in touch with the ground of our being, with the ultimate meaning of our lives, with our very identity and the truth that defines our existence. Because so much is at stake, reaching into that level of interiority leaves us extremely vulnerable. It is so easy to identify with St. Augustine, who recognized he was fleeing from that deepest interiority, "You were within me, but I was outside, and it was there that I searched for you."[2]

St. Augustine says he fled from the encounter with God in his deepest interior because of his "unloveliness": "In my unloveliness I plunged into the lovely things which you created."[3] When we delve more deeply into our interior, we encounter parts of ourselves (or we are afraid that we will encounter parts of ourselves) that appear unlovely to us. For various reasons, we have exiled

---

[1] "*Interior intimo meo et superior summo meo.*" St. Augustine, *Confessions*, bk. III, chap. 6, no. 11.

[2] Ibid., bk. VII, chap. 10. Translation from the *Roman Breviary*.

[3] Ibid.

parts of ourselves, and we are afraid to look on the naked poverty
of our weaknesses and limitations. In the language of Genesis, "I
was afraid, because I was naked; and I hid myself" (Gen 3:10).
Thus, St. Augustine is describing a basic, human dynamic: out of
fear for what we will discover within ourselves, we go out of ourselves and live superficially, plunging ourselves into created things
like food, drugs, work, a multitude of material possessions, endless
entertainments, video games, or other preoccupations. St. Teresa
of Ávila commented similarly in her great work on prayer, *The
Interior Castle*, "there are souls so ill and so accustomed to being
involved in external matters that there is no remedy, nor does it
seem they can enter into themselves."[4]

One man in formation preparing to live the consecrated life
seemed rather rigid and distant much of the time. He was the same
in spiritual direction and often described his own experiences as
if he were describing someone else's. The spiritual director never
had a sense that this young man was really sharing his interior
life. This problem became so severe that the young man began
having memory lapses during which he acted out with strange
behavior. Finally when this behavior was confronted, the young
man revealed that his father had died when he was only a boy,
and his mother had told him that he should not cry. She told him
that he had to be the man of the family and provide support for
everyone else. She had told him that crying was something only
girls and little children did. The man told his spiritual director he
could not remember crying ever again. However as he began to
talk about the loss of his father and other losses and fears in his
life, he did begin to cry and became able to share much more of
his interior life.

It takes great courage to delve into our interiority. In some
cases, it is a journey to a place we have never known. In other
cases, we have carefully buried those places under certain defenses.

---

[4] St. Teresa of Ávila, *The Interior Castle*, found in *The Collected Works of St. Teresa of Ávila*, vol. 2, trans. Kieran Kavanaugh and Otilio Rodriguez (Washington, DC: ICS Publications, 2001), 286.

In any event, we need help to delve more deeply into our original solitude. St. Augustine teaches, "Urged to reflect upon myself, I entered under your guidance the innermost places of my being; but only because you had become my helper was I able to do so."[5] Note the importance of St. Augustine's qualification for going deeper: "*only* because you had become my helper was I able to do so."[6]

The key to entering into the innermost places of our being is knowing that we are loved unconditionally. Even those seemingly ugly and exiled parts of us, poor and weak as they are, are truly loved—indeed, are especially loved. God is the only one who can love us unconditionally, who can show us this love perfectly, and He does this most explicitly in Jesus Christ, especially in His crucified love. St. Augustine affirms the importance of Christ giving us the strength to encounter God in the depths of our interiority: "I looked for a way to gain the strength I needed to enjoy you, but I did not find it until I embraced the mediator between God and man, the man Christ Jesus, who is also God, supreme over all things and blessed for ever. He called out, proclaiming I am the Way and Truth and the Life."[7] Likewise, we get a glimpse of this in the story of Adam's original fear. Although he hid himself when he heard God in the garden, he responded to the word of God, who called out, "Where are you?" (Gen 3:9). Jesus Christ is the Word of God who seeks us out and calls after us. His Incarnation is the deafness-shattering cry that St. Augustine speaks about: "You called, you shouted, and you broke through my deafness. You flashed, you shone, and you dispelled my blindness. You breathed your fragrance on me; I drew in breath and now I pant for you. I have tasted you, now I hunger and thirst for more. You touched me, and I burned for your peace."[8] The encounter with God in Jesus Christ gives life "a new horizon and a definitive direction."[9]

---

[5] St. Augustine, *Confessions*, bk. VII, chap. 10.

[6] Ibid., emphasis added.

[7] Ibid., bk. VII, chap. 18.

[8] Ibid., bk. X, chap. 27.

[9] Pope Benedict XVI, *Deus Caritas est*, no. 1.

A man who complained that he was not able to enjoy life or get excited about anything came into spiritual direction. He was not sure whether he was called to pursue a vocation to the priesthood or to marriage. He could not seem to feel any zeal about either possibility and had never dated seriously or developed a deep relationship. Likewise, the sharing of his interior life tended to be quite shallow. When they reached a point of mutual frustration, the spiritual director and the directee continued searching to find out what was giving him the difficulty in deeply feeling things and experiencing any deep desires in his life. Eventually he became able to talk about the fact that he was addicted to pornography. It turned out that this wound made him feel disqualified for any vocation. He had hidden his wounds under a covering of hopelessness by which he had concluded that this addiction would never be overcome and that he simply had to live with it. He had not realized how much this had clouded over his entire interior life and caused him to shut down emotionally. His relationship with God had likewise been stunted, but began to grow along with his other relationships as he began to address his addiction.

The love of God always initiates, always takes the first step, to give us the courage to continue going deeper and unearthing more and more of our "unloveliness." "In this is love, not that we have loved God but that he loved us and sent his Son to be the expiation for our sins" (1 Jn 4:10). When we are confident that what we discover in our nakedness will be loved, we will have the courage to see it and even to share it. Furthermore, this is where the greatest healing takes place. St. Augustine's conversion took place in exposing his unloveliness to the Lord. Likewise, Adam's recovery began with his response to God's voice (Gen 3:10). Even without uncovering himself, he called out to God honestly from his hiding place, admitting his fear. With divine tenderness, God did not exploit his nakedness and did not even leave him exposed, but gave him a new, warmer, softer covering and also gave him hope and a path forward (Gen 3:21, 15, 24).

The spiritual director has the privilege to witness and facilitate this journey of deepening interiority and the accompanying purifying and healing experience of self-discovery. In the one-on-one context of spiritual direction, the director becomes a loving face and a listening ear that represent God's unconditional love for each person. The director becomes the loving voice of God that calls out to the hidden and exiled parts of the directee, reassuring him that he is loved and that God is with him and helps him to come out of hiding.

A nun who was crippled by her fears found that they made her very indecisive. She was afraid that her spiritual director would become angry with her and reject her. A previous spiritual director had told her that she was always praying her "Rosary of fears" with one fear leading to another like one bead of the Rosary leads to another. Though she recognized her fears she had no idea how to stop them. One day she became very indecisive about whether to take an opportunity to see her spiritual director or to pursue another spiritual opportunity. When she and her director began to talk about her fear of rejection, she described her indecisiveness by saying, "It's like I have two doors. Behind one door is a lion and behind the other door is a bear. Either way I am afraid." Her spiritual director told her, referring to himself, "But there is no lion behind this door." Her fears originated in severe neglect early in her life, but very slowly she began to be less afraid, particularly in her relationship with God and also in her relationship with her spiritual director and other important people in her life.

This helps us understand a principal dynamic of spiritual direction, namely that as the directee comes to trust the director, the directee is able to delve further into his interior by sharing with the director. If the directee never begins to trust the director, spiritual direction bears little fruit. But, as the examples above show, as the inability to trust is explored and transformed, it may open up the very core of the interior life. Because our interior life deals with the most fundamental parts of our being, the parts that answer the questions "Who am I?" and "What is the meaning of my life?" these areas are extremely vulnerable. When lies reach these parts of us, the damage can be extremely painful and lasting; this is at the heart of trauma and abuse. For this reason, our natural, human behavior is to protect these vulnerable, interior areas of ourselves. Our basic protection is to ensure that we are sharing these areas of our hearts only with those who will not hurt us through harshness or lies. *Thus, for spiritual direction to be effective, the director, for his part, must earn the directee's trust through patient, prayerful listening with loving attention.*

The Heart: The Center of Interiority

When we speak of interiority, we often refer to the "heart." The Catechism assists us in understanding what this means:

> The heart is the dwelling-place where I am, where I live; according to the Semitic or Biblical expression, the heart is the place "to which I withdraw." The heart is our hidden center, beyond the grasp of our reason and of others; only the Spirit of God can fathom the human heart and know it fully. The heart is the place of decision, deeper than our psychic drives. It is the place of truth, where we choose life or death. It is the place of encounter, because as image of God we live in relation: it is the place of covenant. (CCC 2563)

Above all, as the Catechism expresses, we want to open our hearts to God in prayer, "Yet it is most important that the heart should be present to him to whom we are speaking in prayer: 'Whether or not our prayer is heard depends not on the number of words, but on the fervor of our souls'" (CCC 2700). It is from this same part of the soul that we speak in spiritual direction.

The Holy Spirit dwells in the depths of our hearts and is our true Director. As the directee discovers his own interior and opens that interior in spiritual direction, the Holy Spirit directs also through the spiritual director. "In this very special move-

ment [of sanctification], the Holy Spirit takes up His abode in
the deepest, most intimate, and most active part of our being. He
constitutes Himself the immediate Director of the soul, which in
its full strength and freedom moves only under His inspiration."[10]

The philosopher Dietrich von Hildebrand offered a compel-
ling analysis and teaching on the heart and summarized that "we
must realize that in many respects the heart is more the real self
of the person than his intellect or will."[11] He reflected further,
"The heart is here not only the true self because love is essentially
a voice of the heart; it is also the true self insofar as love aims at
the heart of the beloved in a specific way. The lover wants to pour
his love into the heart of the beloved, he wants to affect his heart,
to fill it with happiness; and only then will he feel that he has
really reached the beloved, his very self."[12] For the same reason,
the heart is the focus of spiritual direction. The spiritual director
is interested in seeing the heart of the directee and helping the
directee to receive "God's love [which] has been poured into
our hearts through the Holy Spirit which has been given to us"
(Rom 5:5).

Aspects of the Interior Life

There have been many formulations of a spiritual anthropology to
describe the interior composition of the human person. Monastic
theologians described an interior consisting of a *psyche* that is in
touch with the world, a ground of the soul (or *nous*) that is in
touch with God, and a spirit (or *pneuma*) that is the intentionality
of the person and could move between the *psyche* and the *nous* or
be in contact with both at the same time. The monastic spirituality
of the Desert Fathers (see Evagrius Ponticus, John Cassian, etc.)
recognized the impact of the *pathe* (though literally translated as

---

[10] Luis Martínez, *True Devotion to the Holy Spirit* (Manchester, NH: Sophia Institute Press, 2000), 42.

[11] Dietrich von Hildebrand, ed. John Henry Crosby, *The Heart: An Analysis of Human and Divine Affectivity* (South Bend, IN: St. Augustine's Press, 2007), 67.

[12] Ibid.

"passions" we would translate it more accurately as "attachments")
which act like hooks coming in through the *psyche* to hold down
the *pneuma* and prevent contact with God. They prescribed a
process of detachment leading to *apatheia* (though literally translated as "apathy" we believe it would be more accurate to describe
it as "interior freedom") in which the *pneuma* is "unhooked" and
free to be in touch with the depths or "ground" of the soul (*nous*)
where the person is in contact with God.

Expanding on this image, other schools of spirituality describe
the soul as the composition and interaction of the powers of the
imagination and the memory, the senses, the sentiments, and the
will. The soul is moved by passions. "The term 'passions' refers
to the affections or the feelings. By his emotions man intuits the
good and suspects evil" (CCC 1771). Consistent with monastic
spirituality and contrary to a spirituality that would eliminate the
passions, as found in other religions, philosophies, or Christian
heresies, Christian spirituality has always sought to transform the
passions, shaping them under the influence of reason such that
the soul forms an habitual character which we call "virtue."[13] For
each virtue, there are corresponding vices in which there is a lack
or suppression of passion or an excess or exacerbation of passion.
Virtue lies in the middle.[14]

In the modern day, schools of psychology have also sought
to define the elements of the interior life. Freud called our base,
irrational instincts and impulses the *id*, and the product of organ-
izing the *id* under the influence of reason, held up to reality, he
called the *ego*.[15] Two Catholic psychologists, Conrad Baars and
Anna Terruwe, adopted a more traditionally Catholic, namely
Thomistic, description of the soul together with its concupiscible
and irascible appetites.[16] Another school of psychology, Internal

---

[13] See St. Thomas Aquinas, *Summa Theologiae*, II-I, q. 55.
[14] See Aristotle, *Nicomachean Ethics*, 2.4.
[15] Sigmund Freud and James Strachey, *The Standard Edition of the Complete Psychological Works of Sigmund Freud* (London: Vintage, 2001).
[16] Anna Terruwe and Conrad W. Baars, *Psychic Wholeness and Healing: Using All the
Powers of the Human Psyche* (New York: Alba House, 1981).

Family Systems, takes another approach, seeing the soul consisting of various "parts" each with its own dynamics.[17]

The Inner Circle: Seat of Intuition and Desire

One particularly helpful and simple description of the interior life of the soul distinguishes between an "inner circle" and "outer circle" of the interior life. This provides a foundation for an understanding of contemplative prayer and the dark contemplation which is not accompanied by images or words. This is an important part of the process of passive purification that we take up in Chapter 6 in the passages on prayer. For now we will simply note that, according to St. John of the Cross, active purification is initiated and pursued by the self while passive purification is undergone in self-surrender to events outside one's own control. The following is a description of the inner circle and outer circle:

> The outer circle is what we normally use in the thinking process: the reason, which is that part of the intellect which goes step by step from one thing to another, and our inner senses, particularly the imagination and the memory, which we also use to help our thinking. For our purposes, the inner circle is only a certain aspect of the intellect and will. It is the intellect, as it is able to know by intuition alone, and the will, as it is able to love by a single act, prolonged without making one act of love after another.
>
> God Who can do all things can make Himself known in this inner circle without going through the outer one. The soul can perceive Him in the intuitive intellect without visible images, without words, and without

---

[17] Jay Earley, with a Foreword by Richard C. Schwartz, *Self-Therapy: A Step-By-Step Guide to Creating Wholeness and Healing Your Inner Child Using IFS, A New, Cutting-Edge Psychotherapy* (Larkspur, CA: Pattern System Books, 2009).

individual acts. God is able to plant Himself, so to speak, in this part of the soul which knows Him best when it does not know that it is knowing, that is, when it does not reflect on the fact that it knows or what it knows. It simply knows Him and is delighted beyond all other delights in just knowing. This is, of course, the essence of all contemplative prayer, but the soul must not expect delight from dark contemplation. [18]

In spiritual direction, we are interested in hearing the directee's sharing about the outer circle of the interior life, but the effort to share what is happening in the inner circle is sometimes possible in more advanced stages of spiritual direction. In addition to the above-described aspect of intuitive knowledge and prolonged love, another aspect to add to the inner circle is the dynamic of desire. In dark contemplation, in which no images or words are forthcoming, we may learn to discern a deeper desire that is not satisfied by any earthly thing. This is not a mere physical craving for chocolate cake or just an interest in going to the movies or even a zeal for social work. A typical criterion of the passive purification, which St. John of the Cross called the Dark Night, by which we enter into the unitive way, is that this desire is not satisfied by an earthly thing. It is a longing for prayer, but even more, prayer does not leave us fully satisfied and often even increases this deep desire. We could say that such a desire is rising up from the "inner circle" of our interior life.

In a certain sense, all of spiritual direction is a means by which the director helps the directee to come to a place of full interior integration, "to mature manhood, to the measure of the stature of the fulness of Christ" (Eph 4:13). This involves an awareness of what is happening in the outer circle of our imagination, reason, and memory as well as learning how to bring our passions under the direction of reason. Sometimes we are aware of our passions

---

[18] Dominic M. Hoffman, OP, *The Life Within: The Prayer of Union* (New York: Sheed and Ward, 1966), 12.

(that we are angry, for example) but we do not know *why* we are angry or *how* angry we are. Our interior is a mystery to us. This includes the inner circle of our deeper selves where God abides, but also aspects of our memory and imagination that rise up from instinct or are exacerbated by experiences we do not take note of and thus do not have active access to. As the directee trusts the spiritual director enough to open up these mysterious areas of the interior, then order, understanding, and integration will take place and the directee will experience a deeper interior peace despite whatever else he may be experiencing outwardly.

Having offered these descriptions of the interior life of the human person, it is important to note that these do not constitute dogmatic definitions. Each model has something to offer as we consider the complex reality of the human soul, or what in the Bible is most often called "the heart." Above all we realize that all of our models, while offering some insight, also fall short. As the Catechism affirms, "The heart is our hidden center, beyond the grasp of our reason and of others; only the Spirit of God can fathom the human heart and know it fully" (CCC 2563).

Interiority: A Multifaceted Reality

We speak of interiority as a place, but we might say, to be more precise, that there are many interior places in each of us. St. Teresa of Ávila described the soul as a "castle made entirely of a diamond ... in which there are many rooms, just as in heaven there are many dwelling places."[19] This matters when understanding the dynamic of spiritual direction as a shared exploration of the interior life of the directee. Each person has a multifaceted interior that cannot be shared and known in one session. Different events, memories, prayers, challenges, and relationships can lead to different places in our interior life. One of the signs of evangelical freedom is

[19] St. Teresa of Ávila, *The Interior Castle*, in *Classics of Western Spirituality*, trans. Kieran Kavanaugh, OCD and Otilio Rodriguez, OCD (Paulist Press, 1979), 36.

being able to move unencumbered through the interior mansions, finding God in each of them.

St. Teresa of Ávila describes a journey through the interior mansions that begins with entering the interior and deepens to the level of mystical marriage in the seventh mansion. This deepening is not described strictly as seven steps, as if each step leaves the previous one behind or as if they were a merely linear progression, but they are rather seven levels of our interior, each with many mansions. And they are all meant to be accessible to us. The challenges of vulnerability, honesty, and radically facing our own poverty are what generally prevents us from going deeper. St. Teresa of Ávila is also very clear about how important a spiritual director is in this process of progressive interior development and freedom.

St. Teresa described the interior castle knowing very well that few approach the deeper mansions. All the same, she considered it to be an important motivation and point of navigation to describe the basic levels of interiority: "Let us now imagine that this castle contains many mansions, some above, others below, others at each side; and in the center and in the midst of them all is the chiefest mansion, where the most secret things pass between God and the soul."[20] Having personally come to that center mansion, St. Teresa wanted very much for others to enjoy this fulfillment of their redeemed humanity. She lamented, however, that "many souls remain in the outer court of the castle which is the place occupied by the guards; they are not interested in entering it and have no idea what is in that wonderful place, or who dwells in it, or even how many rooms it has."[21] It is notable that the Second Vatican Council reinforced St. Teresa's conviction and emphasized that "mystical treasures," "an abundance of contemplation," "an experience of Divine things," and "an assiduous union with God in prayer" are meant for each and every person in the Church.[22]

---

[20] Ibid.

[21] Ibid.

[22] See Ralph Martin, *The Fulfillment of All Desire: A Guidebook for the Journey to God Based on the Wisdom of the Saints* (Steubenville, OH: Emmaus Road Publishing, 2006), 1–9; Second Vatican Council, Dogmatic Constitution on the Church *Lumen*

"The gate of entry to this castle is prayer and reflection . . ."[23] This guidance echoes that of St. Augustine. "Urged to reflect upon myself, I entered under your guidance the innermost places of my being; but only because you had become my helper was I able to do so."[24] It also echoes the first step of the basic teaching of St. Ignatius in the process of discernment: *be aware*, judge, act.[25] It requires silence and reflection to enter into the interior. When we take the time for silence, we begin to discover layers of images and words, ideas and memories that flow within us. This is the first step of prayer. Simply sharing this with a spiritual director can also be a good first step of spiritual direction. As we take more time in silent prayer, we become familiar with our interior and can sort through the distractions and start to explore different areas.

An Existential Description

When we speak of our interior as a multi-faceted reality, how does that correspond to our experience? To start with, we can recognize that the way we see God, the way we see ourselves, and the way we see others can change situationally. A slightly different version of myself comes out in the locker room than in the Church, or in the home, or in the office. I might see that when I am with one person, I can be confident and feel like myself, but when I am with someone else, I am hesitant, unsure of myself. If I have everybody convinced that they are seeing me the way I want them to see me, I can be comfortable; or maybe I don't know how I want people to see me. We put on different masks, develop different personas depending on whom we are dealing with. This is normal, especially in adolescence, and then over time we tend to consolidate a presentation of ourselves that is more consist-

---

gentium (November 21, 1964), no. 11, http://www.vatican.va/archive/hist_councils/ii_vatican_council/documents/vat-ii_const_19641121_lumen-gentium_en.html.

[23] St. Teresa of Ávila, *The Interior Castle*, 38.

[24] St. Augustine, *Confessions*, bk. VII, chap. 18.

[25] St. Ignatius of Loyola, *Spiritual Exercises*, trans. Louis J. Puhl (Westminster, MD: Newman Press, 1960), no. 313.

ent. There will be some appropriate differences depending on the setting and individuals with whom we are interacting, but there should be stability.

As an example, one young lady had a very strong prayer life but many problems in her relationship with her parents and some other dimensions of her life. In her prayer life she could bring her best before God and receive His grace, but that grace was not reaching and transforming the other parts of her life. Her spiritual director asked her to share the parts of her interior life, including the relationships and self-perceptions, that were causing her difficulty. She shared about her highly ambivalent relationship with her mother and feelings of being abandoned by her father. Her mother's domineering, controlling personality and the perception of restrictive expectations from her father undermined the young woman's confidence and hampered her efforts to strike out on her own. The spiritual director was able to affirm her goodness as she shared her struggles and helped her bring these troublesome aspects of her life before God. Her spiritual director also encouraged her to deal with her isolation by forming a young adult group and helped her persevere through some difficulties in getting it started. This helped the grace of her prayer start to flow into the troubled areas of her interior, and she experienced healing that blossomed into confidence and the courage to take some necessary risks. That confidence also brought healing to her relationships with her mother and father.

Interiority has to do with what a person thinks and feels inside about himself, about the world, about others, and about God. Normally this will correspond with how we present ourselves in various situations. We would say that a person whose interior corresponds directly with his exterior presentation is transparent. What you see is what you get. A person who outwardly presents himself very differently from his interior self is duplicitous or can be hypocritical. A person who acts in an extremely different way, even in a contradictory way, in one situation or another is duplicitous, although there is a question of whether he even realizes the difference or whether his interiority is equally duplicitous. Sometimes people who are wounded, unsuccessful, or feel themselves to be failures can become very unstable and chameleon-like. They may be equally unstable interiorly with drastic swings from the heights to the depths. They may feel rejected and as if life is not worth living. They may be dreadfully ashamed. At other moments they might be elated and wildly optimistic. A person with a broad range of external presentation may not know who he is and feel very dependent on how other people see him, playing too much to others' expectations.

From these descriptions we get a sense of the complexity that occurs in the person and even in the external behavior of the person. "The heart is deceitful above all things, and desperately corrupt; who can understand it? I the Lord search the mind and test the heart" (Jer 17:9–10). With God's help, patient listening, and some time, the spiritual director can get a reasonably good idea of how a person sees himself, others, and God; how they present themselves in different situations; what others think them to be; and who they want to be.

As mentioned, interiority has to do with what a person feels inside about himself. Some people have a very negative view of the world and themselves. Some people are more positive. Some people are more stable and not always shifting; they are in touch with their core self and not blown by every wind. Getting a window into this interior reality of the person is an important part of spiritual direction. The spiritual director seeks to understand the interior world of the directee and then he can help the directee open that interior world more fully to the Holy Spirit.

An important part of the interior world is the way that we see God. From the moment of our conception, we have a relationship with God inside ourselves. We may be more or less in touch with that relationship and we may not have spent much time trying to articulate that relationship or describe it in words. Even the process of looking at our interior relationship with God and describing it in words is a positive fruit of spiritual direction.

Our view of ourselves and our view of others can change according to the situation; so also our approach to God. In some settings I may see God as loving and approving, in other cases I avoid Him because I fear He is judgmental and disapproving. I may acknowledge the tenets of the Christian faith about the Trinity, divine mercy, or carrying my cross when I am in Church, but doubt or deny those statements when I am in a secular environment. I may simply forget about God when I am at work or shopping or at a football game. Especially in our highly secularized world, there are strong forces that push us to keep our relationship with God to ourselves and not bring Him into our everyday activities. Expressions of religious faith and talking about God are highly scorned in our modern, western world. This may influence us to develop a different approach to God in the church building than outside of the church building, or in our family setting, or at work.

Furthermore, there is the question of what I think about God in a quiet moment alone, in my interiority. When I am honest with myself, I might think about God as harsh and judgmental, even though all the language of my faith tells me He is merciful. I can converse about His mercy with others, but when I try to meet God in myself, I fear Him as judgmental. These interior and exterior spheres behave differently. How does my spiritual life express itself in practice, in the way I live, the various spheres of my life? I may even live out contradictions between one sphere and another—between business and church, or between friends and family. An important goal in life is to integrate all these spheres, interior and exterior. We should strive to relate what is happening inside ourselves with what is happening in our relationships, our work, and our prayer. We strive to integrate what is happening in our thoughts with what is happening in our feelings and with what is happening in our actions across all the spheres of our lives.

Reflecting, talking, and most importantly praying about all these things makes a critical difference. In regard to talking, spiritual direction is a precious place to be totally honest and vulnerably share the incongruities we see between our interior and exterior. Ultimately, though, the integration takes place in prayer, in our relationship with God. As discussed in Chapter 1, God is the ground of our being and He is the point at which all these things come together. As the prophet Jeremiah says, he probes the mind and tests the heart. He is the One who can make sense and bring together the complexity that we encounter in our own lives. A spiritual director plays a key role in helping a directee to bring all these things into prayer and into relationship with God.

Interior Pain and Darkness

Within our interior, there are also places of pain and darkness, parts of us that are exiled and that we work hard to keep hidden, even from ourselves in many cases. To protect ourselves from falling into or getting lost in these places, we often form various layers of resistance called defense mechanisms or protectors.

We form those dark places in us, often early in life, but also in traumatic experiences later in life (for example, we see this in refugees, victims of torture, witnesses of atrocities, and victims of abuse and broken trust). When the loneliness, rejection, fear, despair, and pain become too great, an individual can give up, and a kind of personal hell is created deep in the heart that is marked by radical despair and absolute hopelessness. One cannot live in that place. The only way one can climb out of it, especially early in life, is to form layers of defense around those experiences and feelings. These defenses can take the form of perfectionism, anger, denial, avoidance, self-indulgence, overeating, alcohol addiction, drug abuse, workaholism, and more. For one who is unable to develop such protectors or at times in life when they completely break down, even suicide can be the result of falling into that darkness and knowing no other way out.

It requires a great deal of trust for a directee to explore and invite the spiritual director into these dark areas of the interior. Our wounds are profoundly personal and thus profoundly vulnerable. As trust develops, however, and the directee allows God first of all, and also the spiritual director (who can bring the merciful love of God) into some of these dark places, much healing and mercy can reach the deep recesses of a person.

Integration through Prayer

Prayer that takes place interiorly, in the heart, is the place of integration. Vocal prayer in common is an important part of the Church's life, but interior prayer is necessary for the integration of the various spheres of our lives. "Prayer is internalized to the extent that we become aware of him 'to whom we speak'" (CCC 2704). "Where does prayer come from? Whether prayer is expressed in words or gestures, it is the whole man who prays. But in naming the source of prayer, Scripture speaks sometimes of the soul or the spirit, but most often of the heart (more than a thousand times). According to Scripture, it is the heart that prays. If our heart is far from God, the words of prayer are in vain" (CCC 2562).

Bringing our secular life into our prayer has a way of properly relativizing the importance of our everyday activities. It is easy to make a tempest in a teapot, but when we bring those tempests before God's love, they have a way of dissipating and we are able to see more clearly.

A man named Jack had worked at a prison until he had a stroke. The stroke caused him to face his mortality and also prevented him from maintaining his job at the prison. He sought out spiritual direction because he felt the Lord was asking more of him. Sometimes his limitations seemed insurmountable and he could be tempted to think his life was over. His spiritual director repeatedly asked him what happened when he brought these fears before God in prayer. Although at first he struggled to do that, eventually he was able to find confidence in God's love for him and confidence that God still had a plan for his life. As he began to experience God's love in prayer, he became open to new possibilities. In particular, it occurred to him that he could return to the prison as a volunteer and lead Bible studies and other spiritual ministries. His familiarity with the prison and the system gave him a lot of insight that was extremely helpful for the prisoners. He found that he was able to assist them in undergoing a deeper conversion and that helped him also undergo a deeper conversion. From a place of profound uncertainty, he had developed much trust in God and undergone many important changes in his life.

We can bring daily life into our interior life by bringing it into private prayer. In doing so, we start to see what we really believe about God. The way I relate to God when I am alone, in prayer, in silence, may be different than the Creed I profess and the prayers I say. Recognizing this and sharing it in spiritual direction presents a tremendous opportunity for some correction to take place. When I see behavior that is not congruous with my beliefs, then prayer and spiritual direction can bring harmony between belief and behavior. The things we are most unsure of may be the things we were taught when we were young and we have not understood how they correspond with the experience of life. In other cases, our failure to live out our beliefs may result in rationalization or dismissal of our childhood faith. Harmonizing belief and behavior is a massive task in adolescence as we take responsibility for what we believe and the choices we make. However, there are many things that can only be worked out as life advances.

When we are totally honest with ourselves, we view God differently from how we pretend we do. That may not even become apparent, however, until we reflect on and talk about our beliefs. In spiritual direction, the director listens carefully and may point out incongruities we did not recognize. This process of sharing and having someone reflect back what we are saying can help us to get a better grasp on what we truly believe.

In this book, we are discussing spiritual direction in the Christian context where the director and directee share a common heritage of belief. This common heritage allows them to presume a lot. However, it is important for the director to see whether the directee's conscience is well formed or whether there may be distortions about the faith and about God that need to be adjusted. By working with the interior world of the directee, the spiritual director has the opportunity to help the directee make fundamental changes in his beliefs so that not only his beliefs, but also his actions, in all the spheres of his life, can correspond more perfectly with the teaching entrusted by Jesus to His Church. The spiritual director can guide the directee through prayer, study, and practices of the Christian life to harmonize the various areas of his interior and to bring them into a single whole around a relationship with a person, Jesus Christ, who is the Truth.

Spiritual direction is a safe place to grapple with areas in which the directee may not have been well formed in the faith or in which the wounds of the past may interfere with and distort his vision of God. For example, a directee may believe that God is merciful but struggle in applying that mercy to himself. The directee may read about God in the Scriptures, but what he reads does not sink in. The directee may be confused about the moral teachings of the Church or wonder how they connect with the God he learns about in the Scriptures. These are all areas where a spiritual director can help a directee to work through disparate concepts and teachings about God. A spiritual director can help to integrate all of that into the directee's decisions and actions and especially show how to allow those teachings to unfold in the directee's interior life.

A young seminarian named Ted could have given the right answers on an exam about God's mercy, but struggled to apply that mercy to his own life. He would not have even articulated the contradiction, however. The way it manifested itself in spiritual direction is that he always refused the invitation offered by his spiritual director, who was a priest, to go to Confession. He simply stated that he had already been to Confession recently. After several months in spiritual direction, he finally declared, "I guess I am going to have to talk about this sooner or later." That declaration is music to the ears of a spiritual director, even though it will always make him feel his own poverty, not knowing how he will be able to respond to this new, deeper plunge into vulnerability.

Ted proceeded to talk about his struggles with pornography and masturbation. As is often the case, just talking about it provided Ted with tremendous relief. There are no quick solutions or easy answers, but Ted was able to open up a new area of his life and take a step forward in trusting God and in trusting his spiritual director. The mercy and understanding he received from his spiritual director helped him to believe in the mercy of God as well. He probably needed those first months to build up enough trust in his spiritual director to open up this shameful self-revelation. There is no reason to be ashamed of struggling to be more vulnerable. At the same time, if a spiritual directee knows that he is holding something back, it can slow down the whole process of spiritual direction and so it is of the utmost importance to build trust between director and directee. It is worth noting here that such experiences should be received by the spiritual director from a place of poverty, in which he knows that he is poor, weak, sinful, and profoundly loved and held by God's mercy. If a spiritual director is not aware of those parts of himself he needs to do some work in his own process of spiritual direction before moving forward too much in meeting with others.

Spiritual direction should help a directee to live his whole life in the presence of God and to become more vulnerable to God in that relationship. The Catechism asserts that the life of prayer consists in living always in the presence of God, as made possible by our Baptism, "Thus, the life of prayer is the habit of being in the presence of the thrice-holy God and in communion with him. This communion of life is always possible because, through Baptism, we have already been united with Christ" (CCC 2565). The Catechism elaborates further on how radically dependent we must become on God, letting Him guide our hearts at every moment: "Prayer is the life of the new heart. It ought to animate us at every moment. But we tend to forget him who is our life and our all. This is why the Fathers of the spiritual life in the deuteronomic and prophetic traditions insist that prayer is a remembrance of God often awakened by the memory of the heart: 'We must remember God more often than we draw breath'" (CCC 2697).

The Christian life is not merely a matter of knowing about God by talking, thinking, and reading about God. The Christian life consists of an encounter with God and a personal relationship with Him. As our relationship with God develops, it flows into and even transforms every area of our interior world of thoughts and feelings as well as the exterior world of how we present ourselves to others—the things that we say and the decisions that we make.

Letting our relationship with God flow into and direct every area of our lives is a process that continues to unfold over a lifetime. "As God gradually reveals himself and reveals man to himself, prayer appears as a reciprocal call, a covenant drama. Through words and actions, this drama engages the heart. It unfolds throughout the whole history of salvation" (CCC 2566). This is why the first call of Jesus, "Repent, and believe in the gospel" (Mk 1:15), is repeated again and again each Ash Wednesday, throughout the Lenten season, and throughout our lives. There is a lifelong need for ongoing conversion. This is true for everyone.

The process of transformation in Christ unfolds naturally as we live out our relationship with God. In fact, God is more intent on this process than we are. He wants us to enjoy the blessing of His continual presence, love, and support in our lives. We are more receptive to His loving initiative as we open our hearts in greater trust and vulnerability. By being vulnerable with Him in our prayer, in spiritual direction, as we read Scripture and attend the Mass, and as we take in the teachings of the Church, we will be more supple in His Hands.

Exploring the Interior

Exploring the interior life of the directee requires vulnerability on the part of the directee (a dynamic explored more thoroughly in Chapter 3) and a prayerful, empathetic listening we call "vulnerable attentiveness" on the part of the director (we explore this more fully in Chapter 4). The director must listen in such a way that he seeks to enter into the interior world of the directee and the directee must trust him enough to allow him in.

Everything in the life of the directee is important. Over time the spiritual director discovers many things about the directee's interior life, namely how the directee sees the world, others, himself, and God. The spiritual director has the opportunity to notice and gently identify incongruities. While providing hope and love by always reminding the directee of the presence of and merciful love of Jesus, the spiritual director will see many challenges resolved simply in the process of letting the directee share them and leaving the directee room to work out the incongruities.

Basic Pattern of Direction

We will explore in detail later the process of listening and communicating that will help a directee become more vulnerable and better able to see and share his interior life. We give a brief overview here, however, of a basic process that can facilitate exploring interiority.

First, the director should provide the directee with a safe space in order to see what the directee can discover and share on his own about his interior life. Second, the director can point things out and then carefully observe how that direction is received. Even when pointing something out, the director will do best to let the directee himself discover as much as possible. Third, it is important to know that everything cannot be worked out in the spiritual direction meeting and the director should encourage the directee to take points of reflection into prayer. Lastly, some action is advisable whenever it is possible to provide some concrete steps that can be taken by the directee.

For example, it may become evident in spiritual direction that a directee only speaks to God in rote, memorized prayers. The best case would be if a person figures this out on his own and is able to raise that point in direction. For example, the director might ask about his prayer life and get the response, "I just pray a novena to St. Joseph and a Rosary and the Divine Mercy Chaplet, but it seems like the saints in the movies are able to talk with God in their own words. How do people just talk to God like that?"

The second step would be for the director simply to point out, "It sounds like your prayer time consists primarily in reciting prayers. Is that right?" This leaves a lot of space for the directee to decide how to proceed. The directee might ask then, "How else am I supposed to pray?" Or he might bring up the problem himself, "I have always wondered how I could speak more personally with God." He might even refer to a particular incident, "One time I was on retreat in adoration and it was like God was speaking to me and I was speaking to Him." Such a revelation from the directee provides a great opportunity to invite him to explore this further by asking him to share more about that experience.

The third step is to encourage the directee to take these points to prayer and speak with God about them. He could start with the words of the Apostles, "Lord, teach us to pray" (Lk 11:1). He could reflect on whether he has ever experienced a more personal encounter with God. The next spiritual direction meeting will likely involve exploring how it went when the directee tried to pray in this new way. Some persons will do it easily and just begin talking to God like they talk to a friend or like they talk to the spiritual director. Other persons will be stymied by this. They will need examples. They might need to be encouraged into imagining God as a friend or they will need to look to a crucifix or a statue or icon while praying. Likewise, it is important for a person to find time to listen in the quiet of their hearts for God's response to their prayers, particularly their more spontaneous prayers. Some persons will return after receiving this recommendation and will readily understand the patience required to continue returning to silence from any distractions that may occur. Some will be discouraged because they did not hear anything and complain that they did not know what they were supposed to be listening for. A spiritual director has to observe, in cases like these, how well a person is able to follow such directions. Some people are very literal and it can be helpful to explain to them that God does not always speak in words that we can hear. Sometimes God speaks to us in words that come to us in our own thoughts, but which we somehow know are coming from beyond ourselves. The words attributed to St. Francis to justify remaining silent in the proclamation of our faith can also be turned around to describe the silence of God—God speaks always, but only uses words when necessary.

When the point of exploration is something other than prayer, a fourth step is to ask a directee to take up a concrete action. A directee might be encouraged to make a work of mercy, or to complete an assignment, or to reach out to a particular individual from whom he has been estranged. He might be asked to reflect on a particular Scripture passage or to make several journal entries. These concrete actions can become part of the discussion for the next meeting of spiritual direction. The director is always looking to see whether the directee follows through and then gently explores what happened or why the directee did not follow through.

We are describing an iterative process that proceeds step by step with the directee leading, moving back and forth between directee and director, and also being brought to prayer and deeper reflection between meetings. In this way, the spiritual direction goes ever deeper into the directee's heart. The director always lets the directee first explore his own interior life through his sharing in spiritual direction. In response, the director makes observations and asks questions. The directee may explore his interior life further in direction or take the questions and observations to prayer and some concrete actions that can be taken up in subsequent meetings. An important part of this process is that the spiritual director is very patient and gentle. The spiritual director must be watching and listening for the movement of the Holy Spirit and leave plenty of space for the directee to move at his own pace.

Cultivating Interiority

In summary, interiority is the key to spiritual direction. Spiritual direction explores the interior life of the directee. It is in the interior of a person that the one-on-one relationship with God develops. The interior life is mysterious and complex, a multi-faceted reality that can even be internally contradictory. Wounds in the interior life can distort a person's view of reality, including himself, others, and God. In addition to being distorted by wounds, the interior life can simply be insufficiently examined or developed in the directee. Because our culture does not foster interiority, there are many people who live unexamined lives. Delving into the interior life can be awkward or intimidating for some people. For others it may be a welcome change of pace and even an adventure. In either case, it will require vulnerability, and the spiritual director must be very gentle and patient, always maintaining reverence for the directee's free will in order to develop trust and allow the process to unfold in the Lord's time.

3

Vulnerability

I N JESUS, God has shown us that divine power, God's very
omnipotence, is manifested in infinite vulnerability. From the
first moment of His human existence, in the womb of Mary, Jesus
shows us that God dwells in vulnerability. Jesus moves from the
helplessness of being in the womb to the helplessness of being
in swaddling clothes in Mary's arms. He is exposed to hunger,
cold, violence, and hateful threats. He cannot defend Himself or
provide for Himself. He is radically vulnerable to the harshness
of the world and the sinfulness of man. Jesus teaches again and
again, by His actions and by His words, that to be childlike is to
be Godlike (Lk 2:12). The Kingdom of Heaven belongs to little
children (Mt 18:3–4). Little children, in their vulnerability, are the
ones who understand best the wisdom of God (Mt 11:25). At the
same time, those who exploit the vulnerability of children receive
the most severe curse: "it would be better for him to have a great
millstone fastened round his neck and to be drowned in the depth
of the sea" (Mt 18:6).

Vulnerability radiates the beauty of God Himself. The vulnerable human heart is the most beautiful thing there is. When a big,
hulking man starts to cry; or when a strong, successful businessman awkwardly communicates tender love to his wife; when a
little child looks with big, hungry eyes at one who can feed her;
or a little boy bursts into song, it pierces our cynicism and reaches
our hearts. It is so beautiful when people who are powerful in

this world—whether a military general, or a nation's president, or a CEO of a large corporation—humbly kneel before God with folded hands and pray.

Spiritual direction can open us to the beauty of vulnerability and help us to start thinking and acting in a more Godlike way. A natural development in spiritual direction is for the director to be thought of, and even referred to, as a father or mother. The dynamic of spiritual direction provides a safe setting for childlike vulnerability to emerge. This brings out the most beautiful things for both the director and the directee to see and cherish.

Interiority: A Journey of Vulnerability

The journey of deepening interiority is a journey of vulnerability. In the depths of our interiority, we come face to face with the Truth. This includes the truth of our identity—who we are uniquely—and of the meaning of our lives. These truths define the value of our person. Consequently, they are extremely sensitive. When rejection and distortion enter into that realm, it is damaging and painful. Every person knows the pain of wounds that have been inflicted when we let someone into those intimate places and they did not have sufficient reverence for what they encountered in us. This pain may be caused intentionally or unintentionally, but it hurts in a deep and lasting way all the same. Many times, such wounds are inflicted at a young age when we are naturally more exposed. Because we are inherently disposed to trust, and because we do not have sufficient capacity to discern whom to trust nor sufficient context and knowledge, we can easily take in lies and experience some abuse of our trust. This can be the experience of a small child who overhears his parents talking about him being worthless because he did badly in school and so a lie enters into that sacred interior place and he begins to associate personal value with academic performance. This can be the experience of a five-year-old girl who innocently and joyfully tries to share her latest artwork with her father who, in his frustrations over work, dismisses her and unintentionally leaves a wound of rejection.

How do we find the vulnerable areas within us? The unfinished parts in us are vulnerable and they can be found by reflecting on our weaknesses, our failures, and our sins. We also find unfinished parts in our actions, which look ugly to us, or in our reactions, which we are afraid will make us unlovable. Our hopes and dreams, our memory and imagination, our feelings, our experiences of God, and the words we hear in prayer are all areas of our interior life which are naturally hidden from others. Exposing these interior places is very vulnerable. Also vulnerable are the places where we have been hurt before and remain tender.

When we open our interior to someone, which is the basis of all intimacy, we can be wounded by their response. From the Latin *vulnus*, which means "wound," we derive the word vulnerability, meaning "wound-ability." Becoming more intimate goes hand in hand with greater vulnerability. There is a risk of being wounded. At the same time, with intimacy and vulnerability, there can also be significant healing that takes place. When we can see and expose those intimate, vulnerable places in us and receive love there, we are affirmed at the deep level of the goodness of our person and the value of our lives. When we can experience intimacy with and affirmation from a person, it helps us also to experience a deeper intimacy with and affirmation from God.

We see in the Gospel the reverence that God has for our freedom and the way He values the vulnerability of those who expose their wounded bodies and hearts to Him. For example, Jesus invites the man with the withered hand first to come before everyone and then to take another step of vulnerability, "Stretch out your hand" (see Mk 3:1–6). The next verse seems to imply that it is this act of vulnerability itself that caused or at least allowed his healing—"He stretched it out, and his hand was restored" (Mk 3:5). Similarly, healing comes to the man at the Pool of Bethzatha in his willingness to get up and begin to walk (Jn 5:1–9). The blind beggar at the Beautiful Gate of the temple finds healing in taking the risk of responding to the call of Peter: "in the name of Jesus Christ of Nazareth, walk" (Acts 3:1–10). Before he heals the blind Bartimaeus, Jesus elicits the beggar's vulnerable, interior desire in asking, "What do you want me to do for you?" (Mk 10:46–52).

Spiritual direction is a privileged context for exploring the interior of the directee, because the relationship with God is explicit in spiritual direction and our relationship with Him is the deepest part of us. This requires much vulnerability and thus fosters much intimacy between director and directee. Such vulnerability and intimacy have the power to bring healing and to help God's love reach the deepest places in the directee. Furthermore, vulnerability always moves toward totality in opening up the full depths of the person. As stated previously, it is not uncommon for spiritual directors eventually to hear those cherished words, "I have never shared this with anyone." Note that this intimacy creates a bond between the director and the directee that can be very intense and requires some care and attention so that proper boundaries are maintained.

In short, a directee should share everything with his spiritual director. This wisdom goes back to the Desert Fathers and has been repeated throughout the ages. St. Benedict directed his monks in that way, and St. Ignatius reiterated this principle in Rule 13 of the First Week rules for discernment of spirits.[1] St. Francis de Sales, St. John of the Cross, and other masters of the spiritual life agreed on this point. At the same time, the level of vulnerability required for full disclosure is not normally a psychologically safe starting point and is rather something to grow into as trust develops organically between directee and director.

---

[1] For example, see St. Benedict, *RB 1980: The Rule of St. Benedict in English*, ed. Timothy Fry (Collegeville, MN: The Liturgical Press, 1982), chap. 7, v. 44; St. Ignatius, *Spiritual Exercises*, no. 326.

The Vulnerability of the Director

Spiritual direction is not a relationship of equality or mutuality like friendship or marriage. The focus of spiritual direction is always on the interior of the directee. The directee is the one who shares intimately, while the spiritual director is in a position of listening and receiving. At the same time, *the quality of the spiritual director's listening must still be vulnerable.* The director's loving attention and reverence for the interior of the directee must be such that the directee feels truly heard and loved. This will only happen from a posture of vulnerability and genuine compassion, to the point that the director allows his heart to be moved, even pierced, by the vulnerable sharing of the directee. Vulnerability elicits vulnerability. This kind of vulnerability on the part of the spiritual director helps him to enter into the directee's world and bring the grace of God there and the Holy Spirit's gifts of wisdom and counsel. Such vulnerability is never burdensome. This can be seen as a mystical participation in the Incarnation—the way Jesus entered into our world and our individual human conditions.

One way to illustrate this is through an experience that was shared in spiritual direction. One woman shared a memory from when she was a little girl. She had done something wrong and felt so guilty and afraid that she hid under her bed. She hid so well that her parents had a hard time finding her. When her father finally found her, he was understandably upset and called her to come out from under the bed and reprimanded her. His reproach piled more shame on the shame and fear that she already had. The spiritual director takes a different approach. He humbles himself and becomes little and vulnerable and waits for an invitation to enter into the hiding place with the directee. If the spiritual director remains vulnerable by being unarmed—both unintimidating and safe—he can draw close to the most vulnerable places in the directee, right into the directee's hiding places.

This is the image that Jesus gives us in His own wounds. His wounds are truly our wounds. He has been pierced with our wounds in the very same places in which we have been pierced.

"It was our pain that he bore, our sufferings he endured. . . . he was pierced for our sins, crushed for our iniquity" (Is 53:4–5).[2] "He himself bore our sins in his body upon the cross . . . " (1 Pet 2:24).[3] Jesus' free choice to bear our wounds and to be pierced by our sins was God's way of bringing love into those most intimate places in us. He enters into the hiding place of Adam, sharing the pain, and bringing everlasting, unconditional love. This experience transforms us: "By his wounds we were healed" (Is 53:6,[4] cf. 1 Pet 2:24). The spiritual director shares in this healing ministry of Jesus by entering into the interior of the directee, at the directee's invitation, and sharing the pain through genuine compassion, and bringing the love of God. The director does not do this in the same radical way as Jesus did, but by listening vulnerably he becomes a face and a voice for Jesus' healing love in the heart of the directee.

In the example of the young woman given above, the spiritual director was able to facilitate a process of healing in the directee. That experience of hiding from her parents out of shame and then being found and reprimanded had inflicted a wound that was coupled with the lie that when she does something wrong, she is bad. Furthermore, she had an unspoken vow to never do anything wrong. This turned into a pattern of perfectionism. When she was able to share her fear and shame as a little girl with her spiritual director, she was able to experience something new in that part of her. Her spiritual director, unlike her father, responded with mercy, tenderness, and compassion, and she was able to live that memory in a different way. That started a process of healing that had wide-ranging ramifications in her life.

All vulnerability leads to participation, in a unique way, in the Cross of Jesus. The wounds of Jesus are the signs of vulnerability that He shows to the Apostles. In the Upper Room, on the third day, they recognize Him by His wounds. Note that, except for

---

[2] NABRE.
[3] NABRE.
[4] NABRE.

John, they never previously saw the wounds of His pierced hands, feet, and side, because the Apostles were not present at His crucifixion. But they identified Him by those wounds because they represented the totality of His love.

When Thomas cried out, "My Lord and my God!" (Jn 20:28), he recognized Jesus as Lord and God because he recognized his own wounds, of which his doubt was a symptom, taken up and transformed in the glorified wounds of Jesus. The vulnerability of Jesus is prominently evident in His glorified body, and it was thus that they "saw" Him.

That same total love was then expressed in the way He approached them after their betrayal. Without a word of accusation or condemnation, He greeted them with peace, saying, "Peace be with you," and extended to them the gift of forgiveness: "If you forgive the sins of any, they are forgiven" (Jn 20:23). This is the model for the spiritual director, who will hear vulnerable admissions of guilt and shame from directees, but who must always respond with the crucified love of Jesus—full of mercy, peace, and forgiveness. When the spiritual director is a priest, it is quite fruitful for this to take the form of sacramental Confession. It can be particularly helpful to end each session by enfolding the exposed parts of the directee into the merciful embrace of God, as that embrace is communicated through the Sacrament of Confession.

As the spiritual director enters more fully and vulnerably into the role of Jesus, he shares more personally and intimately in the crucified love of Jesus, who weeps with those who weep and rejoices with those who rejoice (Rom 12:15). The spiritual director will also discover sentiments of love filling his own heart and the mercy of God being expressed through him. The sentiments of God, as expressed in the prophets—"My heart recoils within me, my compassion grows warm and tender" (Hos 11:8)—become the sentiments of the spiritual director as well. This free gift of mercy, expressed through spiritual direction, can be a profound source of healing. Our sins and failures are some of the most intimate places in us, where we can experience profound shame. We can often expend a great deal of energy in hiding them. When we have the courage to uncover them and receive the free gift of God's mercy, it is a profoundly healing and freeing experience. The spiritual director is a privileged communicator of divine mercy, because he represents God in a special way and is privileged to see those places in the directee that are often hidden out of fear and shame.

Also related to the spiritual director's vulnerability is the fact that he is fallible and will make mistakes. Spiritual directors can be tired at times and have bad days. Sometimes those weaknesses are evident and, though a spiritual director should not dramatize or draw attention to those weaknesses in a way that distracts the attention from the directee, it may sometimes be a valuable example for the spiritual director to take ownership of his weaknesses. Often the spiritual director can be held in such high esteem by the directee and can create the impression that he has all the answers or even reads the soul of the directee. The spiritual director may be tempted to foster or validate these illusions, but he is better served by quietly dispelling these illusions and humbly admitting at times that he is not sure what direction to take or not sure if his guidance is on the mark. This is not a "technique" but should rise up naturally from a spiritual director's self-awareness. It may be that the humble admission of weakness—when a spiritual director starts to doze off, or forgets an important part of the directee's sharing—can be precisely what is needed to help the directee become more vulnerable as well.

We will continue to elaborate on this process of prayerful, vulnerable listening and responding with God's merciful love in subsequent chapters.

A Process That Requires Patience

God always reverences our freedom and, like we see in the Annunciation, He always awaits our permission before incorporating us into His plan of salvation. He also chooses to work through human mediation, because part of His ultimate goal is that "they may all be one" (Jn 17:21). For this reason, God typically brings about healing and transformation in a way that is slow and requires patience. He moves at our pace. Vulnerability does not develop instantly, but it requires time to discover and open up the depths of our hearts. It takes time to respond to God's call to Adam, "Where are you?" (Gen 3:9). This is true both in spiritual direction and in prayer. We learn to trust, over time, that the intimate places in our hearts will not be rejected and further wounded, but will be accepted and cherished with love.

God does not act contrary to our human nature, but shows tremendous reverence for our human nature by building on it and perfecting it with His grace.[5] He works with our human psychology and personality and is patient with our natural hesitation to trust. He does not undermine or subvert natural human processes by zapping us with grace, but is ready to pour His healing into our hearts as we develop the courage to open up those places to Him. Grace builds on nature. His grace purifies, perfects, and elevates our nature, rather than destroying it or ignoring it or simply substituting something else for it.[6]

For example, one young man named Steven, who was very active in the Church, was held back by struggles with his identity, including questions about his sexuality. Over several years, the continual affirmation of his spiritual director reinforced his dedicated life of prayer and helped him to set aside those issues. They were not completely resolved, but they were no longer hindering the free and generous offering of his other gifts. He had some behaviors that were exaggerated as a result of his identity struggles. He had a propensity to be overly fashionable and had a desperate need to be liked and affirmed that led him to be

---

[5] ST I, q. 1, a. 8.

[6] See CCC 1839: "The moral virtues grow through education, deliberate acts, and perseverance in struggle. Divine grace purifies and elevates them." See also Pope Francis, Homily on the Occasion of the Closing Mass for the Sixth Asian Youth Day (August 17, 2014): "As Asians too, you see and love, from within, all that is beautiful, noble and true in your cultures and traditions. Yet as Christians, you also know that the Gospel has the power to purify, elevate and perfect this heritage" (https://w2.vatican.va/content/francesco/en/homilies/2014/documents/papa-francesco_20140817_corea-omelia-gioventu-asiatica.html).

the center of attention. He also had some very beautiful, sensitive qualities and a capacity for developing deep and committed friendships, but those qualities were overshadowed by the attention-seeking behaviors. Through the process of healing, his natural gifts were freed and empowered through grace as his anxiety gave way to greater confidence in God's love for him.

Patience is never easy. The director's patience with the directee and the directee's patience with himself and the whole process of growing and healing simply takes time. Pope Benedict XVI observed how God's patience makes us impatient, but that we should give thanks that He is patient: "We suffer on account of God's patience. And yet, we need his patience. God, who became a lamb, tells us that the world is saved by the Crucified One, not by those who crucified him. The world is redeemed by the patience of God. It is destroyed by the impatience of man."[7] Spiritual direction trains us in the practice of God's patience and we learn to stand in awe as we see the power of His redemption gradually unfold.

This is illustrated in the etymology of the word patience itself. The word patience comes from the Latin verb *patior*, which means to suffer or lie open (be vulnerable), and from which we derive the words passion, passive, and suffering. Patience implies that we are being acted upon. Spiritual direction ultimately helps us place ourselves before God to allow His grace to act upon us.

Because the process can be slow, it may sometimes seem that nothing is happening. Thus, it can help for the spiritual director periodically to take the opportunity to reflect back to the directee the progress that has been made. Likewise, it can be helpful to invite the directee to self-reflection, so that he may see the progress that has been made. Taking time for reflection and thanksgiving is an important way to consolidate the process of growth and healing.

---

[7] Pope Benedict XVI, Homily at the Mass for the Beginning of the Petrine Ministry of the Bishop of Rome (April 24, 2005), https://w2.vatican.va/content/benedict-xvi/en/homilies/2005/documents/hf_ben-xvi_hom_20050424_inizio-pontificato.html.

What Makes for Vulnerable Sharing?

Some of the most painful questions that can plague us in quiet moments are, "Does my life matter?" "Does this experience have any meaning?" "Will this relationship ever get better?" "Will I ever be happy?" "Does anybody love me?" These questions tie into the two foundational elements of our personhood, namely identity and mission. "Who am I?" "Why am I here?" "Where am I going?" These dimensions of our person are more important than everything else.

Unfinished

Every human being is a work in progress. Every one of us is unfinished. Even Jesus, in His humanity, grew "in wisdom and in stature, and in favor with God and man" (Lk 2:52). Human beings are always becoming. This fact is most obvious in little children, and one of the most refreshing aspects of children is their humble acceptance of their limitations. They know they are a work in progress. As adults, however, we get the idea that we ought to be finished products already.

For example, a man may still struggle with procrastination at age fifty. He is embarrassed that he has had trouble with this problem since he was a teenager. Out of fear of being unfinished in that area, however, he may try to cover it up or justify it or even deny that it is a problem in his life. A thirty-year-old woman may be afraid of being in a crowd, just as she was when she was ten. Instead of admitting that she has this limitation, however, she covers up her anxiety by eating and makes excuses for why she cannot go to social gatherings. A forty-five-year-old woman might be embarrassed as she triple-checks everything she does because she is afraid of failure and irrationally fears her kind and loving boss. A religious sister of many years might find herself struggling in her relationship with God and second-guessing her decision to enter a convent. A very successful and well-loved priest may get overwhelmed with the responsibilities in a new parish and start coping with his fears in embarrassing ways.

As adults, we have a tendency never to allow for limitations in our lives. The discovery that we have unfinished parts tends to scare us. These may be parts that got stuck and stuffed away through some painful experience in our past. They may be parts that never had the chance to develop for lack of opportunity, as in the case of a little girl who lost her mother and consequently lost her childhood because she had to take on adult responsibilities. They may be parts that developed in a friendly environment but are now exposed to hostility for the first time or in a more prolonged way. We may find ourselves confronting fundamental questions for the first time, or on the verge of failing for the first time in our adult lives. Whatever the situation, it always requires vulnerability to expose the parts of our lives that are unfinished.

The Fear of Being Unfinished

Why do we get scared about our unfinished parts? We tend to measure the value of our lives by how finished we are. We are afraid that it is precisely the unfinished parts of our lives that define us, and then at the deepest level we fear that our lives are less valuable than others'. It also makes us fear what we might become as those parts develop. As a result, we hide the parts that are unfinished, and we avoid activities and interactions that would expose those parts.

We often start to form the idea at a young age that being perfect is synonymous with being lovable. For example, one little girl, Jill, who was the youngest of five children, experienced a strong inner drive to make things perfect for her mother. Her parents had hit hard times financially and her mother had to go back to work. Jill found that if she did the chores, cleaned the house, and had everything in order when her mother got home from work, her mother was more cheerful and affirming. When things were a mess, however, Jill experienced her mother's disdain and impatience. Jill's sensitivity to her mother's moods left her little room for being unfinished. Any mistakes she made were costly. It was too painful for her not to receive her mother's affection and attention. As she grew up, she subconsciously transferred this on to her relationship with God. She had a constant drive to please God by leaving no loose ends and nothing overlooked. The price of being a work in progress was too high and she was very demanding of herself. Through spiritual direction she came to see this dynamic, and although it required frequent reminders from her spiritual director, she was eventually able to be more open to God's mercy, allowing Him to look with loving patience on her shortcomings and limitations.

Spiritual direction thrives on the vulnerability that comes from exposing the unfinished parts of ourselves to the spiritual director. The spiritual director is in a privileged position to reverence and affirm the unfinished parts that are revealed by the directee. The spiritual director may also be able to offer some wisdom to help the directee develop certain parts of himself. Above all, the director should love the directee right in the midst of where he is unfinished and reassure him that God loves him there even more. Just as a mother does not disdain the helplessness of her baby, but holds him even more gently and tenderly, so the director will always be most helpful by tenderly handling and spiritually holding the unfinished parts in the directee.

The areas of greatest vulnerability in the human heart are tied to our identity and destiny. Those two realities are always played out through relationships, most especially our relationship with God through prayer and our relationships with others through work or ministry or service. Furthermore, because we cannot enter into relationships except in a bodily way and our bodies are male or female, sexuality always enters in at some level. The major things that threaten our identity and destiny are also vulnerable—namely suffering, guilt, and death. These are all good areas to explore if the directee is unsure of what to share in spiritual direction: prayer, relationships, ministry, sexuality, suffering, guilt, and death.

One man, Robert, came to spiritual direction feeling very inadequate and unfinished in his masculine identity. He could not articulate these feelings at the beginning of spiritual direction, but they emerged over several meetings. The spiritual director played an important role in naming the dynamic that was playing out, the unfinished part in the man's life: "It sounds like you are struggling with not feeling like you are 'man enough.'" Being able to express his feeling and fear of diminished masculinity helped Robert be able to place that part of his life before the Heavenly Father and feel loved, even as a work in progress. It helped him to focus on that part of his life as well. Instead of wasting all his energy on hating himself for his inadequate masculinity, he was able to redirect that energy to growing in his masculinity.

Robert had come to spiritual direction because some things were coming unhinged in his life. He had always been quiet and reserved, simply going along with the stronger personalities that were around him. Over time, however, he became resentful and developed a stubborn, recalcitrant attitude that started to emerge in passive aggressive behaviors that caused problems in his relationships. He baited people to make them angry and got under their skin. He did not like this in himself and it turned inward in addictive behaviors as he buried his problems in alcohol.

In spiritual direction, the director learned that Robert had grown up on a farm and had a very loving father and mother, but then he burst into tears and revealed, "My father gave us everything, but I didn't want everything. I wanted him to give us himself." As he realized this dynamic, he became more compassionate toward himself and learned to accept himself. He was able to forgive his father, who was a very good man but was simply not the father Robert needed him to be. This opened up his relationship with God the Father and his spiritual life moved to a new level. This developed in tandem with receiving fatherly love from his spiritual director.

As they started spiritual direction, the director had a sense that Robert did not have a very high opinion of himself. The spiritual director learned this as he affirmed some of Robert's childlike qualities and sensed that Robert was unfamiliar and a little uncomfortable with the affirmation. As Robert became more confident, it helped him to face his deficits and to accept them. By listening and noting Robert's good qualities, the spiritual director was able to recognize and affirm those qualities, and Robert came to value those qualities as well and gained more self-confidence. That self-confidence helped Robert admit some of his deficits and also gave him the courage and patience to work on those deficits in prayer and spiritual direction.

Identity and Destiny

In gaining the courage to look at and share the vulnerable, unfinished parts in us, Christian theology offers two critical reassurances to dispel our fears. The first is that we are not defined by our unfinished parts. At the deepest place in us is the *imago Dei*, the image of God. Furthermore, through the Sacrament of Baptism, we are brought into a relationship with God that is even deeper, leaving a mark on our very being and changing us in a way that can never be removed. This defines our *identity*. In particular, through Baptism, we become beloved children of the eternal Father. "You have received the spirit of sonship. When we cry, 'Abba! Father!' it is the Spirit himself bearing witness with our spirit that we are children of God" (Rom 8:15–16). This love relationship with God is unconditional and infinite: "I am with you always" (Mt 28:20). "If we are faithless, he remains faithful— for he cannot deny himself" (2 Tim 2:13). And so, no matter how much of a person is unfinished, the most important part is finished—our foundational and indestructible identity as beloved children of God. We have been taken into God's own heart and He always holds a sacred place for us there.

The other critical reassurance that Christian faith provides is in what we are becoming: our *destiny*. Fear arises when we look at our unfinished parts and wonder what will become of all this. Perhaps we look at others and make judgments about the quality of their lives and we fear that we may disintegrate into people like them—failures, criminals, the poor, addicts, or others whom society deems "losers." We might try to convince ourselves that by keeping our unfinished parts hidden, or under control, stuffed away and safely separated from our daily functioning, we can prevent this potential for falling apart. In the face of such fears, we do well to remember that God has made each one of us to be saints. St. Paul sees this call to holiness as a consequence of our identity, of having a spirit of adoption: "It is the Spirit himself bearing witness with our spirit that we are children of God, and if children, then heirs, heirs of God and fellow heirs with Christ" (Rom 8:16–17). We are made to inherit the Kingdom. No matter how unfinished we may seem to be, each one of us is made to be a saint. "For this is the will of God, your sanctification" (1 Thess 4:3). We are made to be holy and called by Jesus, to love one another: "A new commandment I give to you, that you love one another; even as I have loved you, that you also love one another" (Jn 13:34). Each person is called toward that summit in different ways, through particular vocations and with unique challenges at each step of the journey, but the intended destination is the same for everyone.

The Christian truths about everyone's identity and destiny can be a profound help in spiritual direction. To revisit the example of Robert given above, the spiritual director could affirm these fundamental truths in Robert's life. The spiritual director found particular qualities in Robert to affirm, but he could also say with confidence to Robert that he is a beloved son of the Eternal Father. Affirming that identity could give Robert some strength to face his deficits without fear that those deficits define him. He is, rather, defined by the Father's love for him. Likewise, those deficits might cause Robert some fear that he will never amount to anything or that they will diminish his whole life. To the contrary, the spiritual director can affirm that Robert is made to be a saint and God will give him everything he needs to become one. It is never too late and God will never settle for anything less than holiness and the happiness that goes along with it. This was beautifully taught by St. John Paul II when he spoke to the young people at World Youth Day in Toronto: "We are not the sum of our weaknesses and failures; we are the sum of the Father's love for us and our real capacity to become the image of his Son."[8]

In the end, love makes us like the beloved: "we know that when he appears we shall be like him, for we shall see him as he is" (1 Jn 3:2). This means that as we open our interior more and more to love, we are transformed from within to take on qualities of the beloved. This makes us more Christlike as we open our hearts to the Lord in prayer. If we are confident in God's intention and His power to achieve it (only with our cooperation, of course), our attitude flips from anxious concern over how unfinished we are to a hopeful excitement to see how God will make something beautiful out of this "mess" of our lives.

In the end, if we allow God's loving action to transform us, we will become uniquely what we were created to be. Every human life is unrepeatably unique. In our insecurity, we fear that we are broken when we are different. The most distinctive parts of us are the most vulnerable. But when we stand before God face to face, we will be completely at home and the most distinctive parts of us will be the ones that are most like God. Then we will see God in the mystery of the uniqueness of the life we have lived. We will be able to see our own paths and the paths of everyone else and how they all meet in God. Our lives are being directed by God towards a completeness, as St. Paul said, "I am sure that he who began a good work in you will bring it to completion at the day of Jesus Christ" (Phil 1:6).

Sharing Vulnerably

Spiritual direction requires vulnerability for it to be effective. If the directee only remains on the surface and does not share the more intimate parts of the heart, spiritual direction will remain shallow and lack the power of healing and transformation that it should normally have. For this reason, the directee will be well served if

---

[8] Pope St. John Paul II, Homily for the Closing of World Youth Day (July 28, 2002), https://w2.vatican.va/content/john-paul-ii/en/homilies/2002/documents/hf_jp-ii_hom_20020728_xvii-wyd.html.

he starts the spiritual direction session with the things he wants to avoid or that are most difficult to share (rather than leaving those things until the last five minutes of the meeting, which is not uncommon). The directee should avoid the temptation to simply report superficially on what is happening in his life.

If the directee chooses to report superficially, vulnerability can be facilitated by questions that lead to deeper areas of the heart, like: "How did that make you feel?" "How did you handle that struggle?" or, "What happened when you brought that to God in prayer?" The directee may be tempted to make excuses or offer only self-justification, but that is like sinful Adam remaining in his hiding place and only showing God the fig leaves rather than revealing what they were covering up. The directee needs to come out of hiding and be vulnerable. It is only in that way that healing and transformation can take place. The directee might try to focus on what everyone else has done, but gently the spiritual director should redirect the sharing to focus on what is happening in the directee. As one priest said before hearing the confessions of a large number of penitents, "It will help to move things along if you focus on confessing only *your own* sins."

One young man named Andy seemed regularly unprepared for spiritual direction. He was pleasant, but he made small talk and fished for things to bring up in meetings. His spiritual director initially thought he was not taking spiritual direction seriously and asked him to journal and bring notes to spiritual direction, but his request was unheeded. Andy often brought up topics that seemed inane and unrelated to spiritual direction. His spiritual director felt frustrated but was careful not to express that frustration. When he finally had a breakthrough, he was very grateful that he had not expressed his frustration. In one of their meetings as Andy talked about movies, his spiritual director's first impulse was to move on to a deeper topic, thinking this was a matter of small talk. He waited, however, and noted that Andy opened a door to a more interior reality, although he made the comment nonchalantly and somewhat jokingly: "People don't seem to like the movies that I choose." His spiritual director took that opening to ask a deeper question, "What is it about the movies that you like that other people do not seem to appreciate?" Andy replied, "I guess I like movies that are a little darker. The characters struggle with things. Sometimes with depression, sometimes with despair. I like to see that side of humanity." The director continued to probe: "Do you struggle with those things?" "Sometimes," Andy answered. Next, the director asked, "And do you feel alone in that?" To which Andy responded, "Definitely." As the spiritual director asked, "Can you share with me what that is like for you?" he opened the door for Andy to share struggles that he was afraid to share because he was afraid people would react to his darkness like they reacted to his choice of movies.

How do we find the vulnerable areas within us? The unfinished parts in us are vulnerable and they can be found by reflecting on our weaknesses, our failures, and our sins. Jesus taught us that rotten fruit comes from rotten trees (Lk 6:44). Our soul is like an orchard with a lot of different trees. When some rotten fruits emerge in our words and behaviors, we benefit if we find the tree and bring that to Jesus by bringing it to spiritual direction. Our hopes and dreams, our memories and imagination, our feelings, our experiences of God and the words we hear in prayer are all areas of our interior life which are naturally hidden from others. Exposing these interior places is very vulnerable. As a class exercise, seminarians were asked to write down what was happening in their interior lives at that moment. It was made clear that the sheets would *not* be collected. After a few minutes, the professor said, "Now share what you wrote with your neighbor." The professor quickly repealed the request, but waited just long enough so that the seminarians felt the vulnerability in that request. Just talking about an experience of abuse is very vulnerable. Talking about rejection or betrayal is very vulnerable. To protect ourselves, we often talk about those experiences with some strong expressions of anger or blame, but the hurt that lies underneath is the most important part to expose to Jesus' healing love.

Sometimes it can seem pointless to share one's interior experience, feelings, or prayer. However, when the directee has the courage to share vulnerably, many things happen in the sharing itself. In the very process of expressing one's feelings or experiences out loud, there can be new insight and profound healing that take place. It is not uncommon for the director to hear, "I am just realizing this as I am saying it." Likewise, simply by listening and loving, even without saying much, the director can lovingly receive the intimate experience of the directee in a way that brings about much healing. Something powerful happens simply through putting into words the intimate places in our hearts. We discover the power of self-expression, the power of the word, as expressed at the beginning of John's Gospel: "In the beginning was the Word, and the Word was with God, and the Word was God" (Jn 1:1). Through the Word, who is also the Son of God, God is able to express His entire Self, His deepest interior, "No one has ever seen God; the only-begotten Son, who is in the bosom of the Father, he has made him known" (Jn 1:18). In spiritual direction, the directee can discover that Godlike experience of deep self-revelation as well.

Jesus Heals Exposed Vulnerability

Throughout the Scriptures, Jesus heals those whose unfinished parts are exposed. He heals the lepers who draw His attention to their leprosy by crying out, "Jesus, Master, have mercy on us" (Lk 17:13). He heals Zacchaeus who stood there, exposed before the crowd, and who essentially admits his extortion and dishonest wealth even as he promises it as a gift to the Lord (Lk 19:8). He raises the son of the widow of Nain, who is exposed in her sorrow and moves Him with her pitiful tears (Lk 7:13). He heals the woman who was exposed in her adultery by forgiving her and expressing His belief that she could avoid sin in the future: "Neither do I condemn you; go, and do not sin again" (Jn 8:11).

When we are unfinished in our knowledge, we can hide our ignorance out of embarrassment. It is better to expose it. When the Apostles were willing to expose their ignorance, as when they asked, "Lord, teach us to pray" (Lk 11:1), they and we received the great gift of the Lord's Prayer and the invitation to call God our Father (Lk 11:2–4). The exposed ignorance of Nicodemus brought us a foundational teaching on Baptism and a clear, profound expression of God's great love for us: "For God so loved the world that He gave His only Son" (Jn 3:1–21).

Another unfinished part of us is tied up in doubt. When we vulnerably expose this doubt, the Lord can heal us with reassurances of His love. We have observed this in the experience of Thomas, who wanted to see the nail marks in Jesus' hands and the wound in His side. We see this in the two disciples on the Road to Emmaus, who were willing to share their doubts and disappointments with Jesus as they walked along the way. They were eventually healed as their eyes were opened through the vulnerable self-giving of Jesus in the breaking of the bread (Lk 24:30–32). The doubts of the Apostles, expressed by Philip—"Two hundred denarii would not buy enough bread for each of them to get a little" (Jn 6:7)—were healed through the great miracle of the multiplication of the loaves. But note that this only took place after they were made vulnerable by Jesus urging them, "You give them something to eat" (Mk 6:37). When they began to distribute the little they thought they had to the expectant, famished crowd, this miraculous multiplication became a sign for an even greater miracle—the Eucharist.

As mentioned earlier, our sexuality is a particularly vulnerable area of our lives. It is so private that we tend not to talk with anyone about it, but it is deeply intertwined with our identity and it is involved in all of our relationships. If there are distortions in our self-perception or struggles with sexual sin, it can be profoundly difficult, but profoundly healing, to open up that area of our lives. A spiritual director is not expected to have all the tools of a psychologist to handle some of these human problems, but a spiritual director has a tool that can sometimes be even more powerful: prayer. By encouraging a directee to bring struggles to prayer and then talking through the process and experience of prayer, the director can help provide a vehicle for much healing in the directee.

To illustrate this point, consider Fr. Hugh, a priest struggling with same-sex attraction. He never acted upon his temptations but was ashamed of having that tendency. Furthermore, he had a lot of problems with his weight and his physical appearance. He was never athletic or attractive. As he was growing up, he came to hate his body and hate his sexuality. He had the courage to speak about this in spiritual direction. The spiritual director helped him first of all to see that he had these feelings about himself. Then the spiritual director encouraged Fr. Hugh to bring all of this before Jesus in the Blessed Sacrament. He suggested that Fr. Hugh go before Him in the Tabernacle, very aware of his bodiliness, and particularly his sexuality, and just to stay there before God's loving gaze. At first, because of his self-loathing, Fr. Hugh could not bring himself to do this. It was too difficult to see himself in his mind's eye, let alone to see God seeing himself. At the same time, the effort itself allowed God's grace to work in him for healing. After some time, he reported that he had been able to place himself in God's presence with an awareness of his body, and believe that God looked on him with love. This helped him to integrate more effectively, and his poor self-image and self-preoccupation diminished along with his shame over his sexuality.

When we go through intense things, such as feeling angry or hurting intensely, we often go through them apart from God. It is a significant sign of progress when a person can go through those things in the presence of God and let the Lord show him how He sees what the person is going through. Allowing ourselves to be loved, especially in those areas that seem most out of control, most broken, most poor, and most unlovable, brings about a powerful encounter with a God who is infinite love. This helps our theology to become real and experiential in our lives.

Resisting Vulnerability

The only unhealable wound is the one that is intentionally hidden from the Divine Physician, just as the only unforgivable sin is the one that is intentionally withheld from the mercy of God. Resisting vulnerability is the greatest hindrance in spiritual growth. When we do not admit our limitations, share our pain, confess our guilt, admit our ignorance, express our doubts, and, in general, ask for help, we cannot receive the healing power of Jesus. Hiding our unfinished parts behind an iron fortress that is impenetrable to love will prevent those parts from developing in the beautiful way that God intends. Sometimes it helps to ask if the directee is aware of anything he is deliberately withholding. If he is not able to name it, it can still be valuable at least to try to uncover why it is so hard to talk about or even name certain things. Sometimes the spiritual director can even take a step further and speak of the tragedy of having to hide a secret we feel we have to keep.

We resist vulnerability in a variety of ways. Sometimes a person will move into anger rather than remaining in the pain. Sometimes a person expresses indignation rather than feeling and speaking about the shame. People often turn outward to speak about or blame others. The spiritual director can press in gently by asking about a significant experience, "What did you go through inside yourself when that was happening?"

Sometimes the spiritual director can name the problem and that will be the key that opens the door to the heart. We are more comfortable being vulnerable when we know that we will be received with love. When a spiritual director can name a problem and, in naming it, show acceptance and love for that problem, it can give a person courage to admit it. For example, a man went into a deep depression after his girlfriend broke up with him when he had to move away due to the demands of his work. When his spiritual director asked him to describe how the depression felt, the directee could only give clinical, objective descriptions. As the man continued to share the experience he mentioned how he had received a number of going away cards and had opened all of them, except for the one from the woman with whom he had been in the significant relationship. At that point, the spiritual director offered an explanation: "Perhaps the depression is caused by the fact that your feelings, especially the most significant ones, never get opened up, but they remained sealed up, like that envelope.

Now those feelings are catching up with you and drawing you in, shutting you down." That helped to open the man up and enabled him to see that he had buried his painful feelings of shame and regret. It can sometimes be particularly powerful for the spiritual director to actually name the closed-up feelings as well. This may be sensitive territory, but it can give the directee the courage to see and acknowledge important feelings.

A lack of vulnerability can close up important parts of a person and they can lose access to those exiled parts. They might be able to tell that there is a fire burning them up inside—they smell the smoke—but they cannot figure out where the fire is coming from. Sometimes a person can even tell that the fire is spreading in his life, causing him to act out, even by punching someone or going into a rage or a binge, and yet he cannot tell where this is rising up from. In extreme cases, someone who is psychopathic can be totally disconnected from his own feelings. In general, there is a deficit of empathy in our society and additionally there seems to be a growing incidence of persons on the autism spectrum. These individuals can be difficult to work with in spiritual direction if they are unable to get in touch with their feelings and expose their hearts in a more vulnerable way. In this case, the spiritual director must support the directee as best as possible. By naming some feelings, and even helping the directee to experience them in the context of spiritual direction, perhaps through the foundational opportunity of having a spiritual father or mother for the first time, there can be developmental advances in the directee. The relationship with a spiritual father or mother can be effective in backfilling developmental holes that were left from childhood. This can even be the case for people who had very good parents. Even the best of fathers and mothers still have imperfections. Additionally, the experience of being loved by a spiritual father or mother who *chose* to love (rather than just being "forced" into it due to biological relations) can touch a deep place in the heart.

Setting the Pace

While it sometimes may seem that a directee is resisting vulnerability, he may actually just be setting a pace that he is comfortable with. If a question is too probing, if the area gets too tender, he may back off or compensate. Sometimes people will control the pace by constantly correcting the spiritual director. When the spiritual director suggests that the directee always seems to be angry at someone, the directee might clarify, "No, not angry . . . more like frustrated." The next time the spiritual director might suggest that the directee was feeling frustration and gets corrected, "More like anger." There is nothing wrong with the directee setting the pace and a spiritual director should always be reverent and gentle when initiating greater vulnerability.

In other cases, the directee might be overly eager to agree with whatever the spiritual director says. In those cases, the spiritual director must be careful not to lead the directee excessively and thus shut down the process of the directee freely opening his interior life and sharing vulnerably. Nor should the spiritual director get into a contest to get to the right answer first or dominate the process of sharing, but rather he should let the directee take the lead and express himself in his own words. These will be the words he is best able to hold onto as he continues to be aware of the dynamics at work in his interior life.

In this way, the spiritual director can be a good spiritual father or mother. As a spiritual directee grows, he gains freedom to differentiate himself from the spiritual director. Like a father whose little child sometimes wants to hold his hand and other times wants to run ahead, the spiritual director should always strive to provide a stable and safe sanctuary for the directee to open up and share his heart at his own pace, in his own way.

Cultivating Vulnerability

In spiritual direction, a directee should be able to share everything, where *everything* need not include what he had for breakfast so much as it includes the deepest fears, longings, shame, or other vulnerable, interior places. When a directee is able to be vulnerable, he touches on and shares the parts of his interior where God is already present or where He wants to be more present. In this way, the directee is able to get in touch with Christ in the very process of spiritual direction and also open up areas of his life to Christ that unfold outside of spiritual direction. A spiritual director who is able to guide his directee into vulnerability will witness much growth and healing. This process of guiding a spiritual directee into vulnerably sharing deeper areas of interiority requires a vulnerable openness on the part of the spiritual director that comes through more in the way he listens than in what he says.

4

Listening

T HE JOURNEY OF deepening interiority, which unfolds through vulnerability, always involves another person (sometimes that person is God alone). That other person plays a critical and active role in facilitating the journey of interiority. As described in the chapter on vulnerability, there is a possibility of harming a person deeply when that person's vulnerable self-revelation is received poorly. There is also the potential for tremendous healing and the opening of a deeper relationship with God when that self-revelation is received with reverence and love. The difference lies primarily in the quality of listening. Listening is the human means by which the vulnerable self-revelation of one's interior is received and loved. (We say listening is a "human means" because we can speak of God "listening" only by analogy. His vision already penetrates the depths of our souls.)

Jesus, in His humanity, models a quality of listening that penetrates deep into the interior of the person. With His divine prerogative He apparently does not need to sit in an office and spend hours at a time listening to clients. At the same time, He does not simply read everyone's minds and tell them everything about themselves. He leaves room for them to speak, and through their self-revelation and with the assistance of the Holy Spirit, He sees deeply into the souls of those He encounters. For example, this is what causes the Samaritan woman to exclaim, "He told me all that I ever did" (Jn 4:39), when in fact He said very little to her. Likewise, He sees through the protests of Martha as He says, "Martha, Martha, you are anxious and troubled about many things" (Lk 10:41). He sees the deeper needs of the paralyzed man when He asserts, "Your sins are forgiven" (Mk 2:5), and He listens to and responds with love to the blind man's desire, "Master, let me receive my sight" (Mk 10:51). He hears the good thief's cry, "Jesus, remember me when you come into your kingly power" (Lk 23:42). And He even leaves room for His critics to ask questions (regarding the greatest commandment, the practice of fasting, and the nature of marriage, for example)[1] which He then answers in ways that will best serve them. Although we know Jesus as the Teacher, He is a teacher who has first listened to and loved those whom He is teaching.

The Psalms speak to this reality as well: "O Lord, you have searched me and know me! You know when I sit down and when I rise up; you discern my thoughts from afar. You search out my path and my lying down, and are acquainted with all my ways. Even before a word is on my tongue, behold, O LORD, you know it altogether" (Ps 139:1–4). Another way to express what the psalmist asserts in Psalm 139 is "you listen to me and you under-stand me." This is the example for all of our listening to each other and especially for the listening that is the principal activity of the spiritual director. The most significant difference between God's listening and our listening, of course, lies in our inability to see and understand as quickly as God does. Our listening normally stretches over a longer period of time than the examples of Jesus' listening that we see in Sacred Scripture.

When we listen like God, in a manner that penetrates to the interior of the person and makes a person feel heard, understood, and loved, profound healing can take place. Again, the examples from Scripture are manifold and we see the way Jesus is able to listen deeply, such that He can identify the pain and brokenness of those He encounters. When He then speaks a word of love or

---

[1]   See Mt 22:34–39; 9:14–15; 19:1–12.

makes a gesture of tenderness, it directly touches the wound and heals it from within.

This posture of listening is not just for spiritual directors. Every Christian is called to form a culture of encounter and accompaniment:

> We need to help others to realize that the only way is to learn how to encounter others with the right attitude, which is to accept and esteem them as companions along the way, without interior resistance. Better yet, it means learning to find Jesus in the faces of others, in their voices, in their pleas. . . . never tiring of our decision to live in fraternity.
>
> There indeed we find true healing, since the way to relate to others which truly heals instead of debilitating us, is a *mystical* fraternity, a contemplative fraternity. It is a fraternal love capable of seeing the sacred grandeur of our neighbour, of finding God in every human being, of tolerating the nuisances of life in common by clinging to the love of God, of opening the heart to divine love and seeking the happiness of others just as their heavenly Father does.[2]

Indeed, Pope Francis has expressed hope that not just Christians but everyone can take up these attitudes that come from listening: "I would like to encourage everyone to see society not as a forum where strangers compete and try to come out on top, but above all as a home or a family, where the door is always open and where everyone feels welcome. *For this to happen*," the Holy Father writes, "*we must first listen*. Communicating means sharing, and sharing demands listening and acceptance."[3]

If compassionate listening is a requirement for everyone, it is

[2] Pope Francis, *Evangelii gaudium*, nos. 91–92.
[3] Pope Francis, "Communication and Mercy: A Fruitful Encounter," Message for the 50th World Communications Day (January 24, 2016), https://w2.vatican.va/content/francesco/en/messages/communications/documents/papa-francesco_20160124_messaggio-comunicazioni-sociali.html. Emphasis added.

above all a necessity for the spiritual director. He should be an expert listener. As the spiritual director listens vulnerably to the directee and to God, the presence of God becomes more palpable, and with His presence comes a healing love that transforms lives. In calling us to listen, Pope Francis described the manner of listening he had in mind:

> Listening is much more than simply hearing. Hearing is about receiving information, while listening is about communication, and calls for closeness. Listening allows us to get things right, and not simply to be passive onlookers, users or consumers. Listening also means being able to share questions and doubts, to journey side by side, to banish all claims to absolute power and to put our abilities and gifts at the service of the common good.[4]

Building on our reflections on vulnerability given in the last chapter, we describe this kind of listening as vulnerable listening or *vulnerable attentiveness*. It is vulnerable because, as Pope Francis described, it sets aside "claims to absolute power" and it draws close to the other, sharing the condition of the other, even when the other is suffering. It also elicits vulnerability from the other, making it safe to share questions and doubts. Pope Francis explained further:

> Listening is never easy. Many times it is easier to play deaf. Listening means paying attention, wanting to understand, to value, to respect and to ponder what the other person says. It involves a sort of martyrdom or self-sacrifice, as we try to imitate Moses before the burning bush: we have to remove our sandals when standing on the "holy ground" of our encounter with the one who speaks to me (cf. Ex 3:5).[5]

---

[4] Ibid.
[5] Ibid.

Indeed, spiritual direction can sometimes seem like a thankless task, tucked away in an office out of sight—which has led Pope Francis to compare this ministry of vulnerable attentiveness to martyrdom, which is the Church's highest form of sanctity! "Knowing how to listen is an immense grace, it is a gift which we need to ask for and then make every effort to practice."[6]

Jesus Listens by Entering Our Pain

As the Fathers of the Church expressed, "For that which He has not assumed He has not healed; but that which is united to His Godhead is also saved."[7] By taking on our human nature and entering into the full depths of our human misery, Christ touched everything human with His divine mercy. Without going into the details of when Christ experienced cancer or old age or paralysis or brain damage, we can say simply that He took all human suffering on Himself in His Passion and death. He never kept our wounded humanity at arm's length, but drew close, touched us, and shared in our experience. It is in this way that He extended His healing power to every area of human suffering. A good spiritual director allows himself to be drawn into this experience of redemption by drawing close and, through compassion, entering into the human misery of his spiritual directees. A spiritual director listens and guides his directees in a way that will lead them into greater vulnerability and he allows himself to be drawn into that vulnerability with them.

In spiritual direction, content is often less important than process. When people are vulnerable it is hard not to love them. When we can see the fragility of what is being shared, it brings out a tenderness in the one who listens. This is a little taste of

---

[6] Ibid.

[7] St. Gregory Nazianzen, Letter 101 to Cledonis the Priest Against Apolinaris in *The Nicene and Post-Nicene Fathers*, vol. 2, no. 7, ed. Philip Schaff (Buffalo, NY: Christian Literature Company, 1886; reprint, Peabody, MA: Hendrickson, 1994), 440.

heaven, where we will know everything about each other. When we open ourselves to the vulnerability of others we begin to feel the tenderness of God, who is always protecting His little ones. We feel what they are feeling. This empathy is an essential part of spiritual direction. Ultimately God's empathy for us is so powerful that He enters right into our pain; He feels our shame and hurt. In spiritual direction, with vulnerable attentiveness to the directee, the spiritual director can enter into the directee's pain and share in the Cross with him. By our willingness to empathize and share in the Cross, the spiritual director also opens himself to God's mercy. By communicating that mercy to the directee, it fills what is missing and helps the directee grow in awareness of God's mercy. What is most often missing in our anguish is an awareness of God's mercy.

There are people who have experienced horrible abuse or lost innocence and have a fractured understanding of their own bodies and their own identities. The spiritual director can allow himself, with vulnerable attentiveness, to be drawn into the directee's story, allowing himself to feel the directee's pain in compassion. This should all be done in Christ. Feeling it, in Christ, brings it to a new level. To do this, the spiritual director can make himself aware of the presence of Christ, identify with the compassionate movements of His Sacred Heart, and imagine His pain as He witnessed and shared in the suffering that is being described by the directee. There are many temptations in this process, for example, to fix the problem, talk the directee out of it, to try anxiously to fill any silences, or to find the perfect words with which to respond. The spiritual director will do best if he simply remains attentive, vulnerable, authentic, and poor.

Spiritual direction helps people to process their pain and work through it, in Christ. Sometimes a directee will feel stuck because he keeps reliving a painful memory. Sometimes this will be played out in spiritual direction with the same painful stories being brought up again and again from one session to the next. The key is to take all those feelings, whether they are flashbacks or memories or other felt effects of past painful experiences, and bring them to Christ and to feel them while focusing on Him. Knowing that Christ has shared in all of it, it is possible to focus on Him by focusing on the way He carries our own pain in His body, in His heart. One directee described an image of Christ's heart bearing the knife wound of betrayal, the searing pain of failure, the scrape of being misunderstood. He could see his own pain on Christ's heart and found so much comfort by pressing his wounded heart against Christ's wounded heart, pressing the wounds together, and simply feeling the pain with Christ.

The spiritual director can effectively guide people to bring their pain to Christ. Instead of deflecting the directee away from the spiritual director, when the spiritual director feels the trauma, the ache, the piercing pain of sins and failures, he can express to the directee the way that Christ also carries all that pain in His own heart. The spiritual director's empathy can greatly help the directee to believe that Christ truly shares the pain as well. This process can bring up questions and even anger. As a directee opens up a painful area, anger may flare up as he protests God's apparent absence: "Where was God in the concentration camps or in the death camps?" Though the spiritual director might be tempted to try to answer such questions or dread that he has no answer, the only adequate answer is the Cross. Christ Crucified is united with all human suffering. He is in the most forsaken corners of the prisons, in the interminable feeling of being beaten, and in the smoke of the crematoria. It is hard for people to see that right away, but when a person feels deeply heard and believes that the listener understands their pain, the director has more credibility when expressing the closeness and the loving mercy of God.

In our day, there is a cult of "victims" which has become so widespread that many of us now belong to it. It entails an interminable, unforgiving exhibition of one's wounds, as opposed to exposing them vulnerably. In such flaunting of wounds there is often a failed attempt at catharsis, doomed by a determination never to forgive, never to forget. For people who refuse to break out of this pattern, only a superficial healing is possible, at best. God's place in all of this needs to become very explicit at the right time.

The first thing is to let a person tell his story and express his pain. A spiritual director should listen lovingly, with vulnerable attentiveness, and then he will be in a position to speak on behalf of God to the directee. A person who has experienced trauma might be very angry at God. Once a person articulates how angry he is at God, however, he can start to get over it. A person often needs to enter into the dark valley, and sometimes become even more angry as he allows himself to feel the pain more deeply, before he can pass through it and come out a different way than before.

The Challenge to Listen Well: Entering into the World of the Other

Listening in a penetrating way has great power to heal, but also places great demands on the listener. The listener must set aside his own curiosities and self-interest to stay focused on the one who is sharing. Through a self-emptying listening, the listener can open his heart to an empathy with the one who is sharing himself, even internally feeling what is being expressed by the directee. He enters into the world of the other to try to understand from the inside. At the same time, the spiritual director can be open to the "feeling" of God, allowing compassion to well up in his heart, making it even easier to express the mercy of God in response to the directee's experience. "Mercy," Pope Francis described in his Bull of Indiction for the Extraordinary Jubilee Year of Mercy, is "the fundamental law that dwells in the heart of every person who looks sincerely into the eyes of his brothers and sisters on the path of life."[8] When we listen deeply, we are looking sincerely into the eyes of our brothers and sisters, and mercy, which originates in the heart of the Trinity, is the law that is at work in our hearts. Looking into the eyes of our brother or sister is a precious oppor-

[8] Pope Francis, Bull of Indiction of the Extraordinary Jubilee Year of Mercy *Misericordiae vultus* (April 11, 2015), no. 2, https://w2.vatican.va/content/francesco/en/apost_letters/documents/papa-francesco_bolla_20150411_misericordiae-vultus.html.

tunity for the spiritual director to savor the moment of intimacy and to savor the beauty of this unique soul.

This merciful, vulnerable attentiveness can be quite demanding as the narrative may seem boring at times or the spiritual director may have many other duties that compete for his attention. The decision to focus full attention on the directee, which sometimes must be made repeatedly throughout a session, is in itself an act of love that provides so much healing. Sustained listening should be preferred to jumping in, problem solving, or chasing after curiosities. The directee may find all he needs in simply sharing himself, sharing his relationship with God, and being heard.

Another challenge to vulnerable attentiveness is the possibility of feeling useless or helpless. The spiritual director may feel like he does not know what to say or what to do to help the directee. In this he may feel useless. Likewise, he may find himself together with the directee facing an overwhelming situation—such as a broken marriage, an experience of persecution or injustice, or a struggle with sin—and feel helpless to rescue the directee from these trials. The failure of a directee to apply what has been discussed in spiritual direction can be a source of frustration and leave the director feeling helpless to assist his directee. In the feelings of uselessness and helplessness, the spiritual director must learn to remain poor and united with the poor, crucified Christ, praying and entrusting the directee and his struggles to the mercy of God. The decision of the director to remain with the directee and accompany him in his own poverty and then to speak the mercy of God into that poverty can be profoundly healing and strengthening, even without resolving the circumstances described by the directee.

Sometimes it is best for the spiritual director to remain patient and simply persevere through difficult meetings. Other times it is important to remain patient, but also to challenge the directee and even to raise the question of whether spiritual direction is helping. In any case, it is always important to remain very gentle.

Jason came to spiritual direction after having an emotional breakdown. He had borne a great deal of stress for many years and finally broke down, quit his job, and went into a depression. After a year, he was recovering in some ways. He had been too anxious to drive his car after the breakdown, but he was slowly recovering his ability to drive. He was reading the Bible and was working through his issues, including his anger toward those he felt had mistreated him at work.

However, when he started spiritual direction, he was still unemployed. That was a source of frustration and confusion for his family. They did not understand why he did not simply get a job. In fact, they even started to blame spiritual direction for enabling him by only encouraging him in his unemployment and not challenging him to get back to work. The spiritual director started to wonder, as well, if this was an accurate description of what was happening, and so during one meeting he raised the question about the effectiveness of spiritual direction for Jason. He asked whether spiritual direction was providing a security which was allowing him not to move forward.

Jason reacted quickly with great anxiety. The shock gave him energy to go deeper and admit how strong his fears were in regard to being stuck in another job where people would take advantage of him. He also vulnerably expressed his fear that the spiritual director would abandon him and this would send him back to square one. As Jason emotionally dissolved and shared vulnerably, this moved the spiritual director's heart to compassion and he could see that his challenge was motivated by the pressures he felt from Jason's family and from his own impatience since nothing seemed to be changing. He softened at Jason's reaction and they were able to work on bringing Jason's deeper fears to Jesus. The challenge turned out to be very beneficial in the end. Jason was able to express his fear—"I don't know when I am going to go back to work"—and the spiritual director was able to love him there and make God's love present, advising him simply, "You are going to go back when you can."

For healing, a directee must make decisions and do as much as he can. At the same time, every little bit helps. Jesus did not simply zap people and fix them. He gave them little tasks such as, "Take up your pallet, and walk" (Jn 5:11). And this led them to further challenges, such as to witness to their faith, like the Samaritan woman who proclaimed after her encounter with Christ, "Come, see a man who told me all that I ever did" (Jn 4:29). The spiritual director, likewise, cannot fix a directee by saying some magical words, and he cannot make decisions for the directee. But he can help the directee to take steps, even baby steps, and he can accompany the directee in that process.

To illustrate how spiritual direction invites a directee to make gradual progress, consider the situation of a woman who had an accident riding a horse because the horse panicked. She was badly injured in the accident. Her trainer gave her time to heal physically, then put her back on the horse. At first he led the horse around. Then he rode with her. Lastly, he let her ride on her own. This is analogous to what a spiritual director does. When do we need to challenge or be patient? When do we need to push and pull? When do we need to wait or to hasten? When might an opportunity be lost?

The spiritual director must learn to be comfortable in feeling helpless and poor. At the same time, the spiritual director has access to divine power due to his relationship with God, and through this power he can be instrumental in bringing healing. Calling on the power and love of God, through prayer, to bring healing is something that the spiritual director can employ in the context of spiritual direction. Even when he does that, though, he must learn to be comfortable with feeling poor and helpless because the power is not his but God's, and the spiritual director is never in control of the outcome. When he truly enters into the poverty of his directee, though, he may find that prayer for healing accelerates the directee's process of growing in freedom and grace.

The approach recommended by Jesus to His Apostles applies very well to spiritual direction: "Settle it therefore in your minds, not to meditate beforehand how to answer; for I will give you a mouth and wisdom, which none of your adversaries will be able to withstand or contradict" (Lk 21:14–15). Likewise, the way that the Lord sent out the disciples with minimal possessions and yet supplied for their needs applies also to spiritual direction. "He said to them, 'When I sent you out with no purse or bag or sandals, did you lack anything?' They said, 'Nothing'" (Lk 22:35). The Lord blesses most what we offer from our poverty, as with the poor widow, when he said, "Truly I tell you, this poor widow has put in more than all of them; for they all contributed out of their abundance, but she out of her poverty put in all the living that she had" (Lk 21:3–4).

In the discomfort of feeling poor, the spiritual director will often face the danger of trying to move too quickly to a resolution rather than exploring the depths of what is happening. The directee can also face this temptation, as he will feel as awkward or even more awkward than the spiritual director with exposed, unresolved questions about what is happening in his interior. However, both directors and directees must learn to sit in this discomfort and let the Holy Spirit do His hidden work. Like the benefit of airing out an open wound, our exposed interior can be ugly to look at and painful to expose, but the very process of airing it out, with both the director and directee sitting in the mess, can be powerfully healing. The only communication from the spiritual director may be simply that he is staying with the directee and not afraid to be in the pain, confusion, embarrassment, shame, or failure with him. Spiritual directors should learn to cherish the high praise that can come from a grateful directee, "I am so thankful that you are willing to sit in my mess with me."

A spiritual director can also be challenged or even attacked by a spiritual directee. An important point to keep in mind is that this is often not about the issue that is being raised but may be a smoke screen disguising some other issue, or a way of seeking attention, or even of manipulating the spiritual director. For example, one young woman named Stephanie started a spiritual direction meeting with the accusation that the spiritual director had broken her confidence. This immediately caused an interior reaction in the spiritual director, because he took confidentiality extremely seriously. Although his first impulse was to defend himself, he had the wherewithal to ask her to explain the situation. As she described the situation, it became clear that she was afraid of the reaction of one of his other directees, who happened to be a boy whom she had a crush on. She had read into that boy's response to her and assumed that he responded a certain way because the spiritual director had told him something about her.

As he began to understand the situation, the spiritual director had a choice to defend himself or to go deeper into her sharing. Remembering that spiritual direction is not about him, he chose to go deeper into what she had opened up and said simply, "You really like this boy, don't you?" That led her to move completely away from her initial accusation and begin to share her feelings about the boy and her fears about her own lovability. Although the spiritual director was still stinging a bit from the accusation, he realized that Stephanie had completely moved on from it and he chose to affirm her and speak truth into her fears about her lovability. Eventually he was able to show her that she had no basis for her concern about him breaking confidentiality. She saw that her own fears had made her overreact to something that was said. This allowed her to think about her identity as a beloved daughter of the eternal Father. The spiritual director affirmed her strengths and built her up and gave her confidence to bring her feelings to God in prayer and to consult with God about how to move forward in the relationship. She did all of that and was able to reach out to the boy she liked and discover that he also liked her. They both ended up growing through that relationship and it helped them move into their respective vocations—he entered into marriage and she entered into religious life.

Affirmative Listening

Dr. Conrad Baars developed an approach to psychotherapy that depends heavily on affirmation. He held that the deprivation of affirmation has caused much pain in the world today, sometimes resulting in a psychological malady he named Deprivation Disorder, but more broadly resulting, to various degrees, in an inability to relate with others and form intimate friendships and in feelings of uncertainty, insecurity, inferiority, inadequacy, and depression. As the word itself communicates, affirmation "firms up" one's being, giving the confidence to be open to more of reality.

The core of affirmation is not about saying something (and thus it is best introduced in this chapter on listening), because merely saying something can result in a pseudo-affirmation which is unhelpful. The core of affirmation is in taking the other into one's heart to affirm his basic goodness. Dr. Baars described this in the following way:

> Your affirmation, your feeling firm and strong, your pos-sessing yourself in joy, your feeling worthwhile, starts with and is dependent on another human being, who:
>
> 1) *is aware of, attentive, and present to* your unique good-ness and worth, separate from and prior to any good and worthwhile thing you may do or can do, and
> 2) *is moved by, feels attracted to, finds delight in* your goodness and worth, but without desiring to possess you, or use you, or change you, and
> 3) permits his being moved by and attracted to you *to be revealed* simply and primarily by the psychomotor reac-tions—visible, sensible, physical changes—which are part of his "being moved."
>
> These changes constitute the tenderness and delight in his eyes, his gaze, his touch, his tone of voice, and choice of words. They cause you to *feel*, sense, see and hear that you are good and worthwhile—good for the other and good in and of yourself. You come to feel and know who and what you are.[9]

[9] Conrad W. Baars, *Born Only Once: The Miracle of Affirmation* (Chicago: Franciscan Herald Press, 1975), 22–23.

We speak about taking the directee into the heart, allowing the spiritual director to be moved by the directee, vulnerable to what is being shared. Dr. Baars offers a beautiful image for that:

> The affirming process can be compared in a certain sense to the effect water has on an object immersed in it. The water surrounds it perfectly and adjusts itself faithfully to the exact contours of the object without destroying it. It allows the object, if a living one, like fish, coral, or plant, to grow and develop without hindrance by adjusting its own weight in relation to it. The water cushions with its mass and density any shocks or blows it might receive and thus protects the object. The tiny baby in the water bag of the pregnant mother is an excellent example. Finally, water may hide from view any defects the object may possess.[10]

The Basic "Grammar" of Interaction

In the attentive listening called for in spiritual direction, there can be a basic "grammar" of interaction that forms between the director and the directee. The principal goal is to keep the flow of the sharing moving. This grammar of interaction is not artificial and should not be forced, but it is, rather, profoundly human. Spiritual direction is a human interaction with the particular focus directed toward the one-on-one relationship between the directee and God.

The interactions between the spiritual director and directee can be expressed in such basic human forms as eye contact and head nodding, smiling, and small acknowledgments of what is being shared. Small comments can be helpful to encourage sharing, but each person is unique and the spiritual director has to be sensitive to what is most helpful. Some directees do not need much assistance in sharing themselves, while others may require some recognition that what is being shared is also being

---

[10] Ibid., 27.

received by the spiritual director. This may also develop over time as the trust between director and directee develops. On the other hand, the spiritual director must be careful not to put up road-blocks to the directee's sharing by asking too many questions or interrupting with unhelpful comments. The spiritual director should do what he can to make the directee feel loved, cared for, and supported.

Primarily, the spiritual directee should be the one talking. If, at times, the directee tries to get the director to do the talking, as if trying to interview him, it could be for various reasons. The directee might be trying to build trust and the director can facilitate this by answering questions sincerely, although he should be somewhat brief and look for the opportunity to invite the directee to lead the sharing. It is also possible that the directee may be avoiding something and so turns the attention back to the director. Sometimes the directee is feeling vulnerable and pushing the attention away from himself. In each case the director can gently shift the attention back to the directee, affirming what has been shared and working to build trust by sharing a little bit in a way that will help the directee be more confident that he will be received with unconditional love. This can happen, for example, if the directee invites the director to ask questions or tell the directee how the director is doing, or if he asks the director for personal self-revelation or to accommodate many special needs. While not necessarily problematic, these behaviors may indicate evasion or signify that the directee is testing the director. The director can respond by saying, "I can answer that question, but could you share with me why you are asking it?"

As much as possible, the spiritual director should let the directee share vulnerably what is in his heart. As he listens, he may want to mentally tag certain points to return to. The spiritual director's response to the directee will be most powerful if it comes after the directee is convinced that he has truly been heard and his narrative is resonating in the director's heart. This response will often come out best if it is offered closer to the end of a session. At the same time, it can be important in some cases to offer feedback earlier to see how the directee receives it. If the response is left to the end of the meeting and if it is misunderstood, the directee might suffer between sessions over the misunderstanding. Obviously, as the director notices any shifts of mood in the directee that might indicate misunderstanding or some other dissonance, he should always encourage the directee to share whenever it occurs.

This is what Pope Francis calls "accompaniment," and he stresses the importance of the whole Church entering into this relational posture with others:

> The Church will have to initiate everyone—priests, religious and laity—into this "art of accompaniment" which teaches us to remove our sandals before the sacred ground of the other (cf. Ex 3:5). The pace of this accompaniment must be steady and reassuring, reflecting our closeness and our compassionate gaze which also heals, liberates and encourages growth in the Christian life.[11]

The less we think we know, the better we can listen. As soon as we think we have things figured out we close our minds and hearts and our listening is diminished or stops completely. By remaining poor and ignorant, we listen more deeply, allowing the directee to teach us about himself. It can be hard to remain poor like this. It can be tempting to size a person up and apply preformulated answers and solutions. But ultimately, such a mechanical approach to spiritual direction will leave the directee feeling unaccompanied on his journey.

Self-Monitoring While Listening

While prayerfully listening to the directee, it is important for the spiritual director to monitor himself and his internal and exter-

---

[11] Pope Francis, *Evangelii gaudium*, no. 169.

nal reactions. We cover this important topic of self-awareness in more detail in Chapter 9, but it is fitting to mention it here in the context of listening as well. As the spiritual director opens himself to the directee in his listening, there is a strong potential for him to be triggered by the directee. In psychological terms, this is known as counter-transference. The more the director is aware of this, the more he can be careful not to react to it. It is important to take note of those reactions for the sake of his own growth as well, and even to bring it up with his supervisor or his own spiritual director.

For example, the directee's complaints about the Church or members of the clergy may trigger reactions in the director that make him defensive. The directee might also try to solicit a director's opinion or agreement, as well as his emotional support, for a variety of issues, including things like politics, the behavior of a spouse, or even commentary on a mutual friend. What the directee is sharing may touch on something that the director is also going through or has experienced in the past. The director may acknowledge understanding from personal experience and even share some insight, but he should always be careful to ensure it is for the directee's best interest and that it does not interfere with the flow of vulnerable sharing.

Maintaining a Dynamic Tension with Silence

In attentive listening, there is value in maintaining a certain tension that helps the directee to keep sharing and even to become more vulnerable in the sharing. This tension can be facilitated simply through openness and eye contact, without saying anything. Even as the directee may come to more vulnerable moments and may hesitate or pause in a few moments of silence, the director must be careful not to jump in simply to fill the silence. Silence can be a powerful invitation to go deeper. The silence should never be a cold silence, but remain warm and loving through posture and eye contact that welcomes further sharing from the directee. Again it is worth mentioning how important it is for the director to continue praying throughout each spiritual direction session, especially while listening. The silence, through the director's love and prayer, should be pregnant with the divine presence and divine love.

If at times the silence becomes too much (sometimes causing the directee to ask a question or even vulnerably to ask for feedback), the director can ease the tension slightly by asking questions that communicate loving care, "How are you feeling as you're sharing this?" or, "Are you doing okay?" or, "Is it hard to share this?" Affirmations can be very helpful as well, such as, "I really appreciate your honesty," or, "Thank you for being so vulnerable," or, "Thank you for trusting me." The tension may also draw out tears from the directee and an encouragement, such as, "Don't be afraid to cry—tears can be very healing," can give the directee permission to release the tension through tears. Even a little kidding with the directee can help to release the tension, but one must be careful not to derail the sharing completely. The director also has to be careful not to make the directee self-conscious or feel he is being made fun of, since the sharing has already made him very vulnerable.

Developing Working Models

As the spiritual director is listening, he may also be forming working models and theories as he seeks to understand the directee. These working models will be filled out and greatly enhanced by the spiritual director's own experience. There are patterns of human behavior that often repeat themselves. When a spiritual director is listening to a directee launch into a story about what happened recently, he is wondering, "Why is the directee sharing this story? Where are we going with this?" It may lead to sharing some pain. It might be constructed by the directee to justify himself or set up some excuses for why he has not kept up his prayer life or why he committed a particular sin. A directee may offer an advance outline for what points he plans to cover and that can help the director stay focused on where a particular story is heading. At the same time, the spiritual director must listen attentively to the points of the story that do not adequately support the outline or topics for reflection. These are points he may want to bring out when the directee is finished. If the spiritual director is able to hold on to some highlights or details in the story, he can bring those up later to affirm or guide the directee. In this listening, however, the best thing is to love and appreciate the directee as much as possible. By letting one's heart be moved by the sharing that one is receiving, it will be easiest to love the directee and refer back to anything that has been shared.

When listening, it can be helpful to form a mental sketch of the directee, getting a basic sense of his motivations and the development of his virtues. Models such as the temperaments or personality types can be of assistance here. It can also be worthwhile to note how developed one's relationship with God seems to be. Is the directee a committed believer? Is he a casual Catholic? How developed is his prayer life? Does he have daily, lengthy, personal periods of prayer or does his prayer consist simply of a few rote prayers once or twice a day. Does the directee have a robust sense of the communion of saints? Does he have a love for the Church? What is his practice of the sacraments like? None of these evaluations should become judgments or condemnations, but only connecting points for knowing how best to guide someone. A person who has a less developed relationship with Christ is going to need more coaching on how to bring things into prayer. A person with a strong, choleric personality might be better equipped to confront a coworker than a person with a timid, phlegmatic personality. A person with a melancholic personality will be more likely to torture himself with unrealized ideals and the spiritual director might need to be especially encouraging of that directee.

Although we form working models of the directee during our listening, we must always leave them open ended to let ourselves continually encounter the real person in front of us rather than our preconceptions or misconceptions. Furthermore, our openness will allow our directee to grow and change over time without being forced by the spiritual director back into old models:

> Every *genuine human encounter* must be inspired by poverty of spirit. We must forget ourselves in order to let the other person approach us. We must be able to open up to the other person, to let that person's distinctive personality unfold—even though it often frightens or repels us. We often keep the other person down, and only see what we want to see; thus we never really encounter the mysterious secret of their being, only ourselves. Failing to risk the poverty of encounter, we indulge a new form of self-assertion and pay a price for it: loneliness. Because we did not risk the poverty of openness (cf. Mt. 10:39), our lives are not graced with the warm fullness of human existence. We are left with only a shadow of our real self.[12]

A Path for Vulnerability: Information, Interpretation, Affectivity, Spirituality

In listening, the spiritual director is looking for ways to lead the directee to greater vulnerability. A general path to vulnerability moves from the level of information to the affective and then to the spiritual. Information is an important part of spiritual direction, because the experience of the directee is rooted in a concrete reality. Our lives unfold through real, lived experiences. This level of sharing is often the least vulnerable, however, and can be reduced to merely reporting the facts. In spiritual direction we want to explore the interior. To go deeper, the spiritual director can invite the directee to reflect on the meaning of what happened and give an interpretation to the events. Another avenue to going deeper is to invite the directee to share how he felt in the course of what happened. Though it has become somewhat cliché,

---

[12] Johann Baptist Metz, *Poverty of Spirit* (Glen Rock, NJ: Newman Press, 1968), 45.

the question "How did that make you feel?" can be a valuable invitation to go deeper. Lastly, the spiritual aspect is the ultimate goal and can reach into the deepest levels of vulnerability. In this regard, questions such as, "Where do think God was in that experience?" or, "What happens when you pray about that struggle?" or, "How has God been speaking to you in prayer?" can be helpful invitations for the directee.

Distinguishing between these different categories of sharing can be helpful while listening to a spiritual directee. For example, the spiritual director might want to return to certain points in the directee's narrative and invite him to share more deeply about his feelings in various ways: "It sounds like that made you angry," or, "Were you afraid when that happened?" or, "It sounds like you have some affection for that person," or, "You are really zealous to proclaim the truth!" or, "Is it fair to say that you don't like your job very much?" After exploring feelings, it may be possible to go deeper into the spiritual interpretation with an open-ended question like, "Why do you think God has allowed you to be in this job right now?" or, "Where do you think God is when you are feeling afraid?" or, "How do you think God feels about your zeal for evangelization?" It is always better to focus or highlight by using questions in spiritual direction, such as, "And what was it like when you brought those feelings or that experience to the Lord?" If the directee has not explicitly done what is asked, it can serve as a reminder or encouragement to do so.

Being aware of these different categories of sharing can also help to provide some starting points for sharing if the directee seems stymied. Sometimes a directee says, "I don't know what to say today." In this case, he is providing information; a question from the director that invites an answer or interpretation can move the directee to a deeper level of sharing; for example, "Is there a reason you don't know what to say?" Likewise, an invitation to look inward and share what is happening in the moment can be helpful: "Is there anything you are feeling as you talk with me?" Especially if the spiritual director is picking up on some anger or resistance, this can be a better way to gently lead the directee rather than asking the direct question, "Are you angry right now?" These kinds of questions allow the spiritual director to show that he is attentive and empathizing, that he is there with the directee.

To repeat a general principle: as much as possible, let the directee be the one to speak. Whether on the affective or interpretive or spiritual level, if the directee can be the one to make a step and can claim something on his own, he will be more vulnerable and see the most powerful results. This mirrors God's own approach as Jesus tells us, "Ask, and it will be given you; seek, and you will find; knock, and it will be opened to you" (Lk 11:9). Even though "your Father knows what you need before you ask him" (Mt 6:8), this approach engages our freedom more fully. Likewise, Jesus asks the blind man to be vulnerable and speak his desire: "What do you want me to do for you?" (Mk 10:51) and sometimes even reduces it to a yes or no question, "Do you want to be healed?" (Jn 5:6). The more that the director can help the directee to draw conclusions and uncover interpretations and insights about his situation, the better. For this reason, rather than making a pronouncement, "I think that . . ." it is better for the director to ask a question such as, "Do you think that . . . ?"

Primacy of Listening

It has already been said and it is worth repeating that in spiritual direction primacy must be given to listening. It is a great temptation to become a kind of oracle or wise man who provides the answers to all of life's questions. Some people will be only too happy to place the spiritual director into this role, but at best this will be a revelation of the spiritual director's own personal path and a monologue of projection onto the directee. To the contrary, the spiritual director should be reluctant to speak too soon. The director will always benefit from more listening. If the directee is hesitant to open up, then the spiritual director should assist him in going deeper through encouragement and clarification rather than taking over for him. The directee will benefit from the director's hesitancy to start providing answers and all kinds of sage advice without first taking time to understand what is happening in the directee's interior life.

To illustrate this point, consider a parable told by Taylor Caldwell in the book *The Listener*.[13] In the parable, a man endowed a center where anybody could come and be heard. Any person who longed to be heard simply entered into a room to speak to "the man who listens." The listening man was evidently behind a curtain where he could not be seen. Upon entering a room the person simply saw the curtain, but after a period of silence usually seemed to feel a silent presence and began to talk. Sometimes the person railed at the man for his silence, but eventually poured his heart out, came to some sense of what the silent listener was saying, and left in peace, often with resolution. Many spoke at length and left feeling consoled and healed. Eventually one person came in and, after sharing deeply and being transformed in the process, pulled back the curtain to discover who the excellent listener was. Behind the curtain was simply a life-sized crucifix on the wall.

This story illustrates the importance of listening. It also provides a particular nuance to the qualities needed in the listener. It shows why God usually speaks through silence, and how eloquent that silence is. It illustrates that the most powerful listening is truly to share in the experience of the one speaking. The most radical sharing happens in Christ, as He takes on the depths of our pain caused by our own sins and the sins of the whole world. In doing this, He also provides hope by showing a way forward to a new life of sharing with Him in His Resurrection, for "if we have died with Christ, we believe that we shall also live with him" (Rom 6:8). This is the picture of how spiritual direction should also operate; but again, it is important to emphasize that the foundation for this transformation comes in the vulnerability of the directee facilitated by the compassionate listening of the director.

---

[13] Taylor Caldwell, *The Listener* (Garden City, NY: Doubleday, 1960).

A Look of Love

The first response of the spiritual director comes through loving attention. God's love for each person is unique and total. There can be no comparison of who is loved more or less. In earthly terms, we often experience this first in the love of a mother who can love each of her children uniquely and totally as if each child is the only one. Pope Francis' mother described her love for her five children by saying each child was like a finger on her hand.[14] This capacity for love can be communicated to the spiritual director by the Holy Spirit if the director opens his heart to it.

This fundamental disposition of the spiritual director, to be a communicator of God's gratuitous love, highlights the necessity of prayer on the part of the spiritual director. During spiritual direction, the director may feel helpless, overwhelmed with compassion, moved to tears, or uncertain of what to say next, and so in all of it he must learn to be in prayer, opening his heart and opening the dialogue to the Holy Spirit who is, Himself, the love of God and can work very powerfully through the spiritual director's own person.

The unique and total love of God is expressed in a primary way through the eyes, as a *look of love*. Without saying anything, the director, through sustained attention and openness to the love of God poured into his heart through the Holy Spirit (see Rom 5:5), can communicate that love to the directee most powerfully through his eyes. Like Jesus, who first looked at the rich young man and loved him before He went on to challenge him, it is important for the director also to learn this look of love before responding vocally to the directee. This look of love can have a powerful impact that can open a directee even to a challenge like Jesus gave to the rich young man. Pope Francis challenged newly ordained bishops to do this with their flocks: "Look the faithful

---

[14] Pope Francis, General Audience of February 11, 2015, https://w2.vatican.va/content/francesco/en/audiences/2015/documents/papa-francesco_20150211_udienza-generale.html.

in the eye! Not crosswise, but in the eye, in order to see the heart. May your faithful, whether presbyter, deacon or lay person, be able to see your heart. Always look them in the eye."[15]

Looking sincerely into the eyes of a directee already summons forth mercy in a heart that is open. This self-emptying gaze of the director is precisely what opens his heart to the love of the Holy Spirit for the directee. The Holy Spirit enters into the heart of the director as a gift and moves him, when he looks sincerely into the eyes of a directee, with grace for a kind of empathy. This empathy can be accompanied by a knowledge of what the directee needs most. When a director is really engaged in listening, he can get a sense, under the influence of the Holy Spirit's gifts of wisdom and counsel, for what is happening in the other person. That is revealed most powerfully in the eyes. The director should not be looking at the directee with glazed eyes or out the window, but intently in an empathic and compassionate way. This warm gaze can elicit trust from the directee. Note, though, that this is not a technique, but comes from the fullness of the heart and is shaped by the gifts of the Holy Spirit. At the same time, the director must be careful to remain sincere and authentic, because, as he becomes more transparent to the directee, his distraction, dissatisfaction, or disinterest can show through as well.

St. Thérèse of Lisieux was confident in the power of God's "Divine Glance" to cleanse the soul and consume its imperfections. She reinforces the power of a look, even without any words to accompany it: "If through weakness I sometimes fall, may Your Divine Glance cleanse my soul immediately, consuming all my imperfections like the fire that transforms everything into itself."[16] Similarly, Pope Francis identified Jesus' look of love upon the rich young man: "Jesus perceives this desire that the young man bears

---

[15] Pope Francis, Homily for a Mass for Conferral of Episcopal Ordination on Msgr. Peter Brian Wells and on Msgr. Miguel Ángel Ayuso Guixot (March 19, 2016), https://w2.vatican.va/content/francesco/en/homilies/2016/documents/papa-francesco_20160319_omelia-ordinazioni-episcopali.html.

[16] St. Thérèse of Lisieux, "Act of Oblation to Merciful Love," available at https://www.ewtn.com/therese/readings/readng4.htm.

in his heart; for this reason his response is expressed in an intense gaze filled with tenderness and love."[17] At the same time, this loving gaze leaves us free: "The young man did not allow himself to be conquered by Jesus' loving gaze, and thus was not able to change. Only by accepting with humble gratitude the love of the Lord do we free ourselves from the seduction of idols and the blindness of our illusions."[18]

Sometimes a directee can be so shy as to avert his eyes, and it can help to invite him eventually with words like, "I don't want to make you uncomfortable, but why don't you look at me?" And later the director might ask, "What difference do you notice when you look at me while talking to me?"

As the spiritual director opens up to God's unique love for each person, he can become charmed by the little, unique qualities in each person. As he focuses on these qualities, the love for that person will naturally grow in his heart. These are not qualities that he should normally point out, lest he make the directee feel self-conscious, but they can move the heart of the director to a greater love for the directee. That greater love can elicit greater freedom and vulnerability from the directee as he feels uniquely and unconditionally loved.

Encouraging Vulnerability

A spiritual director who was a bit uncomfortable with his role and with remaining quiet so as to listen began to say "Uh huh," to affirm the directee. The directee, inadvertently, began to mimic the director by punctuating his discourse in the same way with "Uh huh." At other times, a director who is trying too hard might wind up staring at the directee with a forced grin. It is better just to relax and wait. However, along with the foundational postures

---

[17] Pope Francis, Angelus Message (October 11, 2015), https://w2.vatican.va/content/francesco/en/angelus/2015/documents/papa-francesco_angelus_2015 1011.html.

[18] Ibid.

of listening, looking, and loving, the director can also do a great deal simply by reverencing vulnerability with tender responses. Vulnerability might be recognized through the way the directee looks away, how his voice falters, or when tears are shed. If the directee is struggling to express something, he might even explicitly say that it is hard to share. The director should be careful not to spoil this, but should be gentle, patient, and reverential. This is not a matter of flirting or seducing, but reverently holding and supporting the vulnerability, touching the tender places with tender responses. If this does not come easily to the spiritual director, our Lady, the Blessed Virgin Mary, can teach us this. As Pope Francis said, "Whenever we look to Mary, we come to believe once again in the revolutionary nature of love and tenderness."[19]

The director can make some brief comments to encourage the vulnerability and to show that he is reverencing and loving, not judging or dismissing, the vulnerability. "I'm listening." "It's safe to share this here." "I can see this is hard to talk about." "You're doing great. Thank you for sharing this." "Don't worry—I wouldn't hurt you for the world." Another sign of vulnerability can be the directee seeking feedback, asking what the director thinks. Although the director might be tempted to take over, he may be better served by first saying, "I'm listening," or, "I'm appreciating what you are sharing." Then he can see if the directee, being encouraged by the affirmation, will continue to share more. The director might also encourage with words like, "The Lord can give you more healing when you open this up more." Of course, the director should be content simply to support the directee and must be careful not to make him feel self-conscious or afraid.

The spiritual director can also invite the directee to go deeper by acknowledging his pain, offering comments like, "I can tell it really hurts in that place," or, "You sound really broken-hearted about that." The director can also guide the directee with words like, "Tell me what hurts the most about this," or, "What would you say is the most painful part about that?"

---

[19] Pope Francis, *Evangelii gaudium*, no. 288.

Sometimes the vulnerability gets more painful before the love and healing are experienced. If the directee is struggling, the spiritual director can confidently provide some encouragement, such as, "This is going to get easier as we go along," or, "I know this is painful now, but the Lord is going to give you a deep sense of peace." The director can say this with confidence from his own experience and he can also trust in the testimonies of countless people who speak simply of their experience of Confession and how good it feels after they are finished, saying things like, "I felt so much better afterward," and, "I felt more sure of myself and ready to move forward." These testimonies can give the spiritual director what he needs to encourage those who might be distressed in the midst of vulnerable sharing.

In encouraging vulnerability, the director must avoid the temptation to problem-solve too simply or prematurely. Vulnerability itself is healing and solutions will arise from it. The director can make recommendations and suggestions, but it is better for the directee to come to these himself. The more that the directee can discover through his own sharing, the more impactful it will be for him. As the director gets more experience, patterns may begin to emerge for him, but he should always be careful not to get ahead of the directee. Likewise, he should avoid asking confusing questions or interrupting out of his own curiosity or for the sake of information gathering. The director will do best by loving with his eyes, holding the directee in his heart, entering into the story, and allowing the love of Christ to come forth through listening.

The Beloved Disciple gives us a good example in this regard. After hearing Mary Magdalene's announcement about the empty tomb, he ran ahead of Peter, but waited for Peter to enter first (see Jn 20:4–8). Then he entered, saw, and believed, but apparently did not explain to Peter, who would need his own time and personal experiences to come to belief in the Resurrection. A slight variation on this dynamic took place in the third encounter with Jesus when John recognized Jesus first and announced, "It is the Lord!" (Jn 21:7). Then the Beloved Disciple allowed the Prince of the Apostles to race to the Lord and have the encounter of reconcil-

iation and commissioning that he needed. The Beloved Disciple
models some elements of good spiritual direction in seeing,
understanding, waiting, and announcing at the appropriate times.

At the same time, the director must always respect appropriate boundaries. Although he may want to hold a directee who is
crying or take the person's hand, this is not advisable. Rather, he
can hold the person in his heart and even express, "I am really
hurting with you right now. I am holding you in my heart. I really
wish I could take away your pain or help you carry your cross."
This is not a technique. It must be said and felt sincerely. What is
appropriate and helpful for one person would be inappropriate
and unsettling for another. These situations may bring about some
challenging feelings for the director (see Chapter 9 for more on
this). Sometimes there are no words and the director should learn
how to hold a steady gaze and simply love in the silence. And it
also helps if the director blesses the vulnerability by expressing
how loved the directee is and how close Jesus is at that moment.

Blessing Vulnerability

A man named Joe spoke with his spiritual director about how
angry he was that his wife always put him down. He was seriously
questioning whether he wanted to be with her anymore. He said
they were so different and she didn't get it; she didn't get him. "All
I want is a wife who will love me. Am I so wrong to want to be
loved?" His spiritual director recognized that there is often hurt
beneath anger and so he did not respond directly to the question
but blessed Joe's more vulnerable place—the hurt. "I don't think
you are so much angry as you are hurting. You certainly are not
wrong to want someone to love you and to want your wife, in
particular, to love you." The spiritual director then explained how
the angry response not only makes the pain worse by masking
it but can bring out worse reactions from his wife as well. The
spiritual director blessed Joe's pain, acknowledging how hard it
is to be put down, especially by someone so close whose love is
very important. As they were able to focus on the pain that Joe

felt, Joe gained confidence and felt some consolation. His spiritual director was able to encourage him to speak vulnerably with his wife about the pain. "When she says something that hurts you, perhaps you could tell her, 'That really hurt. Did you mean to hurt me?'" As Joe considered this response, he recognized that she probably did not realize she was hurting him. She had had a hard life growing up and a lot of her reactions were defensive. Joe had gone around and around with her, trying different things, but he had never tried simply to be vulnerable with her. By showing his vulnerability to his spiritual director in asking the question, "Is it so wrong to want to be loved?" and then receiving the spiritual director's loving response, he was able to imagine being vulnerable with his wife as well.

As the directee vulnerably opens up more of his interior life, a spiritual director can do a great deal of good simply by blessing the vulnerability. If a person is in a very painful place, it can help to say, "God loves you so much in this place where you are right now," or, "This is a very beautiful place in you," or, "This vulnerable place is truly where the Lord lives in you." Afterwards, especially if someone seems uncertain or is still hurting, the director can provide some consolation by saying, "What you just shared was so beautiful."

When a word of affirmation is spoken over a time of vulnerable sharing, it blesses that place, leaving a positive mark that encourages the directee to come back to it. Something like, "Jesus loves you there," can make a powerful impression on a vulnerable place in the directee. People will quickly learn that the spiritual director likes it when they are vulnerable and little, which can encourage them to go there more quickly and even become more transparent. The more vulnerable and transparent a directee is, the more effective the spiritual direction will be.

Mercy

When vulnerability is met with unconditional love, it is an experience of mercy. This mercy puts the directee in direct contact with God. Remember that mercy is "the bridge that connects God and man, opening our hearts to a hope of being loved forever despite our sinfulness."[20] The director gives the directee a taste of mercy and, in doing so, shows the directee the bridge to God. The director's love, of course, is limited in many ways, but by also naming God ("Jesus shares your pain and has a heart full of love for you") and re-proposing His promises ("He will never give up on you; He will never leave you; He wants you to be happy with Him forever where there are no more tears and no more pain"), the director helps the directee make his way to the bridge to eternal, unconditional love. These are, of course, affirmations that the director and the directee make in faith, and in the process, faith is shared and deepened.

---

[20] Pope Francis, *Misericordiae vultus*, no. 2.

5

Communicating

W E HAVE BEEN EXAMINING the very basic, three-part structure of spiritual direction: a very brief initial greeting, a
lengthy period of vulnerable sharing by the directee, and a short
conclusive communication by the spiritual director. Of course,
the second and third parts may interweave as the directee covers
multiple, loosely related subjects, but the basic structure and proportion of time remains. As we've discussed, the spiritual director
should do much more listening than speaking.

Before reflecting further on the spoken response of the
spiritual director, it is necessary to emphasize once again how
important empathic, prayerful, affirmative listening—*vulnerable
attentiveness*—is in spiritual direction. This must be the foundation from which any spoken communication emerges in spiritual
direction. To illustrate the importance of this foundation, Dr.
Conrad Baars elaborates:

> The philosopher-reader may want to go deeper into the
> meaning of affirmation, by comparing processes of "com-
> munication" and "communion." Nowadays much emphasis
> is put on communication as the most effective means of
> greater understanding of one another and thus of better
> relationships and friendships. In communication we share
> with one another what we *have*: material possessions, ideas,
> psychological experiences (e.g. feelings we have), and

spiritual experiences (e.g. our particular religious beliefs).

But what we *are* cannot be communicated. This is so because there is a profound difference between having and being. What I *am* can only be received by the other who gives me his full attention, who is present to me and becomes aware of what I am, and that I am good and worthwhile. The other who wills his awareness of me opens his consciousness to my being, and comes to know, that is, possess my goodness. His evident finding delight in my goodness will be perceived by me. I am revealed to myself as good. I have received from the other what I am. I am no longer alone. I have been linked to another human being in this process of affirmation; not by communication of what I have, but by the revelation, the communion of what I am. In friendship the greatest gift my friend can give me is himself. In affirmation I receive an even greater gift: myself.[1]

A Loving Response

Although the foundational role of the spiritual director is to be a listener, there does come a time when he can and should offer some insight and wisdom. If he has listened well, and through body language and little encouragements and clarifications has communicated affirmative and compassionate love to the directee, he will be able to speak most effectively. The listening gives him credit in the eyes of the directee that will make his words even more powerful. This draws attention to the fact that spiritual direction is not merely about saying the right thing or having the right answer to particular problems. Indeed, the truth spoken at the beginning of a meeting will not have the same impact as at the end of the meeting after prayerful listening. It's not merely a matter of saying the right thing or having the right answer. Although the director

---

[1] Conrad Baars, *Born Only Once*, 28.

might have spoken the same truth or given the same answer at the beginning of the meeting, the directee will be better able to receive it after feeling truly heard and understood. Furthermore, after the directee has talked through what is happening, he may discover that he does not need any response at all.

Affirmation

Spiritual directors are often called spiritual fathers or spiritual mothers. There is a real way in which they can give new life to a directee. This happens by fostering and nurturing the spiritual maturity of the directee in a way that is spiritually lifegiving. This can also happen psychologically through the power of affirmation. Affirmation, according to one school of thought, leads to "psychological birth." Psychiatrist Dr. Anna Terruwe and psychologist Dr. Conrad Baars counseled, studied, wrote, and taught extensively about the power of affirmation. Their basic approach to psychology and insights on the modern state of Catholic life and practice have been greatly appreciated by the Church at many levels. Dr. Terruwe's teaching received acceptance by the Holy Office in 1965 and she was affirmed by Bl. Pope Paul VI in a private audience in 1969. Dr. Conrad Baars lectured and taught throughout the United States in the 1970s and 1980s at the invitation of bishops and religious superiors.

Baars described affirmation as a second birth. "For the one affirmed, it is their psychic or psychological birth; and for the affirming person, it is the opportunity to co-create with God. This is why I called my book *Born Only Once*, because it is dedicated to the millions of people who have not yet received their second or psychological birth, who suffer fear and loneliness because they cannot relate to other persons on an adult level."[2]

Baars presented the key elements of such powerful affirmation

<hr>

[2] Conrad W. Baars, "The Affirming Power of Love," in Conrad W. Baars, eds. Suzanne M. Baars, and Bonnie N. Shayne, *I Will Give Them a New Heart: Reflections on the Priesthood and the Renewal of the Church* (Staten Island, NY: St. Pauls/ Alba House, 2008), 69.

by noting first of all that it must be genuine. It cannot be a mere technique. A person cannot merely use certain words, devoid of genuine love. "At the bottom of affirmation must be a genuine love and affectivity."[3] We gave an initial description of affirmation in Chapter 4 because affirmation can already occur through the way we listen. Affirmation clearly depends on the quality of listening and may be expressed without words—through eyes, gestures, the warmth and tenderness of facial expressions, and physical presence. As the spiritual director learns to detect goodness more and more in everything—a project that Baars notes involves lifelong growth—he is able to use the power of affirmation in spiritual direction more and more effectively to give new life to his directee.

As the spiritual director is able to feel the appreciation of the directee's goodness in his heart, he can learn to identify what he is feeling and simply give voice to what he is appreciating. Often this involves simple, almost obvious observations, which are powerful when spoken with sincere appreciation. Simply affirming the directee's vulnerability, sensitivity, self-awareness, or openness is very important; for example, "Thank you for being so open and sharing. That took a lot of courage." Likewise, the spiritual director can affirm the directee's understanding of his own situation with words such as, "You really have an excellent insight into yourself and what is happening inside of you." Even before searching for further steps to take when handling a particular struggle, the spiritual director can affirm the directee's sincere efforts or even simply his desire to be good and do good, "There is so much goodness in your heart and it comes out in all your efforts to do the right thing." The spiritual director might want to affirm the authenticity of the directee's spiritual life or even simply the directee's desire to have a deep spiritual life by saying, "You have a real gift in your faith and your desire to serve the Lord. Not everyone has that gift." The spiritual director might simply affirm how

---

[3] Conrad W. Baars, "The Secret of Affirmation," in *I Will Give Them a New Heart*, 56–57.

much the directee loves God: "I can tell how much you love the Lord." Such affirmations can cut through a frenetic desire to fix some problem and help the directee step back and see a situation more clearly, putting the problem in its proper context.

The key to affirmation is twofold: first feeling it, then revealing it through gestures and words. We often think of affirmation as words, but words are really the second step. Before saying anything, the spiritual director must first learn to appreciate and be present to the unique goodness of the directee. The uniqueness of each directee becomes more evident as a spiritual director gets more experience with more directees. What one might have taken for granted in a spiritual directee, such as a prayer life or a level of self-awareness, is not always universal. Even the ability to see and articulate what is happening interiorly is a quality that develops over time and is not found in everyone. Some can learn quickly and assimilate well what they realize in spiritual direction or prayer, and others sadly seem to lose almost immediately what they have gained. Affirming these points and so many others can be a true gift to the directee. The affirmation reveals the directee to himself and helps him receive and take possession of the gift of his person. For someone who has never experienced this, it can be a new birth. For a person who has lived an affirmed life, it can still be a powerful way to strengthen and build up certain qualities that may have been less affirmed in other settings.

A spiritual director must earn the right to affirm someone by listening enough and truly understanding the person. "I see a change taking place in you," can be a powerful observation coming from someone who has listened over the course of many meetings and has truly understood and appreciated a directee. The spiritual director could also give specific details about that change that is taking place in the directee. It is a special benefit of spiritual direction that the director sees the directee over a long period of time and has an ability to summarize their development.

This can be particularly powerful with directees who have chronic suffering from addictions, various struggles, humiliation, and shame. Simply stating sincerely, "I can see you are a very good person," can bring hope and courage. These words cannot be said mechanically. They must come genuinely from the heart, but when spoken sincerely, they can have the power to dispel discouragement and communicate strength and hope to the directee.

St. Faustina observed this, as she wrote:

> When I talked to my spiritual director [Father Sopocko] about various things that the Lord was asking of me, I thought he would tell me that I was incapable of accomplishing all those things, and that the Lord Jesus did not use miserable souls like me for the works He wanted done. But I heard words [to the effect] that it was just such souls that God chooses most frequently to carry out His plans. . . . At that instant light penetrated my soul and I understood that God was speaking to me through him.[4]

Overcoming Resistance

Sometimes a directee might resist affirmative words. It is valuable to understand why. A part of the directee has become suspicious of affirmation, perhaps from past betrayal or superficial psychobabble. Finding a way to bypass this defense and speak the loving truth to the wounded part of the directee can be a healing experience. The dynamic of resistance can be explored through an explicit observation, "I notice when I affirm you, you change the subject." Then see what the response is. Sometimes a person has made a home in their shame and is afraid of coming out of it to accept a compliment. Accepting one's goodness can be vulnerable if one has lost a sense of that goodness too many times from sin and failure.

On the other hand, some people bolster themselves too quickly through a false confidence with insufficient reflection on their failures and experience of their shame. They need to remain in their shame a little longer so that the sting of it sinks in and leads to a deeper conversion. As Pope Francis taught in his 2016

---

4   St. Faustina, *Diary*, no. 436.

Chrism Mass homily, "Our response to God's superabundant forgiveness should be always to preserve that *healthy tension between
a dignified shame and a shamed dignity*. It is the attitude of one who
seeks a humble and lowly place, but who can also allow the Lord
to raise him up for the good of the mission, without complacency."[5] Knowing when to let someone sit in their shame a bit and
when to lift them out of it through affirmation is an art that is best
guided by the Holy Spirit. The friends of Job model the behavior
of the one who affirms when they sit and weep with him on his
ash heap and quietly share his misery (see Job 2:13).

It is also important to realize that the spiritual director may not
navigate this perfectly, but making a mistake here is not the end
of the world. A humble spiritual director will be able to correct
unhelpful comments or interventions, perhaps by taking a different direction or opposite approach when one direction does not
bear fruit. The spiritual director must also trust in the Holy Spirit
to cover some honest mistakes and allow some to be corrected or
even become an occasion for clarification. We always bring our
own strengths and weaknesses, our own abilities and limitations
into spiritual direction, but the Holy Spirit is the ultimate director. If the spiritual director remains humble, His action will always
provide the dominant and lasting word and will draw the best
human efforts into the workings of grace.

Affirmation can be a powerful remedy against fear and anxiety
as well. Some people are extremely fearful or anxious. St. John
teaches that "perfect love casts out fear" (1 Jn 4:18). A spiritual
director's love will not be perfect but it can be sacramental, such
that the directee receives God's perfect love through it. The
spiritual director can also help the directee see his fears and anxieties and can help him to bring those fears and anxieties to the Lord
in prayer. Some people are so anxious that they cannot see the
source of their anxiety. They simply act out their anxieties. Many

[5]   Pope Francis, Homily for the Mass of Holy Chrism (March 24, 2016), https://
w2.vatican.va/content/francesco/en/homilies/2016/documents/papa-francesco_20160324_omelia-crisma.html.

times there is an underlying wound and if the directee can be vulnerable in spiritual direction, the wound can be exposed and love can reach that place and begin a process of healing. Ultimately the power of the Sacrament of Reconciliation and the other sacraments is most effective and goes far beyond anything that can happen in spiritual direction.

In summary, after listening attentively for most of the session, the spiritual director will do well to reflect on the aspects of the directee's sharing that he has appreciated. If he can trace these aspects back to certain qualities that are a part of the directee, then expressing them will be a great gift to the directee and help to open his heart to what else might follow. Although a spiritual director might want to forge ahead boldly because of his appreciation of the directee and his sympathy for whatever trial the directee is undergoing or whatever success he is experiencing, he will do better if he can first echo back what he has heard and affirm the directee in a way that relates to what he has shared.

Reinterpreting History Through God's Eyes

Another powerful way that the spiritual director can offer insight to the directee is through helping the directee to reinterpret past memories through God's eyes. Neal Lozano, director of Heart of the Father Ministries, provides an approach to healing based on an important and powerful insight: although we cannot change history, we can change our interpretation of history. This is not just a mind game or a sleight of hand. It is also not a matter of imposing wishful thinking on the past. In fact, when we engage in this spiritual exercise of reinterpreting our own history, we are seeking to open up a fuller truth that was always there but that we missed due to our own narrow perspective.[6]

Our own senses tell us only a small portion of reality. This has been illustrated across various cultural and religious contexts

---

[6] Neal Lozano, *Abba's Heart: Finding Our Way Back to the Father's Delight* (Minneapolis, MN: Chosen, 2015), 127.

through the parable of the blind men and the elephant. When several blind men describe an elephant after touching only a part of its body, they come up with very different descriptions. One, having touched the elephant's head, describes it like a pot, while the one who touched the ear thought it was like a winnowing basket and the one who touched the tail thought it was a brush. The one who touched a tusk described it like a plowshare, while the one who touched the trunk imagined it like a plow.

Our experience of reality is always limited and so we interpret it in a way that allows us to derive a fuller sense of what is happening. We use our own senses, our hearts and thoughts, the feelings of the people we are with, and the interpretations of others to find meaning. Typically, every experience we have generates a story or an interpretation. The first step is to recognize the story or interpretation we have generated about an event. Then we are in a position to rewrite that story or reinterpret that experience according to a more comprehensive truth. One big part that is missing from our interpretations, especially the interpretations that are negatively impacting our lives, is the presence and action of God in our experiences. This process of coming to see the fullness of truth will progressively also set us free (Jn 8:32).

A woman named Jane was thinking about leaving her family. She shared with her spiritual director that she thought her husband was having an affair and did not love her anymore because of comments he had made about another woman. Her hurt and distance was felt by her children, who then complained that she was letting them down. This resonated painfully with Jane, since she had always felt she was inadequate as a mother. Fortunately, she talked with her spiritual director before carrying out her plan to leave and was able to describe what her husband had said. The spiritual director was able to show Jane that his words did not indicate that he was having an affair or even that he was interested in another woman. He had merely expressed something about a woman from his workplace. Jane then proceeded to describe the problems with her children and her spiritual director could see that she was crossing signals with her children. They were having their own problems and wanted to share with their mother, but in the midst of her fears about her husband, she was too caught up in her own problems to help them. In the end it became clear that everyone was in a bad place on the day that she formulated the plan to leave. As her spiritual director showed her the dynamics in play, she was able to gain some perspective and then even see that on the day she wanted to leave, one of her children had written her a note to tell her how much he loved and appreciated her. She had also received a voicemail from her husband telling her how much he loved her and wanted her to stay. As long as her false interpretation prevailed, she was blinded even to those positive signs. A spiritual director can be very effective in helping to remove those blinders so a directee's eyes may be opened to the reality that was previously overlooked. Ultimately she felt much more at peace and decided to stay committed to her husband and children.

In spiritual direction, a reinterpretation already begins to happen in the sharing of an experience. This is so much so the case that sometimes a directee will not want to talk about a situation because he wants to protect his interpretation. We waste enormous amounts of energy when we hold grudges, sustain isolation, or resist help and mercy—but we do so because we are so attached to our interpretations. Some people have identified themselves as innocent victims and they work hard to protect that interpretation. With love they might be shown that, on the one hand they share some responsibility, and on the other hand, to the extent they are truly victims, they can find healing in Christ and the freedom to forgive. In another case, someone might see himself as a failure, but a reinterpretation can focus on the circumstances that might have been taken for granted. For example, in a beautiful video conference with the Holy Father, a woman who had immigrated with her children to the United States expressed her regret over having made mistakes that led to having her children out of wedlock. Pope Francis, in response, focused on her heroic sacrifices: to refuse abortion, keep her children, and raise them lovingly.[7] This reinterpretation produced a dramatic shift in understanding.

Offering reinterpretations is an art that must be guided by the Holy Spirit. The reinterpretations must always be guided by truth, inspired by Christian revelation, and incorporate the lived reality that has been shared by the directee. The directee will not always be able to take in the reinterpretations, but they can offer important insight into the ways that God is present and at work even in very painful and difficult situations. Sometimes reinterpretations do not stick with the directee after the meeting and they need to be reframed, repeated, or rethought at a later time.

Seeing Jesus in Our Story

A simple example of reinterpreting is learning to discover Jesus in our memories. Many times when we experience traumatic wounds or failure, we are so wrapped up in the pain that we are not aware of the presence of Jesus and all that He is doing at the time—and all that He is preparing to do in the future. As a directee reflects on past experience, a spiritual director can find opportunities to invite the directee to see how Jesus was at work. Sometimes it helps to ask the simple question, "Where was Jesus when that was happening?" or, "What do you think Jesus was doing when you were experiencing that?"

Here the spiritual director is helped by some fundamental Christian principles: God is all-knowing, all-powerful, all-loving, and always present. This means that God is always doing the most loving thing for each person at each moment. One must be careful not to express this crassly in a way that would imply that experiences of pain and suffering were dispassionately inflicted by a cold and calculating deity. To the contrary, it is extremely important to

---

[7] Pope Francis, interview by Mariana Atencio, *20/20*, September 4, 2015, http://abcnews.go.com/International/video/watch-abc-news-papal-virtual-audience-mccallen-texas-33519522.

express, through the spiritual director's love and words, the way that Christ suffers together with each individual and the way He was suffering with the directee in the directee's past experience. At that time, He was already at work to bring about a greater good. Sometimes that greater good has already manifested itself in the life of the directee and this can be pointed out. Sometimes it can only be proclaimed in hope.

After St. Thérèse of Lisieux lost her mother to a painful death from breast cancer when Thérèse was only four years old, the little saint was able to see how her older sister quickly stepped into her mother's role. Thérèse also received some extra special attention from her father. That became one of the greatest blessings in her life, because it taught her so much about being a little child in the loving care of the Heavenly Father. Thus, the grace at work through her mother's death laid the foundations of human experience that eventually blossomed into her universally beloved spiritual theology of the Little Way.[8]

In other situations, God seems to be absent during and even immediately following various traumatic experiences. Even in those cases, we can confidently affirm that there is a reason for hope. Before God would ever allow any evil to strike us, He has already prepared a remedy, even if we will not experience it fully until many years later—or in Heaven. God is never simply wringing His hands wondering what He can possibly do to help us. We can trust in St. Paul's assertion: "We know that in everything God works for good with those who love him" (Rom 8:28), and "neither death, nor life, nor angels, nor principalities, nor things present, nor things to come, nor powers, nor height, nor depth, nor anything else in all creation, will be able to separate us from the love of God in Christ Jesus our Lord" (Rom 8:38–39).

A German deacon during World War II named Karl Leisner was delayed in his ordination to the priesthood on account of his poor health. During his recovery, he was imprisoned in the Dachau

---

[8] Marc Foley, OCD., *The Context of Holiness: Psychological and Spiritual Reflections on the Life of St. Thérèse of Lisieux* (Washington, DC: ICS Publications, 2008).

concentration camp, where he suffered even more extreme pains. An experience that inspired great hope in the prisoners came after Karl was in the prison camp for over four years. After the imprisonment of a French bishop and an incredible joint effort by many prisoners, the prisoners arranged for Karl Leisner to be ordained a priest in the prison camp. He had longed to be a priest his whole life. Although he may have wondered many times why God had allowed all of his suffering, he could have rightly affirmed that God was preparing something greater, even though he could have scarcely imagined what it was. Karl was ordained a priest on the third Sunday of Advent, 1944. He was beatified by Pope St. John Paul II in 1996.[9]

Sometimes our suffering is extended to purify us, sanctify us, and make God's intervention even more powerfully evident as a witness to nonbelievers. We can think of the seventeen years of tearful, prayerful waiting by St. Monica for her son St. Augustine's conversion in this way. St. Rita's many years of persevering prayer for her husband moves us likewise. The woman in the Gospels who was hemorrhaging for twelve years (Mk 5:25) and the man who was sitting and suffering by the pool of Siloam for thirty-eight years (Jn 5:5) inspire us precisely *because* of the length of time. The man born blind provides an extreme example of one who had to wait a lifetime for healing, but precisely because of that he was able to reveal the glory of God (Jn 9:3).

In some cases, the experience of spiritual direction is itself the remedy. Healing can come from finally finding a person who can lovingly understand and give flesh to God's compassion. In another case, God may be preparing the remedy at the same time as He was allowing the trauma. For example, at the same time as a woman was suffering the trauma of abortion, God was forming Theresa Burke and Vicki Thorn who founded two post-abortion trauma treatment ministries. He was also preparing the friend who would invite that woman to participate in a healing retreat or

---

[9] For more on Bl. Karl Leisner, see Otto Pies, SJ., *The Victory of Father Karl* (New York: Farrar, Straus, and Cudahy, 1957).

counseling relationship. The radical hope given to us by Christ enables us to always say we will be better off because of what has happened to us, because "in everything God works for good with those who love him" (Rom 8:28), and "where sin increased, grace abounded all the more" (Rom 5:20).

These truths cannot be given as pious platitudes at the beginning of spiritual direction, but they can be lovingly applied to the particular situation of each directee once the directee trusts the director and feels truly loved and understood by him. Sometimes our own clever reinterpretations are completely unhelpful and the directee rejects them and embraces something simpler.

Furthermore, these ways of looking with eyes of faith can be given as an invitation to the directee to take his own experiences into prayer and to try to envision the experience in a way that questions how Jesus was present and at work. With some encouragement by the director, the directee can have powerful experiences of reinterpreting his memories in prayer. In the end it is always most important for the directee to be able to accept a reinterpretation, and that is often facilitated best when he arrives at that interpretation on his own. This can lead to life-changing acts of faith and hope in what God is doing through even the most painful traumas.

Lastly, we must be clear that it is not necessary to work through everything with a fine-toothed comb. Some wounds disappear in ways that we do not understand. Again, this emphasizes the importance of prayer throughout spiritual direction as well as the freedom of God and the powerful work of grace. The spiritual director is never the master of what takes place in spiritual direction, but only God's humble servant.

Seeing Myself in Jesus' Story

Part of reinterpreting our experience is understanding how to connect our personal lives with the mysteries of Christ's life. We have to learn how to fit the little story (of our own life) into the big story (of salvation history). Being able to do this provides many benefits.

One benefit is that it can become a source of strength for us. For example, a young man might experience helplessness at watching his best friend make bad decisions and suffer as a result. Identifying with Mary at the foot of the Cross, as she stands by helplessly watching and praying as her Son suffers from all of our bad decisions, may give him strength. When someone must make a painful offering, like letting go of a child with a religious vocation or letting go of a failed relationship, it can be helpful to connect the experience to Mary in the Presentation of Jesus in the temple. Likewise, when a person suffers from confusion and cannot understand how things got so bad or why something is happening, it can be comforting to know that the Mother of God also experienced this when she lost Jesus in the temple.

Another benefit is that the mysteries give us a reason for hope. When we can connect our experience with one part of the Mystery, the resolution of that Mystery provides hope for the resolution of our own situation. Simply helping someone to see that their struggles, even self-inflicted ones, allow them to share in the Cross of Jesus can be a source of great strength, because we know that the Cross *always* resolves, by God's grace, in the Resurrection. Sometimes one can find hope in making a sacrifice when that sacrifice is compared to that of Abraham. When Abraham demonstrated his willingness to offer up his son Isaac, he received his son back. Of course, he had to carry through with that painful detachment to the extreme conclusion before God returned Isaac to him, and this knowledge may provide courage and guidance to a directee. Providing a directee with Scriptures that connect to his experience can be a powerful way to harmonize his interior life with the life of grace. The Old Testament prophets can be helpful in this regard. Someone who has suffered abuse and battled with low self-esteem may find hope and healing in the words of the prophet Isaiah, "You shall no more be termed Forsaken, and your land shall no more be termed Desolate; but you shall be called My delight is in her, and your land Married; for the Lord delights in you, and your land shall be married" (Is 62:4).

Whether connecting a directee's experience to a descriptive version of a mystery of faith or offering some Scripture that helps a directee make a connection, this cannot be done in an automated way. The Holy Spirit is always in the lead and so the director must be attentive to the guidance of the Holy Spirit in his own heart. At the same time, God is able to work with His Word and His mysteries in a wonderful way that may even surprise the director. Often the director will intend for the directee to make a particular connection, but the directee will come back from praying, as suggested, and a completely different connection emerged from the experience.

The Medicine of Truth

Pain, fear, anxiety, doubts, and questions can cause one's world to close in and prevent one from seeing the forest for the trees. Once the spiritual director has listened attentively and loved and connected with the directee in his struggles, he is then in a position to gently open up the directee's world. This involves showing the directee natural things that he might have missed. It also involves showing the directee supernatural realities that can become distant in the face of immediate problems. This is all part of seeing the fullness of truth.

Truth is a medicine. But there is also a need for spiritual surgery that carefully digs out spiritual tumors—problems, wounds, or lies—that a person finds growing in himself. After surgery, however, by giving a directee the truths that God has revealed, he can continue a process of healing. That truth includes God's providential goodness—He works all things to the good (Rom 8:28). It also includes God's commitment to us, which is so strong that nothing can separate us from His love (Rom 8:38–39).

Part of the medicine of truth involves an honest appraisal of events that may get distorted in the directee's mind. A person may read many things into an event that are not really there. A spiritual director can gently point this out and challenge the judgments that the directee made. Many times these judgments are distorted by the way an individual sees himself, and as the spiritual director helps to reshape a directee's self-image, some of the other distorted perspectives change along with it. As an extreme example, one woman expressed to her spiritual director that she believed when she prayed for the Pittsburgh Steelers and they lost, it was a sign that God was displeased with her.

When our plans do not work out, it is easy to blame God and draw conclusions about how He looks at us. We can create false ideas about God's motives and false interpretations of His actions. The spiritual director can play an important role in helping people to understand the divine logic of God's plan for universal redemption. This is part of the ministry of truth. The spiritual director does not leave the directee in the ignorance of low expectations or a faintheartedness that is afraid to ask much of God. It is easy to fall into the trap of lowering expectations to avoid disappointment, but Christian spirituality encourages magnanimity and the hope that comes with having such a great-spiritedness. "I can do all things in [Christ] who strengthens me" (Phil 4:13). A spiritual director is often in a unique and powerful position to show how God's grace is at work.

At the same time, our interventions must always be tailor-made. It is insensitive to the person who just found out he has cancer to tell him immediately, "God has arranged this." It is important to meet a person in his pain, to empathize and console, and only when the person is ready, to move to a supernatural perspective and help him to see through God's eyes. A valuable way to test whether a person is ready is by asking the question, "How do you think God is at work through this?" The response will guide a course of action in spiritual direction.

The spiritual director needs to maintain a hopeful attitude, but that will not always be expressed the same way. This is not merely an optimistic outlook hoping for good natural outcomes, but a theological hope in God, trusting in His ultimate victory. A spiritual director's unflagging confidence in the goodness of God and His divine loving design for us can shape a directee's attitude

gradually over time. The directee learns to take up the outlook
of the spiritual director. For this reason it is very important that
a spiritual director have a robust and integrated faith, as it will
be imparted explicitly and implicitly. Sometimes a directee asks
a spiritual director outright how he sees a situation. A spiritual
director will do well to answer the question, but it is often better
to start with the directee's position by saying, "I will answer that
question, but first tell me how you see it." That way it gives the
spiritual director a chance to work from the starting point of the
directee's faith and ideas and to avoid long-winded responses that
are off-point. One spiritual directee asked, "What do you think
about death?" The spiritual director was about to respond with a
discourse on purgatory but started by asking where the question
was coming from. He discovered that the directee's main concern
was about claustrophobia, thinking about a corpse being closed
in to a small space underground. The spiritual director's initial
thoughts would not have spoken to the directee's fears in this
instance.

Some Particular Truths of Faith

Some truths, which could be personally applied to a directee in
a particular situation, are presented by Pope Francis in *The Joy of
the Gospel*:

> Faith also means believing in God, believing that he truly
> loves us, that he is alive, that he is mysteriously capable of
> intervening, that he does not abandon us and that he brings
> good out of evil by his power and his infinite creativity.
>   . . . we need an interior certainty, a conviction that
> God is able to act in every situation, even amid apparent
> setbacks: "We have this treasure in earthen vessels" (2 Cor
> 4:7). This certainty is often called "a sense of mystery." It
> involves knowing with certitude that all those who entrust
> themselves to God in love will bear good fruit (cf. Jn 15:5).

This fruitfulness is often invisible, elusive and unquantifiable. We can know quite well that our lives will be fruitful, without claiming to know how, or where, or when. . . . No single act of love for God will be lost, no generous effort is meaningless, no painful endurance is wasted. All of these encircle our world like a vital force.[10]

Such faith-filled statements, coming from a spiritual father who loves us, can be powerful medicines for stirring hope in our hearts and giving us the energy and courage to move forward, even in very difficult situations.

Validation

The central focus in spiritual direction is on the directee and the directee's relationship with God. When communicating in the context of spiritual direction, the spiritual director must always keep this in mind. It is not a platform for him to express his ideas to a captive audience or merely an opportunity for him to wax eloquent about the state of the Church or the world. Moreover, what the directee hears and experiences is more important than what the director says or does. How does one know what the directee hears? To determine that, the spiritual director should seek validation from the directee without drawing attention to the fact that he is doing so.

Validation can take several forms. In each case, the spiritual director is watching to see whether his ministry is resonating with the directee. He will not always get the satisfaction of seeing this instantaneously. A spiritual director is often planting seeds and only sees the plant breaking through after a long dormant period in which germination is actually taking place. At the same time, spiritual direction can also be analogous to massage therapy or chiropractic adjustment, in which there is an immediate response of

---

[10] Pope Francis, *Evangelii gaudium*, nos. 278–279.

relief or a felt relaxation of a knotted muscle. Sometimes spiritual direction can feel like groping in the darkness, feeling one's way through the relationship, and validation—even negative validation when the spiritual director says something unhelpful—can be like a doorway in the darkness as he accompanies the directee through the interior life.

Some ways that the spiritual director can experience validation are through tears, through words, or through postures and facial expressions. In each case, the spiritual director is looking for manifestations of the theological virtues of faith, hope, and love. These are important criteria to distinguish genuine validation from the appearance of validation. Sometimes the directee may speak words or even have tears, but if they are empty of faith, hope, and love, the spiritual director must continue to find ways to reach the heart of the directee.

Tears

The office of every spiritual director should have tissues to accommodate the frequency of tears that are shed in spiritual direction. Tears are a very promising form of validation. They are almost always meaningful signs that the interactions in spiritual direction are reaching the heart of the directee. There are "crocodile tears" and there are people who cry so often and so easily that the tears are less significant, but in almost every case they are meaningful and should be lovingly received and even encouraged by the spiritual director. Often a directee will weep and reveal that they have not wept in a very long time. As noted above, the discernment of whether they provide validation for something the spiritual director has done or said should be in whether the directee is also being moved to an increase in faith, hope, or love.

In one case a woman named Ann was sharing with some distress about how much she was failing to maintain her commitment to daily prayer. It was not the first time she admitted this in spiritual direction and she was expressing her disappointment with herself and all the reasons that she was struggling to keep her commitment to prayer. She expressed her plans to do better the next time, but also some dismay and despair that she was a bad disciple and a bad directee. When she finished talking, her spiritual director simply said what he saw: "I can see how much you love Jesus and how much you are trying to be faithful to Him." That brought forth an immediate response of tears, and she visibly relaxed and then said with tender love for God, "Thank you. It's true. I love Him so much." Her spiritual director could then give her encouragement to do a little better: "You said you were faithful to your daily prayer time for half of the month. Perhaps you could add a day or two to that this coming month." She responded with hope, "You're right. I don't have to do it perfectly. I think I could do a little better this month." Finally, her spiritual director was able to encourage her in her faith that God loves her by saying, "Jesus loves you so much. He is so happy when you are able to spend that time with Him." Ann's response came in the nod of her head and more tears, adding to this series of validation.

Words or Gestures of Agreement

Validation does not always come as clearly as described in the last example, and so it is important for the spiritual director to be listening carefully to the directee's responses. A directee may express agreement with the spiritual director, but some people are simply agreeable people and want to affirm the spiritual director's authority. Validation is found not so much in agreement but in *how* the directee agrees with what the director has said. A directee may nod his head in agreement or he may say, "Right. That's right." The spiritual director can acknowledge that as possible validation, but he is really looking for a bit more than that. For example, it would be more clear if the directee says, "That's right," and then goes further with what the spiritual director just said, even adding something new or revealing something that had not been disclosed before. Obviously, the spiritual director is not focusing on getting a good report card or positive evaluation from the directee, but is sounding the vulnerability and being attentive to the quality of the relationship between the director and the directee.

A seminarian named Henry shared about how isolated he felt. He described how his friends and family were not responsive and the demands at work were weighing him down. His spiritual director echoed back the feelings of the directee, saying, "It sounds like you feel lonely." He received the validation in the directee's response, "Terribly lonely." This was a critical moment in the spiritual direction meeting. The directee was leading the spiritual director into a dark and difficult place in his heart, inviting him to enter the hole that he was experiencing interiorly. The spiritual director listened and loved him to the point of entering that hole with him and he was able to express that through the acknowledgment of loneliness. With that connection, the directee was ready to be led back into the light and the spiritual director sought to take that step with him: "I know, as you always do, that you are taking this into prayer." The directee's facial expression indicated openness and slight relaxation and his posture straightened up a bit. That was the validation the spiritual director needed to take another step and affirm him, "You really have been doing so well. You are moving closer to the priesthood." The spiritual director received another validation at that point as the young man expressed hopefully how his father, who had been very critical of his vocation, had recently been relaxing the criticism and seeing him more and more as a future priest. The spiritual director saw the opportunity to build further on the good foundation and acknowledged what was happening, "You are really becoming hopeful." That comment was met with a smile, showing that it found a home in the heart of this directee.

Subtler Validations

A directee may not give an obvious validation and instead merely remains still and unmoved after the spiritual director speaks. The fact that the directee at least has not objected may be a form of subtle validation. Some people prefer to take things in and process them internally without trying to affirm the director's words. For this reason, a spiritual director must often be satisfied with sowing seeds and waiting for them to bear fruit a month, six months, or even several years later. Similarly, a directee may respond with immediate agreement, but not really take in what was said. The spiritual director must learn to watch out for this. Is there any other evidence that the directee has taken in the spiritual director's help? The main signs to watch for are faith, hope, and love, not mere verbal agreement. Those signs may emerge in other ways, such as the directee's posture or countenance or tone of voice.

A directee may even object to what the spiritual director said and then immediately begin to explain why it is actually true. For example, after a spiritual director says, "It sounds like you are struggling with anger," the directee may immediately object, "Oh no. I don't struggle with anger." Then without a break he continues on to agree, "There was one time when I was angry and . . ." This denial is similar to the negative response a spiritual director will often get to a direct question such as, "Why do you think you got angry in that situation?" People will often respond immediately, "I don't know." As long as the spiritual director does not fill in the space, but waits for a few moments, the answer often follows right afterward, "I guess I always get angry when someone is getting picked on."

To Be Helpful, Not Only Right

Although everyone likes to say the right things and have the satisfaction of analyzing a situation in the right away, it can be just as helpful, or even more helpful, to be wrong and let the directee provide the proper analysis. A spiritual director must remember that the goal is to be helpful, not necessarily to be right. For example, one religious sister was recounting to her spiritual director that she had given a talk to a large group after struggling with the prospect of the task for a long time. Her spiritual director commented, "It sounds like you did a great job!" Her response indicated that she was not convinced she had and she began to object that it did not go the way she wanted it to. She had left out a key point and was very nervous during her presentation. At that point, the spiritual director reflected on whether she was being hard on herself and whether he should persevere with his sense that she had given a good talk, or whether he should accept her resistance. If he were determined to be right, he might have persevered blindly and missed an opportunity to be helpful. He chose to ask her instead, "Do you feel disappointed?" She replied with tears, "Yes." He registered the validation. Then he was able to work with her, "How are you handling your disappointment?" This allowed them both to invite Jesus into the place where she was hurting and discouraged. After that, the spiritual director could return to the point of affirming the merits of her talk and she could acknowledge that there were many good things about it. Then she began to share, with some hope, how several people came up to her afterward and thanked her for specific points she brought out. The spiritual director must always keep his attention on the directee, seeking to make everything an opportunity to be helpful, even when he is mistaken in what he is seeing.

Some Particular Challenges

Communication is necessary throughout a spiritual direction meeting, but most of the time the directee can be trusted to set the stage and take initiative in sharing what is most important. When this is happening, the spiritual director can allow the narrative to unfold. In some cases, however, proactive effort is required by the spiritual director even to facilitate sharing.

A Person Who Will Not Say Anything

Sometimes spiritual direction can be stymied by a directee who seems unwilling or unable to share. It can be tempting to start asking a lot of questions, but this would be a mistake. A spiritual director who has taken control of the session by turning it into an interview with the directee will become overworked and exhausted. The spiritual director can try to move things along by asking a question or two, but he should keep them as open ended as possible. One example is, "Tell me about your spiritual life." Another would be, "Tell me what's on your mind," or, "What did you want to talk about today?" As much as possible, the spiritual director should help the directee lead the conversation. An important fruit of spiritual direction is that a directee grows in self-knowledge, confidence, and vulnerability to the point that he can lead a spiritual direction meeting. This is a valuable skill for prayer as well. Even if the spiritual director has something in mind to ask, he should save it and first see where the directee leads. The spiritual director must be careful not to simply fill the silence with questions. A slightly awkward silence can be helpful in drawing the directee into some vulnerable sharing. At the same time, there is no value in having a staring contest. If the silence is not fruitful, the spiritual director should try to move forward with an open-ended question.

A Person Who Talks Constantly

In contrast to the directee who says too little is the directee who never stops talking. Although the spiritual director may be tempted to interrupt too quickly, it is best to see where the directee leads things. If it seems that the directee is simply filling the space and is circling superficially without going deeper, then it may be time to intervene and ask some questions to deepen the sharing. A person may simply be reporting what has happened without delving into a deeper level of the interior. In this case, the director may prompt the directee to speak about his feelings or the interpretation of what he's reporting: "Where did you see Jesus in that experience?" "How did it feel to participate in that conversation?" These approaches can work well with those who talk easily and excessively and are not even listening to themselves. The spiritual director will learn quickly (after a meeting or two) if the directee fits this pattern.

Sometimes the directee does not know how to go deeper and needs help. Other times, excessive talking may be a result of avoidance. By flooding the meeting with superficial conversation the directee may be avoiding an uncomfortable topic. For example, if the directee is being ordained soon and not talking about that at all, it would be a good topic for the director to raise. The directee's response to the question can bring further insight. A question might be dodged entirely or the directee might start to answer the question and then skid off into a tangent.

In other cases a directee might be trying to get into important things and may even discuss a number of important things without going very deeply into any one of them. In this case, a good question for focusing the directee is "You are bringing up many important things. Which would you say is the most important?" Or, similarly, the director could ask, "Of all the things you are bringing up, is there any particular topic that you would like to discuss further?" A simple insight here is that the spiritual director does not need to have magical powers to figure out what the directee needs to discuss the most. If he has some insight into the most important topic, that may be a movement of the Holy Spirit and he can go with that, but he should also feel free to place the responsibility to pick out what is most important on the directee.

A person who is talking excessively may also like having an audience but is not really *connecting*. In this case, it is necessary to break in more decisively. For example, excessive talking might also be accompanied by looking around at everything except the spiritual director. To break in more decisively and facilitate a connection, the spiritual director can see what happens when he invites the directee to look at him or asks him why he is not looking at him. In another case, a directee might skate over important issues and the spiritual director might intervene strongly saying something like, "I am really concerned about this. What do you think this means?" If the directee skips past the question, it might be necessary to return to it, "I don't think you have answered. Is there something you are avoiding?" For example, if someone whose father just died speaks excessively about the funeral, the spiritual director might ask a pointed question: "Your father just died and you are speaking about the funeral, but how are you handling the loss of your father?" A softer approach would be, "It sounds like you had a really hard day. How are you handling your father's death?"

Above all, the interaction should be natural, not clinical, and the spiritual director should err on the side of gentleness rather than harshness. The spiritual director should also be careful that his interruptions do not stem from irritation or his own disinterest in the subject matter being shared, but that he is really convinced his probing is important for the directee. The spiritual director's interventions should always be in the best interest of the directee.

A Person Stuck in Negativity

A directee can get into a negative cycle for various reasons. Sometimes the person will come out of it on his own once he has expressed his hurt and feels heard. At other times, the spiritual director may get the sense that he is truly stuck. When it sounds, for example, like there is nothing good in the directee's life, he may have become so blended with a negative part of himself that he cannot come out of it on his own. When the spiritual director discerns that this is the case, he can strongly switch directions. He may do this by stepping into the stream of negativity and pointing out some positive things. If he knows the directee well and is aware that he has a beautiful family or that he delights in his children, he may simply insert a question such as, "How are your children?" This can have such an impact that there may be an immediate change on the directee's face as he starts reflecting on his family. Any areas in the directee's life where there is some success or blessing are good places to point out. Relational parts of the life of the directee are generally going to draw him deeper and open up vulnerability more effectively.

Breaking out of the cycle of negativity is not a matter of avoiding the pain or difficulties that the directee is going through, but rather a matter of helping the directee step back and get some perspective. We may need to separate or "unblend" from an emotional part of ourselves before we can see clearly. Once the directee is unblended, he is in a better position to see what was happening to bring about all that negativity.

A Person Who Becomes Clingy or Needy

Spiritual directees naturally develop some attachment to their spiritual directors, but for people who do not form healthy attachments, the attachment can become clingy or needy—qualities that have subverted and worked against them in other relationships. They develop a dread of being pushed away, and so they come to a priest or a religious person thinking he will be bound by Christian charity not to reject them. In some cases, there are professionals who refuse to meet with difficult kinds of people or to handle particular kinds of problems, claiming a certain specialty and sending the person on his way by suggesting that he see a spiritual director or a priest! There is a small margin for this in spiritual direction, because there are so few spiritual directors to whom one may "send a person away." This kind of directee may be watching for every sign of rejection and it can be difficult to stay with him and persevere through dark times, especially when he is really stuck. If this becomes problematic, it is important to get advice from a supervisor on how to handle this (anonymizing in order to protect confidentiality, of course).

At the same time, it is important to recognize that some people who come off as clingy or needy are actually soaking up the affirmation and developing deep bonds with the spiritual director—bonds that can be profoundly healing. As noted earlier, a spiritual director is often known as a spiritual father or spiritual mother and the deep trust that can develop must be treated with great reverence. As Dr. Conrad Baars recognized, some people have not had a sufficient foundation of affirming love and when a spiritual director begins to fill that void, some "clinging" can come out from very deep places within the directee.[11] This is a

---

[11] Terruwe and Baars, *Psychic Wholeness and Healing.*

very delicate moment in the spiritual direction relationship. Great healing or great harm can come as the directee opens up places of vulnerability that are extremely fragile.

One direction that a spiritual director may take is to fortify some boundaries within the directee. For example, a directee may want to have emergency meetings and reach out several times between meetings through phone calls. It may be necessary for the spiritual director gently to set boundaries and help the directee wait for the next session.

Some people are afflicted with borderline personality disorder or other interior distortions that do not give them the strength or insight to maintain proper boundaries easily. People in these situations will likely require professional assistance and the spiritual director should not hesitate to recommend and even urge the directee to get additional help from a trained counselor. A professional counselor has several advantages over the spiritual director in the ability to commit to more regular meetings, the clearer boundaries of the therapeutic relationship, and limiting interactions to an office setting (a spiritual director may not be able to avoid encountering a directee outside of meetings, for example), not to mention specialized training in treating these disorders.

The spiritual director may take another approach as well. If he believes that the directee is learning trust in a fundamental way, and especially if there are missing foundations due to missing or broken parental relationships, he may try to be as available as reasonably possible and respond generously to the directee's additional communications. This should never cross boundaries of appropriate behavior (such as meeting in inappropriate locations or at inappropriate times), but an extra meeting, an extra phone call, or text messaging can provide additional support and prevent a directee from becoming destabilized. Sometimes, when trust has been established, the directee, in a child-like way, may seek to reach out and lean on that trusted spiritual father or mother when certain events or fears start to cause some destabilization. A little additional attention and support can go a long way toward bringing healing. As trust and healing are solidified, then the proper boundaries can also be solidified and the spiritual director can facilitate a new birth of hope and peace in a directee. These situations are very challenging, however, and a spiritual director must be careful. The safest path is to be sure that the director is discussing this with his own mentor or supervisor or spiritual director so as to navigate these situations as helpfully and gracefully as possible.

Wrapping Up a Session

The ending is an important part of a spiritual direction meeting. It is an opportunity to summarize and assimilate what has been discussed. Especially when the directee has been very vulnerable, there needs to be a gentle transition back to normal life. When the topics of spiritual direction have been varied, the closing provides an opportunity to review all that has been discussed and sometimes even resolved. It is a blessing for the directee to hear that the director has taken in and can summarize what has been discussed. Sometimes this can be communicated in summary words; other times it might be expressed through a closing prayer or a blessing. If the spiritual director is a priest, sacramental Confession is also a natural way to end a spiritual direction meeting.

During the spiritual direction meeting, the directee expresses his experience and what is happening in his heart. It is good for that sharing to be received as it is, affirmed, and echoed back without moving too quickly to a spiritualization or interpretation of the experience. At the end, however, once the directee feels that he has been heard, the spiritual director is in a better position to echo back with an interpretation, claiming the action of God in the directee's experience. The director might assert, "I think that was the Holy Spirit," or, "God was really working there." The spiritual director comes to know how bold he can be with his claim and assessment without getting out too far ahead of the directee.

Sometimes a meeting may involve a lot of sharing from the directee with little apparent resolution. Although there does not seem to be a trajectory toward anything significant, the very process of wrapping up can bring out crucial insights. For example, one man spent the majority of a meeting talking about the loss of his sister. It was understandably troubling, but he seemed to be struggling beyond normal grieving. The spiritual director let him talk vulnerably at length. At the end he affirmed the vulnerable sharing saying, "Wow. I really learned a lot about you." Then he focused on a key point of what was shared, "As you said, your sister is your last blood relative—you've lost all your blood relatives." Then the spiritual director emphasized his reverence for the directee's pain by sharing personally, "I have a lot of family left; it must be very difficult to be down to your last blood relative." This brought about the response: "And I don't have much time left either." This was the key insight that the spiritual director was waiting for! Sometimes the directee intentionally waits until the end of a meeting to share the critical point. Sometimes the directee does not even know why he is struggling so much. In any event, the end of a meeting can be a very fruitful opportunity. There may not be time to explore the final insights, but a spiritual director will leave a lasting impression on the directee who will have time in between meetings to continue reflecting on these points, and those reflections can make for a good start to a subsequent meeting.

A director may also offer some point or Scripture for meditation at the end of a meeting as a kind of homework assignment. The ability to fulfill such an assignment depends on personality, temperament, and maturity, but for someone who is able to take an insight, a question, or Scripture into prayer and bring back reflections for the next meeting, this can be a powerful gift for the director to provide. St. Faustina was able to be guided by her spiritual director and reflect on a particular point, and she recorded some of those meditations in her Diary:

November 22, 1934. +On one occasion, my spiritual director [Father Sopocko] told me to look carefully into myself and to examine whether I had any attachment to some particular object or creature, or even to myself, or whether I engaged in useless chatter, "for all these things," [he said,] "get in the way of the Lord Jesus, who wants complete freedom in directing your soul. God is jealous of our hearts and wants us to love Him alone."

When I started to look deep within myself, I did not find any attachment to anything, but as in all things that concern me, so also in this matter, I was afraid and distrustful of myself. Tired out by this detailed self-examination, I went before the Blessed Sacrament and asked Jesus with all my heart, "Jesus, my Spouse, Treasure of my heart, You know that I know You alone and that I have no other love but You; but, Jesus, if I were about to become attached to anything that is not You, I beg and entreat You, Jesus, by the power of Your mercy, let instant death descend upon me, for I prefer to die a thousand times than to be unfaithful to You once in even the smallest thing."

At that moment, Jesus suddenly stood before me, coming I know not from where, radiant with unbelievable beauty, clothed in a white garment, with uplifted arms, and He spoke these words to me, *My daughter, your heart is My repose; it is My delight. I find in it everything that is refused Me by so many souls. Tell this to My representative.* And an instant later, I saw nothing, but a whole ocean of consolations entered my soul.[12]

One additional point that we learn from St. Faustina's experience is that the director should not be overly concerned with being right. In this example, Bl. Michael Sopocko gave St. Faustina a point on which to meditate that actually caused her some distress because his general advice about attachments did not actually apply to her. All the same, her sincerity and holiness made good of misplaced guidance and led her to a beautiful encounter with Jesus totally unrelated to what her spiritual director had in mind.

---

[12] St. Faustina, *Diary*, nos. 337–339.

This serves as a reminder of how God wants to work through the spiritual director's poverty and even make him more poor if he is under the misimpression that he has great wisdom to offer his holy directee.

Spiritual Direction and Confession

Sacramental Confession has a significant relationship to spiritual direction. Indeed, in some eras of the Church's history, Confession provided the primary occasion for spiritual direction, albeit in a limited form. The vulnerable confession of one's sins opens up the right place in our hearts for spiritual direction, manifesting the conscience and sharing some of the darker parts of our interior. It is no surprise that the Sacrament of Confession has been identified as a sacrament of healing, because so much healing can take place between the penitent and the communication of God's mercy in the context of the sacramental ritual. When there is adequate time, the one-on-one celebration of Confession can be an advantageous opportunity for some direction in living the life of grace. St. John Paul II made this observation in his encyclical on Confession, *Reconciliatio et Paenitentia*. "Thanks then to its individual character, the first form of celebration makes it possible to link the sacrament of penance with something which is different but readily linked with it: I am referring to spiritual direction."[13]

At the same time, sacramental Confession does not require an elaborate or articulated response from the priest. It is enough that a penitent has the opportunity to confess his sins and receive the Lord's mercy through the prayer of absolution. The sacrament communicates the power of God's mercy through the ritual without any further intervention from the priest. For this

---

[13] Pope St. John Paul II, Post-Synodal Apostolic Exhortation on Reconciliation and Penance in the Mission of the Church Today *Reconciliatio et paenitentia* (December 2, 1984), no. 18, http://w2.vatican.va/content/john-paul-ii/en/apost_exhortations/documents/hf_jp-ii_exh_02121984_reconciliatio-et-paenitentia.html.

reason, Pope Francis emphasized the difference between Confession and spiritual direction when speaking with women religious. He observed how important it is for a spiritual director truly to understand the special vocation of the consecrated woman, while the confessor need not have as much knowledge or understanding (provided he prudently limits his attempts at offering advice in the confessional).

> A spiritual director is one thing and a confessor is another thing. I go to the confessor, I tell my sins, I feel the flogging; then he forgives me of everything and I go ahead. But I must tell the spiritual director what is happening in my heart. The examination of conscience is not the same for confession and for spiritual direction. For confession, you must search where you have fallen short, whether you have lost patience; if you have been greedy: these things, concrete things, which are sinful. But for spiritual direction, you must examine what has happened in the heart; such as the movement of the spirit, whether I have been desolate, if I have been consoled, if I am tired, why I am sad: these are the things to speak about with a spiritual director.[14]

Spiritual direction considers the interior life in more detail on a wider range of subjects. Although it should certainly include the areas of sin, it is not limited to those areas like Confession is. Furthermore, Pope Francis does not expect much communication from the confessor. Here when he speaks of "flogging," it should be understood that he is speaking euphemistically in light of the fact that he admonished confessors on several occasions never to make the confessional a torture chamber or even necessarily to ask probing questions.[15] It is clear that his primary expectation of

---

[14] Pope Francis, Address to Consecrated Men and Women.

[15] See, for example, *Evangelii gaudium*, no. 44; General Audience of November 13, 2013, *https://w2.vatican.va/content/francesco/en/audiences/2013/documents/papa-franc-*

the confessor is to give absolution rather than to provide spiritual direction. Rather he speaks of the flogging that is inherent in the shame of manifesting our own sin before another person. To do so has a way of flogging the heart.

St. Faustina likewise emphasized the difference between a confessor and a spiritual director and recognized the damage that a confessor can do if he is not careful. In this way she seemed to imply, as well, that a confessor should be careful in his communication and err on the side of saying less rather than more:

> Oh, if only I had had a spiritual director from the beginning, then I would not have wasted so many of God's graces. A confessor can help a soul a great deal, but he can also cause it a lot of harm. Oh, how careful confessors should be about the work of God's grace in their penitents' souls! This is a matter of great importance. By the graces given to a soul, one can recognize the degree of its intimacy with God.[16]

A Work of Mercy Led by the Holy Spirit

The spiritual director has a quasi-sacramental character for the directee, representing God for him in a significant way. This gives the director much power and demands care, gentleness, and responsibility. A negligent director can do much damage. At the same time, this realization should not be a cause for anxiety in the spiritual director. The most important work is done by the Holy Spirit and He is always faithful. Even when the director is having a bad day, is suffering from exhaustion, is worn out by many other burdens, makes an ill-advised comment, or provides bad advice for the directee, God has so much mercy. God works all things to

---

esco_20131113_udienza-generale.html; Interview with Antonio Spadaro, SJ "A Big Heart Open to God."

[16] St. Faustina, *Diary*, no. 35.

the good—even for spiritual directors, who are always beset by human weakness. This highlights the importance of the spiritual director's prayer and trust in God. A fitting prayer for spiritual directors to offer after meeting with their directees is, "Please, Lord, make up for all my deficiencies and help this beloved child of Yours in spite of any of my failures."

While a spiritual director develops confidence from God's faithfulness over the course of many positive experiences, he should never lose a sense of his own poverty and dependence on the Holy Spirit. Spiritual direction is always an art. It never dissolves into an automated science with preprogrammed responses to particular situations. It is only when the spiritual director remains humble and docile to the Holy Spirit, even as he remains humble and open to the directee, that the grace of God will be most free to act in the directee through the director. Then both will be able to rejoice sincerely at the miracles that follow.

A spiritual director will be sensitive to the Holy Spirit best when his heart is at prayer in a posture of mercy throughout spiritual direction. Mercy is the key note that makes the minister of the Gospel most in tune with the Heart of God. Pope Francis attributed all pastoral fruitfulness to this key note of mercy:

> Some plans and projects do not work out well, without people ever realizing why. They rack their brains trying to come up with yet another pastoral plan, when all somebody has to say is: "It's not working because it lacks mercy", with no further ado. If it is not blessed, it is because it lacks mercy. It lacks the mercy found in a field hospital, not in expensive clinics; it lacks the mercy that values goodness and opens the door to an encounter with God, rather than turning someone away with sharp criticism . . .[17]

---

[17] Pope Francis, "Third Meditation: The Good Odour of Christ and the Light of His Mercy" in Spiritual Retreat Given for Priests on the Occasion of the Jubilee for Priests in the Extraordinary Jubilee Year of Mercy (June 2, 2016), https://w2.vatican.va/content/francesco/en/speeches/2016/june/documents/papa-francesco_20160602_giubileo-sacerdoti-terza-meditazione.html.

In the chapters that follow, we will elaborate further on the kinds of communication that take place in spiritual direction, the process of guiding the directee into deeper prayer through the passages of the spiritual life, and mediating the Holy Spirit's powerful, personal work of bringing about healing and holiness in each individual.

Part 2

Particular Aspects of Spiritual Direction

6

Guidance for Prayer

A PRINCIPAL WORK of the spiritual director is to help Christians grow in prayer. Fr. Bennet Kelley, CP, in a wonderful work entitled *Spiritual Direction According to St. Paul of the Cross*, states strongly, "Unless a person is willing to give him/herself to a life of prayer and daily seeking God, they are not yet ready for ongoing spiritual direction."[1] For this reason, it is necessary in every spiritual direction meeting to speak about prayer, and if the directee does not bring it up, the spiritual director should always ask, "How is your prayer?" In a related way, the spiritual director will often do well to ask, following a directee's narrative about a particular situation, "What happened when you brought that to the Lord in prayer?" As noted by Fr. Bennet, prayer is at the heart of spiritual direction and spiritual direction should always be accompanied by the ongoing practice and growth in the life of prayer.

Prayer is not simply a personal practice like stretching or exercising or brushing one's teeth. Christian prayer is a living relationship with God Who has revealed Himself as Father, Son, and Holy Spirit. Thus, talking about prayer is ultimately always a matter of talking about one's relationship with God. In the simple observation of Abbot John Chapman, "the only way to pray is to pray; and the way to pray well is to pray much. If one has no

---

[1] Fr. Bennet Kelley, CP, *Spiritual Direction According to St. Paul of the Cross* (Staten Island, NY: Alba House, 1993), 5.

time for this, then one must at least pray regularly. But the less one prays, the worse it goes."[2] For this reason, checking on the frequency and regularity of prayer is an essential part of spiritual direction. As human beings pray more, they learn how to pray better—just as relationships become more natural with personal investment. We are made for this. We are made for a one-on-one relationship with God and the more we invest in that relationship, the more it will grow.

We tend to make a lot of excuses for not praying. It can be helpful for a spiritual director to gently explore with a directee what he is occupying himself with when he is not taking enough time in prayer. It is often not difficult to find some expendable activities that could be replacing prayer. Hours of television, video games, movies, social media, surfing the Internet, and other forms of entertainment are not as helpful as carving out even fifteen minutes for prayer. The accountability of regular spiritual direction and the relentlessly but gently asked question, "How is your prayer?" or, "How much time are you taking for prayer?" or, "Did you bring that problem up with God in prayer?" can slowly move a directee to claim more time for God. One seminarian genuinely wanted to grow in prayer but was an avid computer gamer. With persistent encouragement in spiritual direction, he eventually eliminated computer games on Fridays and instead spent more time in prayer. He immediately experienced the goodness of that prayer time and started trading more time of his video-gaming time for prayer. During Lent, he gave up video games altogether, and by the end of Lent he gave away his gaming system. He never regretted the additional time spent in prayer.

Of course, one should not use prayer as an escape from other responsibilities—though, frankly, this is a rare, almost nonexistent problem in our time. Furthermore, God will not let us use Him, and so prayer often has built-in discouragements for those who would try to escape from responsibility through the excuse

---

[2] Abbot John Chapman, *Spiritual Letters* (New York, NY: Burns & Oates, 1935), 53.

of prayer. If prayer is genuine, which happens naturally as we pray more, God Himself will send us back to our duties. For this reason, a spiritual director need not fear that he is encouraging his directee to pray too much. The one caveat is for individuals who place too high an expectation on themselves and then beat themselves up over their failure to meet that expectation. For this reason, when quantifying time for daily prayer, it is important to set realistic expectations. Having said that, the encouragement to set aside additional time for prayer (as far as it is possible) will always yield good fruit.

As we dedicate ourselves more and more to prayer, the habitual disposition to unceasing prayer begins to grow in us. The regular effort to recollect and place ourselves in God's presence pays off over time as our awareness of Him steadily grows in our souls. In addition to regular recollection, we need an extended period of time every day for prayer, with a substantial percentage of that time dedicated to silence, simply to be in the Lord's presence and open our hearts to listen to Him. A good rule of thumb is that, like in a good conversation, at least half of the time we spend in prayer should dedicated to silently listening to God. As we come to discover that what He has to say is more important than what we have to say, that silence may become a larger and larger part of our prayer time.

As we spend more time in prayer, our prayer becomes more silent. This is because God Himself often "speaks" in silence, and indeed speaks most eloquently in silence.[3] We have already adapted the words attributed to St. Francis, "Preach the Gospel always, and if necessary, use words," to apply them also to God. He is always speaking to us, and when necessary He uses words. He often speaks through actions and presence more than through words. Listening is an act of trust, and as our trust grows, our listening, receptivity, and passivity (toward God) also grow. It is an act of trust to believe that God is even there. As we become more

---

[3] Cardinal Robert Sarah and Nicolas Diat, *The Power of Silence: Against the Dictatorship of Noise*, trans. Michael J. Miller (San Francisco: Ignatius Press, 2017).

convinced of this and more convinced of His love, we need fewer and fewer proofs, and our capacity to trust and receive from Him grows proportionately. Eventually the silence and learning to trust in the face of His apparent absence become purifying movements that deepen our capacity for union.

An Explicit Relationship with God

In prayer, we need to make our relationship with the Lord as explicit as possible. We don't grow in prayer when our relationship is only implicit. When a spiritual director asks often, "What happened when you brought that to the Lord in prayer?" it serves as an explicit reminder that it is commonly the case that we have various things on our minds, but do not actually bring them into our prayer. They may be set aside during the time of prayer or we think about them during prayer, but we consider them distractions and do not actually speak to God about them. Whether we are praying for other people or thinking about the mysteries of the Trinity, it is better to explicitly carry on a steady, interior dialogue with the Lord about those things that matter to us. We have a tendency to think about or even to talk to ourselves, but we need to learn to turn that conversation toward Christ.

It is an enormous step when we start speaking with God in a way that is real and personal by explicitly telling him what is happening in our lives. One young man, a college student and newly baptized Catholic, took an hour every Friday in the adoration chapel. He took the Church's teaching at face value, accepting that Jesus is substantially present in the Eucharist. He saved up his questions and problems, and during his time of Eucharistic adoration he spoke directly to Jesus about these things. We must learn to say more immediately to the Lord the things that are in our hearts and on our minds. We can lay out our temptations, our distractions, our anxieties and stresses, our joys and successes. We can lift up our petitions to Him, speaking to Him about the people who are hurting. The sisters of Lazarus are a model for this in speaking to Jesus of their brother, "Lord, he whom you love is ill" (Jn 11:3).

In addition to speaking explicitly to Him about what is on our hearts and minds, we must also learn to listen to Him. How does He respond to our concerns? It is important to note that what we hear when we listen will be affected by the way that we imagine God. If we continue to hold up our image of God against the revelation in Sacred Scripture and the Magisterium of the Church, and if we continue to speak in spiritual direction about our understanding of God, that image will become more refined and more accurate. Then we can better discern what God is saying based on that image. If God is a loving Father, then He is going to respond with loving concern to our needs. If God is an all-powerful loving Father, then He is never wringing His hands in fearful concern about how He is going to fix the mess of our lives. If God is an infinitely loving Father, then He is always going to have time to hold us and bring us tender consolation and offer us His peace. As we learn to listen in accord with what we know about God, we become more sensitive to His voice and we discover the grace of a loving response to our concerns. There is always the danger of misinterpretation, but this has a way of working itself out over time, not only through correcting our distortions, but naturally as God reveals Himself more and more in a real, personal relationship with us, which shatters all distortion!

Due to our misconceptions about God, it is better to continue being formed in the Church's teaching about God in addition to speaking explicitly to Him, and it is important to speak with our spiritual director about our prayer. A spiritual director will be able to help us see where we have developed distorted concepts about who God is and can help to correct our understanding. Over time, we become more sensitive to the ways that God actually responds to our efforts, our failures, our joys, and our pains. Over time, that inner circle of our souls becomes more operative, in which the intuitive knowing is dominant, and we have the capacity for a single, simple, prolonged act of love. We can describe this as attentive, loving listening to God, a silent knowing, or also as long looks of love. God wants to reveal Himself in that love in a way that goes beyond and exceeds any of our conceptions of Him.

Praying from the Lowest Place

Jesus instructs us to go to the lowest place when we have been invited to a banquet, rather than seeking a place of honor at the main table (see Lk 14:7–14). The same guidance applies well to our lives of prayer. When I am at the main table, particularly when I worked to get myself there or am worried about getting there, I am preoccupied with myself, perhaps congratulating myself that "I've made it." If I choose the lowest place, I am willing to be unnoticed, uninvited, maybe even totally forgotten. The lowest place is a place of vulnerability, of poverty, of powerlessness, not being seated among those who have influence. We do not come to God as equals but as beggars. Or, more accurately, we come to God as equals when we come to Him as beggars, because He came begging before us first. This is why it is so important to go to the lowest place in prayer, because that is where we will find the God who empties Himself (Phil 2:6–11). When we come with demands and attempts to manipulate God, we waste our time and we do not find Him. When we come to Him in our need, our failures, our inability to solve our own problems or make our own way, then we find the God who made Himself poor in order to meet us in our poverty and make us rich in His love: "For you know the grace of our Lord Jesus Christ, that though he was rich, yet for your sake he became poor, so that by his poverty you might become rich" (2 Cor 8:9). Then the one who invited us to the banquet in the first place calls us up higher.

In our poverty, we may struggle with distractions, sleepiness, and temptations. This is all part of being in the lowest place. In the lowest place, we are not impressive—we do not dazzle God into paying attention to us like we attract the attention of worldly powers. In the lowest place, we are naked and exposed in our limitations and weaknesses. This poverty and humility can be lived out with regard to our natural tendency to wander mentally. The best thing to do with distractions is to gently set them aside and lovingly turn our attention to the Lord. We do not need to be distressed if we do this often. After all, every time we turn our attention to the Lord it is an act of love. If we find we cannot set a distraction aside, and the distraction recurs multiple times, then we can show it to God and ask for His help. In any case, we can be humbled by how little control we have even over our own interior thoughts and feelings.

In the lowest place, we are also in touch with our sinfulness. We know how weak we are, how prone to fall into sin. We do not try to hide our sin or make excuses for it, but poor and naked we come before the Lord with open hands and open hearts. We may discover deep resentments. Beneath those resentments are wounds caused by having been used, neglected, rejected, misunderstood, overlooked, attacked, or accused. We can press these wounds against the wounds of Jesus and find intimacy in those wounds. Ultimately, we do not want to remain focused on ourselves for too long. We all are inclined to return to self over and over, yet all we need to do is to repeatedly look away from ourselves and look to Jesus, aware that we have nothing to offer Him other than our sincere yes to His love. We simply need to keep turning back to Him.

A common question is how to handle temptations that come into our minds during prayer. The best thing is to let them pass on, like a bird flying overhead. The worst thing we can do is to try to banish them, or get frustrated by them, or try to bury them. The more energy we direct toward the thoughts, the more unmanageable they become. At the same time, after letting a thought pass, it can be helpful to investigate its origin. It may have an origin in our failure, our fear, or our past, and can be simply brought before the Lord in prayer. It seems to be common sense to banish the thoughts, but the best thing is to let Jesus in and bring all of our thoughts to Him.

This is all very humbling. But we really feel known and get to know our Lord when we go through all this in His presence, not hiding our struggles or weaknesses. When we actually expose and share our weaknesses and struggles with Him, then we have the freedom of the children of God and we can pray, "O LORD, you have searched me and known me" (Ps 139:1).

Importance of Spiritual Direction for Growing in Prayer

The more explicit our relationship with God is, the more we come to know Him and get the sense that He knows us and is speaking to us. Spiritual direction provides a context for articulating our prayer explicitly. Although we might spend time talking with God in prayer and believing that we are hearing Him speak back to us, it is another level of vulnerability and faith to express that to another person. Our spiritual director is often the first to receive our faith testimony. As the trust builds in spiritual direction, it becomes easier to be very explicit with our spiritual director about our relationship with God. This is very important. It is the heart of spiritual direction and a very vulnerable area of our interior life. The more we share, the more we know. The more we share and know, the more we trust both God and the director.

Spiritual direction also helps to clarify what we believe we are hearing from God. The potential for self-deception is always there, but self-deception grows in the darkness while it diminishes in the light. Simply speaking to a spiritual director already begins to purify us and test our confidence about what God is telling us in prayer. God will generally not let us go too far astray anyway, but the relationship of spiritual direction is intended to be a protection against forming false images of God or forming false narratives about how He is speaking in prayer. It might feel crazy to say, "I believe God wants me to do this." The director should give confidence to those who hear God but doubt themselves. They will be hesitant to express that they are hearing God. The director should be cautious with those who are overly confident that they are hearing God and always be careful that what is being reported is in accord with the Gospels and the teaching of the

Church, and also that the directee is applying the proper levels of self-doubt in discerning the voice of God.

One young woman had a very sensitive heart and had many experiences that made her believe that she was hearing God, but she was afraid to talk about this or to talk about how there was something she could not speak about in spiritual direction. Her spiritual director, meanwhile, was trying to help her open her heart and listen to God. As she learned to trust her spiritual director more, she finally admitted, "Sometimes I believe that I hear God speaking in my heart." The spiritual director asked her to describe this experience and she described it very well. She did not hear audible voices. Rather there was a sense of knowing and she was able to articulate that in words. The words had a certain weight to them even at the same time that there was a degree of fuzziness and uncertainty. After having what she called "little talks" with God, she could state in faith, "I believe He was telling me . . ." She had an appropriate level of uncertainty but also a conviction and she humbly submitted her experience to spiritual direction. These are all very good signs. This was a watershed moment in spiritual direction because it opened up a whole new level of dialogue. After this point, her spiritual director could ask her, "Did you ask God about that? What did He say?" And she knew exactly what he was asking.

Assisting the faithful in listening to God and making their relationship with Him explicit is a major benefit of spiritual direction. This requires a great deal of trust. Sometimes the directee will try to deal with the vulnerability of all this trust by trying to get ahead of the director, or he may even begin to compete with the spiritual director and try to anticipate the director's response: "I know what you're going to say." The director might say calmly, "And how do you know?" Ultimately we know nothing at this level of vulnerability apart from what the Holy Spirit lets us know. This is all part of developing trust. Before sharing with another human being the deep, sensitive interior parts of ourselves, we need to have a lot of trust. At the same time, until we share those places, we cannot access them as clearly ourselves.

God allows this deepening of self-knowledge, and lets us get to know Him in the process.

Formative Steps for Relational Prayer

A spiritual director may be the first or the only person who teaches an individual how to grow deeper in prayer. The guidelines we provide here are not definitive or comprehensive, but will hopefully provide some support for spiritual directors who want to help their directees develop a more explicit, relational form of prayer.

A good starting point for prayer is to think for a while in quiet solitude. Just having silence may already be a blessing in an otherwise noisy and busy life. One priest testified to his experience of exposing the Blessed Sacrament for a large number of high school students. He prayed for a few minutes in silence and then when he turned around to process out of the sanctuary, he saw tears streaming down many faces. We are hungering for silence. Pope Benedict XVI spoke about the importance of silence for our integration of the massive amount of information that surrounds us every day:

> In silence, we are better able to listen to and understand ourselves; ideas come to birth and acquire depth; we understand with greater clarity what it is we want to say and what we expect from others; and we choose how to express ourselves. . . . Silence, then, gives rise to even more active communication, requiring sensitivity and a capacity to listen that often makes manifest the true measure and nature of the relationships involved. When messages and information are plentiful, silence becomes essential if we are to distinguish what is important from what is insignificant or secondary. Deeper reflection helps us to discover the links between events that at first sight seem unconnected, to make evaluations, to analyze messages; this makes it possible to share thoughtful and relevant opinions,

giving rise to an authentic body of shared knowledge. For this to happen, it is necessary to develop an appropriate environment, a kind of "eco-system" that maintains a just equilibrium between silence, words, images and sounds.[4]

He concluded his reflections by bringing out the importance of silence in prayer, "If God speaks to us even in silence, we in turn discover in silence the possibility of speaking with God and about God. 'We need that silence which becomes contemplation, which introduces us into God's silence and brings us to the point where the Word, the redeeming Word, is born.'"[5]

Silent reflection is a good—even essential—starting point, but it needs to develop further and open up into relationship. When mere silence becomes "God's silence" we are meeting Him in prayer. We must learn to approach God in a personal way. One may quickly face a stream of doubts centered around the question, "How do I know He is there?" Building trust in the presence of God develops as the virtue of faith develops—through intercessory prayers such as "God, please help me know you are there," through meditating on Scripture, through reading the Catechism, and also through spiritual direction. These questions or doubts are very good to bring up in spiritual direction and allow our trust in our spiritual director to strengthen our trust in God.

A further step beyond simply being silent or thinking of God is actually speaking with God. This may feel silly at first, but it is important to do it anyway, to try to speak to Him as any other person. As we do this, we start to get indications that He is listening, that He cares, that He loves us. This may be something that the spiritual director can bring out explicitly with a question such as "What was God doing while you were sharing that with Him?" The directee may not have fully thought about that until he artic-

---

[4] Pope Benedict XVI, "Silence and Word: Path of Evangelization," Message for the 46th World Communications Day (January 24, 2012), http://w2.vatican.va/content/benedict-xvi/en/messages/communications/documents/hf_ben-xvi_mes_20120124_46th-world-communications-day.html.

[5] Ibid.

ulates it in response to such a question in spiritual direction. This starting point for our relationship with God may feel awkward, but relationships are always awkward at the outset. The best way to work through it is to persevere and continue to be explicit in speaking with God.

A further step in the relationship is allowing God to respond. Beyond the continuous response of God through His presence, care, and love, it is valuable to allow God to express Himself in words. This dialogue takes place in faith and so there will always be the possibility that we are merely manufacturing it on our own. However, as the relationship develops, we become more attuned to the way God speaks to us. One way to open this dimension of the dialogue is to write it out explicitly. We can write our questions or our concerns to God and we can write out what He seems to be saying in response.

One man prayed very faithfully for many years and was very committed to serving God through His Church. He had spent many years engaged explicitly in the lay apostolate and had a sensitive heart and a good sense of discernment. It was not until he met with a spiritual director on retreat, however, that he took the step of writing out God's half of the conversation. He was very hesitant to "put words into God's mouth" but when he took the risk and opened his heart, he discovered that he was able to hear more from God than he realized. He confirmed everything with his spiritual director, but he already knew, in making the act of faith to write down what he believed God was saying, that he was indeed hearing God.

When we are praying and listening and our mind becomes more empty, we find ourselves thinking things, and these may begin to come out formulated in words inspired by God. There is always the possibility that we can overelaborate what God says because our own will gets involved. We may find ourselves changing our minds or going in a different direction rather than understanding more deeply. As we pray we can try to lay out a decision before the Lord and focus on Him. This focus might involve picturing Him in our imagination and hearing a voice in our mind. These are ways to focus on God and speak to God explicitly.

Sometimes we do not hear or think of words but instead have wordless insights or strong feelings. The meaning of insights or feelings is often unclear at first. It simply has a sense of coming from beyond ourselves. This is because the human mind processes things subconsciously that it cannot handle consciously. People often attend to things in the background. Ideas can percolate when we are not focusing on them. When insights and answers come to the surface and become conscious, this can be God speaking through our subconscious. St. Thérèse said that she did not receive the benefit of prayer during prayer, but rather received the benefit of prayer outside of prayer. It is important to know that we can bring things up in prayer, and though we may not receive any communication during prayer, it may come later—when doing dishes, for example, or driving to work.

Peace is a very strong indicator of God's will. When I consider several options and find that I have more peace with one option, that can be an indication that the Lord is moving me in that direction. When I bring something to God in prayer and do not have absolute peace, I can continue holding it out to Him. I may raise several possibilities before Him and see if one of them stands out more than the rest. Another helpful exercise, recommended by St. Ignatius, can be to make a list of pros and cons for several options. This helps us to hold the full reality of the options before us at the same time.

Sometimes God wants us to rephrase or reformulate our questions. One man, discerning whether to enter seminary, kept asking God, "Do you want me to become a priest?" but kept getting no response. With the help of his spiritual director he finally got an affirmative response when he asked instead, "Do you want me to enter seminary?" Sometimes there can be emotional attachments to one dimension but when we look at the whole picture we get a different sense. For example, in discerning accepting a new job, when we think about the job itself there may be some excitement and some peace, but when we think about the location of the job there is much distress and anxiety. It is important to face both of those dimensions at the same time when we hold that up against another job which is less exciting but is located in a place we are much more comfortable with.

Eventually, when making a decision, there may not be absolute clarity but enough clarity to say to God, "I believe this is what you want me to do. If I am making the wrong decision, please put up some road block or give me some sign." One group was discerning whether to buy a particular building. Collectively they had no strong convictions, but many of the details of the purchase checked out through human reasoning. The building was a good size, in a good location, and for sale at a good price. But the group decided to spend a little longer lifting it up to the Lord in prayer, saying, "We believe this is Your will, but if we are off track, please make that clear." When they went to put an offer on the building, it had already sold. They received the news with gratitude and relief. God's will was manifest.

It is important to check with our spiritual director when we are hearing from God lest we fall into self-deception. It is also important to realize that these communications with God cannot be forced. Sometimes there is just silence in response. God has many reasons for remaining silent. Sometimes God's silence means, "Just keep doing what you're doing."

Most of what God communicates in prayer is not a yes or no answer, or an answer at all. Mostly God simply wants to communicate to us His love and His grace. He is usually giving us gifts we do not even recognize or know how to ask for, or He is answering questions we do not even know how to formulate on our own.

A main fruit of prayer and spiritual direction is trust. Trust grows when we speak to God even though we sometimes feel like we are speaking to a wall. Trust grows when we formulate God's response into words and let those strike our hearts. Trust grows when we share these communications with our spiritual director. Trust grows when we wait and have faith, even though we only hear silence in response. All of this trusting can be difficult, but it is deeply formative and helps to mold our interior life to be more

"God shaped." It opens us to union with God. Trust means I am increasingly myself in a vulnerable way, and this is precisely the way I need to come before God and also the way I need to learn to be in my own interior.

Baptism in the Holy Spirit

A grace of the Church since the Second Vatican Council has been the emergence and development of the Catholic Charismatic Renewal. Although many extraordinary phenomena have been associated with the charismatic renewal, a fundamental grace of the renewal is what has been termed Baptism in the Holy Spirit. This is not to be confused with sacramental Baptism, as if it were in competition with it or even a necessary completion of it. Rather, it can be seen as both a "rekindling" (2 Tim 1:6) of grace already imparted in sacramental Baptism or as a deepening or building on sacramental grace with a new outpouring of the Holy Spirit, possibly accompanied by particular charisms.

The important point, related to the foregoing descriptions of relational prayer, is that the Holy Spirit is, Himself, the relationship between the Father and Son. He is the love between the Father and Son, and so, when He is bestowed upon the individual Christian, He manifests the same love of the Father toward that Christian. He is the relationship between the Christian and the Father, so that St. Paul calls Him the Spirit of Adoption. He is, in fact, the Anointing (Chrismation) that makes a man or woman truly an Anointed One (Christian). For this reason, the development of a life of prayer that is more personal, more relational, is always, in fact, a growth in the Holy Spirit.

The Catholic Charismatic Renewal has been entrusted with a special grace to specialize in this reality:

> If baptism in the Spirit is the normal development of the
> Christian life that begins with the sacraments of initiation,
> it follows that this grace is not something unique to the

Charismatic Renewal. It is present in different forms in the lives of many other Catholics without reference to the specific terminology or style of the Renewal. The special calling of the Renewal is to name this grace, to propose an ecclesial context and a specific pedagogy for receiving it, and to foster the full development of its fruits.[6]

Encouraged by this insight that the special grace of the Catholic Charismatic Renewal is to specialize in the Baptism of the Spirit, we approach the question of developing a personal prayer life again from the perspective of the wisdom gained through the Renewal. In fostering Baptism in the Spirit, the International Catholic Charismatic Renewal Services (ICCRS) has identified six key points[7] that are valuable for a spiritual director to keep in mind as he encourages his directee to develop his relationship with God. Each of these points will continue to deepen in the life of each believer, and so they are not so much rungs on a ladder as they are dimensions of Christian formation that play into the individual's relationship with God.

The Love of God the Father

As we discussed earlier, love of God the Father is the basis for everything else in the spiritual life. It is a love that is a free gift and it is a love for sinners. We grow in this love by coming to know simultaneously two abysses—the abyss of our poverty, weakness, and sinfulness and the greater abyss of God's merciful love. We cannot really grow in our knowledge of one without simultaneously growing in knowledge of the other.

---

[6] International Catholic Charismatic Renewal Services Doctrinal Commission (hereafter, ICCRS), *Baptism in the Holy Spirit* (Locust Grove, VA: NSC Chariscenter, 2012), 71–72.

[7] Cf. Ibid., 77–83.

The Lordship of Jesus

The concrete expression of the Father's love for us is that while we were still sinners, He sent His Son as our Savior (cf. Rom 5:8; 1 Jn 4:10). Here we develop a personal relationship with Christ by making a radical surrender to Him and inviting Him to be Lord of our hearts. Here we learn to trust in divine providence and the belief that God works all things to the good for those who love Him (Rom 8:28). We come to believe more deeply that Christ is alive and He is with us now and always, and indeed He is even within us. In accepting the Lordship of Jesus, we take up the call to a radical discipleship that includes a pedagogy of learning to walk with Jesus on the way of the Cross.

The Power of the Holy Spirit

We discover the power of the Holy Spirit at the same time that we discover our own spiritual poverty. Indeed, apart from Him we can do nothing (Jn 15:5). The Holy Spirit wants to empower us to do great things, bringing forth in our lives the fruits of holiness that we cannot produce by our own power but that everyone desires, namely, "love, joy, peace, patience, kindness, goodness, faithfulness, gentleness, self-control" (Gal 5:22–23). The Holy Spirit wants to empower us with gifts that help us to live out our Christian lives and deepen our communion with God in prayer.

Repentance, Forgiveness, and the Spiritual Battle

We will not make much progress in prayer if we do not learn to embrace a "repentance unto life" and an ongoing *metanoia,* or renewal of the mind (Acts 11:18; Rom 12:2). God is always ready to forgive our failures to live a life in the Spirit and to respond to our heartfelt repentance. At the same time, we cannot receive His grace and forgiveness if we do not learn to forgive as well. A major block in prayer can be both our own hard-hearted resistance to admit our weakness and sinfulness and also an unwillingness to forgive those who have offended us. At the same time, the Christian life is always going to be a battle in which those who are not moving forward are falling back. There is no option for standing still. The battle to pray without growing weary and never to despair of the mercy of God requires an ongoing effort and commitment from each believer (Lk 18:1).[8]

The Charisms

The Second Vatican Council identified the importance of the charisms for the life of the Church:

> It is not only through the sacraments and the ministries of the Church that the Holy Spirit sanctifies and leads the people of God and enriches it with virtues, but, "allotting his gifts to everyone according as He wills," He distributes special graces among the faithful of every rank. By these gifts He makes them fit and ready to undertake the various tasks and offices which contribute toward the renewal and building up of the Church, according to the words of the Apostle: "The manifestation of the Spirit is given to everyone for profit". These charisms, whether they be the more outstanding or the more simple and widely diffused, are to be received with thanksgiving and consolation for they are perfectly suited to and useful for the needs of the Church.[9]

There is no definitive or comprehensive listing of the charisms in the Church, but St. Paul includes first of all apostles, also prophets, teachers, administrators, miracles, the gift of tongues, interpretation of tongues, healing, words of wisdom and knowledge, contribution, song, discernment of spirits, intercession,

---

[8]   St. Benedict, *Holy Rule*, Chapter 4, verse 74.
[9]   *Lumen gentium*, no. 12.

hospitality, celibacy, acts of mercy, and others.[10] In short, there are many concrete ways that God desires to manifest, in the life of each Christian, a response to the needs of the Church. The charisms are always for the building up of the Church. They range from the enhancement of what may be natural to a person to the humanly impossible and miraculous.

Mission

"God's love remains alive in a person only to the degree that it is given away, as water that has no outlet will stagnate."[11] For this reason, Baptism in the Holy Spirit and growth in relational prayer will always involve growth in a sense of mission. Just as an essential part of the Church is mission, so also an essential part of the life of every Christian is mission. This mission can be expressed in many different ways that are summed up by the corporal and spiritual works of mercy. Although spiritual direction has a particular emphasis on prayer, one cause of stagnation in prayer can be lack of a sense of mission. This lack of mission might be caused by fear, indifference, ignorance, or pride. The remedies are as diverse as the causes, but it is an important topic to address in spiritual direction.

Tools for the Spiritual Life

In terms of practical guidance in prayer, many things must be customized according to an individual's circumstances and state of life. Some starting points, however, are to make a substantial amount of time for meditative prayer. A holy hour in front of the Blessed Sacrament is optimal and can allow meditation using thoughts and images to lead to a more contemplative listening to the Lord. Based on circumstances, it is possible to alter the holy

---

[10] See, for example, 1 Cor 12:4–11; Eph 4:11–12; Rom 12:6–8.
[11] ICCRS Doctrinal Commission, *Baptism in the Holy Spirit*, 84.

hour both in length and location. For very busy married couples with children at home, fifteen minutes of mental prayer in a quiet room in the house may be a very good daily regimen. For a priest or religious, a holy hour in front of the Blessed Sacrament can be more manageable, though everyone should try to extend the time allotted in prayer. The most important way to grow in holiness is to attend Mass daily, so far as possible. The Liturgy of the Hours can be a very nourishing and grace-filled way to draw closer to the Church and unite more with her liturgical rhythm. The Rosary is a very valuable prayer and pays dividends during the prayer itself as well as over time. Through the Rosary, the one who prays becomes closer to the Mother of God and is caught up more and more in the mysteries of Christ. Prayers like the Rosary can be offered during the holy hour to start with, but the best approach to making a holy hour is, in addition to rote prayers, allowing the holy hour to become a time to speak with and listen to God.

The holy hour can be initiated and nourished by a prayerful reading of Sacred Scripture and other texts which can in turn lead into meditation and contemplation. *Lectio divina* is a wonderful complement to the holy hour. Pope Benedict XVI emphasized the value of *lectio divina* in his apostolic exhortation following the Synod on the Word of God, *Verbum Domini*: "I would also like to echo what the Synod proposed about the importance of the personal reading of Scripture, also as a practice allowing for the possibility, in accordance with the Church's usual conditions, of gaining an indulgence either for oneself or for the faithful departed."[12] (A half hour of *lectio divina*, like a half hour of Eucharistic Adoration, constitutes a sufficient practice for a plenary indulgence.) *Lectio divina* helps to give words to God that He can speak back to us. The Holy Spirit helps to personalize those words so that they can speak to our own particular insecurities, fears, or trials. *Lectio divina* also has the advantage of attaching spiritual weight to small phrases that can be recounted later in the day as a

---

[12] Pope Benedict XVI, *Verbum Domini*, no. 87.

way of refreshing the grace of an earlier time of prayer. This facilitates the process of praying without ceasing.

The holy hour can be seeded with a simple prayer to Our Lady or by taking up one of the mysteries of the Rosary. It can also be helpful to take a verse from a psalm or the long reading from the Office of Readings and ponder it throughout the holy hour. Likewise, a text from the Mass or a verse from the Gospel can be enough to set the tone for prayer. It is important to avoid turning the holy hour into a checklist. A compulsion to complete readings or say particular prayers can eliminate time for silence or deeper pondering and communication with God. The main thing is to make the holy hour a very vulnerable time of prayer. By starting from the "lowest place" one can become very vulnerable before the Lord and remain there throughout the period of prayer.

The most important thing for a spiritual director to do is to help the directee to take the first steps in trying to pray in these ways. There may be various objections to these spiritual practices. Some people have trouble with the Rosary or they are uncomfortable with silence. Some prefer spiritual reading instead of the Liturgy of the Hours or they find the Mass boring. It can be valuable to talk through the importance or merit of each practice, but the most convincing thing is for the directee just to try it out. When people try these practices and persevere through the initial discomfort (or persevere through the initial fervor that quickly becomes discomfort), they start to discover the value of each of the ways of being with God.

In the process of all this, God becomes more and more real. The most significant moments in prayer we can remember always include those moments when we caught a glimpse of God in which we realized how near, how loving, how personally real He truly is. These are moments we cannot doubt: experiences of receiving the gift of God Himself, moments when time stopped, moments when we understood and knew we were understood in the most comprehensive and personally intimate way. This is the meaning of prayer.

Discerning Extraordinary Gifts

Although many spiritual directors never encounter any persons who are experiencing extraordinary gifts in prayer, it is valuable to consider some criteria by which those gifts are evaluated. Extraordinary gifts include apparitions and locutions from God, saints, or angels; levitation; stigmata; bilocation; and miraculous strength. These phenomena can also be initiated by the devil and so it is important to be able to determine their origin and authenticity. More commonly, individuals may enjoy extraordinary charismata such as those listed by St. Paul in 1 Corinthians 12 and 14, including gifts of wisdom, words of knowledge, prophecy, and miraculous healing.

The criteria by which these can be evaluated are important to keep in mind in general, because they are essentially the metrics by which growth in the Christian life can be measured. Sulpician Fr. Adolphe Tanqueray, in his manual *The Spiritual Life*, divided the criteria for discernment into categories of subject, object, and effects.[13] Reflecting first on the subject or recipient of the extraordinary graces, he noted that an individual who is very advanced in the spiritual life will be more trustworthy when it comes to experiencing, describing, and recognizing extraordinary phenomena. He taught that most authentic extraordinary phenomena occur in those who are advanced in the spiritual life. St. John of Ávila, in a letter to St. Teresa of Ávila in which he evaluated her autobiography and her spiritual experiences, offered a different perspective. He believed that God was more likely to utilize extraordinary phenomena when an individual was in danger or offtrack, as St. Teresa herself experienced when she had a vision of hell that roused her from the mediocrity of her religious life to become a founder and reformer.

In regard to the object of the meditation, the most important point is that the extraordinary phenomena should not deliver

---

[13] Adolphe Tanqueray, *The Spiritual Life: A Treatise on Ascetical and Mystical Theology*, trans. Herman Branderis (Tournai, BE: Desclee and Co., 1932), no. 1497.

any content that is contrary to Scripture or the teaching of the Church. God never contradicts Himself. Tanqueray also pointed out that God seldom intervenes with extraordinary phenomena to settle longstanding theological disputes.[14] Another point regards the means of the revelation. The more interior the revelation, the more trustworthy it is.[15] A purely intellectual revelation (God delivers meaning directly to the intellect) is more trustworthy than an interior locution or vision (one that occurs only in the imaginative faculty of the soul) and more trustworthy than an exterior locution or vision (that enters through the exterior visual or auditory senses).

The effects of the extraordinary phenomena are generally the most important point to watch, because, as Jesus said, a tree can be judged by its fruits (Lk 6:44). "True revelations strengthen the soul in humility, obedience, patience and conformity to the divine will; false ones beget pride, presumption and disobedience."[16] Humility is a very important virtue to consider carefully in one who claims to be experiencing extraordinary phenomena. St. John of Ávila added that visions should never be sought and generally should be resisted initially (although not contemptuously) until it is certain that they are from the Lord. He also made it clear that even when Jesus appears, the image that appears should never be worshipped, but rather only Jesus in heaven or in the Blessed Sacrament. The image should be treated like any painting or statue, as a representation of God rather than God Himself. Furthermore, St. John of Ávila summarized the effects that he looked for: greater love of God, greater knowledge of one's own sinfulness, and an increasing desire for penance and the Cross.[17]

A director should be careful but respectful in handling extraordinary phenomena. St. John of Ávila was disappointed in the rough

---

[14] Ibid., no. 1501.

[15] Ibid., nos. 1491–1495.

[16] Ibid., no. 1504.

[17] St. John of Ávila to St. Teresa of Ávila, 1563, in *Letters of Blessed John of Ávila*, trans. Benedictines of Stanbrook Abbey (London, UK: Burns & Oates Ltd., 1904), 17–23.

way that St. Teresa's experiences were handled by Church officials. At the same time, knowing that God will honor the obedience of the directee to the director, the director can be free to slow down the directee or be conservative with the directee. God will work with the director's sincere guidance. It is also valuable to realize that extraordinary phenomena always remain in the realm of private revelation, which is only potentially binding on the conscience of the recipient and never binding on anyone else. Thus, a directee cannot morally compel a director to act in a certain way based on a private revelation. Any effort at being forceful or trying to control others through private revelation should be strongly resisted and subjected to the director's obedience. A directee may also be told not to reveal anything to anyone except to the director.

In one case a woman was receiving interior locutions from Jesus and Mary and began sharing them with her spiritual director. She was an older woman who was not prone to hysteria. She was advanced in her prayer, including great fidelity to daily Mass, regular Confession, and works of mercy, while also always fulfilling her family duties. She shared the experiences with hesitation and healthy self-doubt, indicating the way that they were humbling her, not making her proud or arrogant. It was clear that the words she was receiving were challenging her to deeper prayer and greater sacrifices. The sacrifices were not extreme, but enhanced her state in life. For example, she received a strong word that she should be more deferential to her husband in a nondramatic way that he might not even notice, but she would know the difference. They had a very good marriage, but she had a strong personality and had become accustomed to ignoring him or overruling him on certain points. As another example, she moved to offer her sufferings for particular intentions.

On one occasion she believed she heard our Lady asking her to contact a particular priest. She knew him, but making contact would have been out of the ordinary. She humbly submitted that to her spiritual director, who advised her to go ahead and simply make the contact sound spontaneous. She emailed the priest and told him she felt called to pray for him, and to her happy surprise he wrote back saying that he was going through a particularly difficult time and her email with the promise of prayers had given him strength. On another occasion, the locutions started focusing on the spiritual director's personal life in a way that made him uncomfortable. He simply encouraged her to keep praying and listening to our Lady, but he chose not to let her get entangled with his personal life. She accepted that humbly and so again gave a positive sign that the interior locutions could well be authentic. Over some time they became normalized and eventually diminished. A significant effect was that they developed the mind of Christ in her and her thinking became even more sanctified.

Up to this point, we have focused on extraordinary phenomena. The Church also recognizes the charismatic gifts, such as those listed by St. Paul in 1 Corinthians 12 and 14. In a document on the relationship between the hierarchical and charismatic dimensions of the Church, Cardinal Gerhard Müller, Prefect of the Congregation for the Doctrine of the Faith, offered the criteria that follows as he also set forth the expectation that the pastors of the Church must help to discern the authenticity of charisms. He recognized that this can be time consuming and arduous, and requires special care and attention, but that it is "nonetheless a dutiful service that pastors are required to fulfill."[18] Spiritual directors are not necessarily pastors, and the intervention of the pastors of the Church, the bishops, may be necessary depending on the magnitude and public nature of the extraordinary gifts. The criteria apply to spiritual directors as well, though, and we can consider them here briefly.

The Primacy of the Call to Holiness

The growth in love and pursuit of perfect charity must always remain foremost when evaluating extraordinary gifts. St. Paul

---

[18] Cardinal Gerhard Müller, *Iuvenescit Ecclesia* (May 15, 2016), no. 17, http://www.vatican.va/roman_curia/congregations/cfaith/documents/rc_con_cfaith_doc_20160516_iuvenescit-ecclesia_en.html.

described love as "a still more excellent way" (1 Cor 12:31), and it is the definitive way in which every charism must be exercised and the primary criterion against which it must be tested. Is the extraordinary gift ordered to charity and does it lead to a growth in charity?

Commitment to Spreading the Gospel

Any gift in prayer that leads an individual to become more isolated must be watched with care. Although an individual might experience a call to greater solitude for the sake of intimacy with God and deeper prayer, this should, at the same time, open the heart to more love for our brothers and sisters. The growth in love and mission might not be immediate, but the directee should be accompanied and helped to develop in prayer, and eventually some signs of deeper compassion, intercession, and even concrete missionary outreach should become manifest.

Profession of the Catholic Faith

Authentic spiritual gifts and growth in prayer do not take one outside the teaching of the Catholic Church. The universal teaching of the Church as it is expressed in the Catechism will always be a metric by which to evaluate supernatural phenomena. "But even if we, or an angel from heaven, should preach to you a gospel contrary to that which we preached to you, let him be accursed" (Gal 1:8). There will be no new Gospel, no additions to the deposit of the faith, and no new teaching that contradicts the Catechism.

Growth in Communion with the Whole Church

Authentic prayer is deeply personal, but at the same time it always roots one more deeply in the universal Church. Participation in the sacraments and in the life of the parish and even a greater awareness of the local diocesan Church and the universal Church naturally develop. A life of prayer or an extraordinary gift that makes one more idiosyncratic, egocentric, arrogant, or divisive is bearing bad fruit and should be pruned. A person who grows in prayer always grows in love for the mother of prayer, who is Mary, and the Church.

Esteem for Other Charisms

No authentic extraordinary gifts will claim to supersede or elim-inate a charism previously recognized by the Church. The Holy Spirit produces many gifts but He harmonizes all of them into a beautiful unity. Charisms that set themselves up as enemies of other charisms are to be reformed and expanded in order to develop harmony. If they cannot be harmonized it is a sign of inauthenticity. Our Lady will not appear in Pennsylvania and con-tradict what she said in Fatima or Lourdes. Our Lord will not speak a word that negates the importance of the approved eccle-sial movements or religious orders. Rather, the authentic charisms, though emphasizing different dimensions of the truth and life in Christ, will always harmonize into a beautiful radiance of the infinite creativity of the one God.

Acceptance of Moments of Trial

Throughout the ages, visionaries and mystics have often had to endure the trials of waiting for ecclesiastical approval. The patient endurance of trials is a good sign of authenticity. St. Teresa of Ávila stood trial while her autobiography was evaluated for authentic-ity and she suffered severe critiques and rebukes. St. John of the Cross suffered at the hands of his own religious community as he sought to carry out the reforms that he believed the Holy Spirit was inspiring in him. A spiritual director should never be harsh or arbitrary in testing the spirits in his directee. At the same time, he need not fear imposing some limits on the spiritual gift as a test of authenticity. The Lord recognizes the authority of the spiritual director over an individual directee and will honor the sincere guidance he offers. It might be prudent to prevent a directee with miraculous gifts from talking about them so as to test obedience and reduce any pride or vainglory that might be in his heart.

Presence of Spiritual Fruits

The fruits of the Spirit, as catalogued by St. Paul, are a good test of authenticity. In summary, "charity, joy, peace and a certain human maturity (cf. Gal 5:22); the desire 'to live the Church's life more intensely', a more intense desire of 'listening to and meditating on the Word'; 'the renewed appreciation for prayer, contemplation, liturgical and sacramental life, the reawakening of vocations to Christian marriage, the ministerial priesthood and the consecrated life'."[19]

Social Dimension of the Gospel

This criterion goes hand in hand with the criterion for fervor for evangelization. Authentic growth in holiness will always lead to "concern for the integral development of society's most neglected members."[20] Here again, too narrow a criterion should not be applied: for example, doubting a spiritual experience because a directee will not work at a soup kitchen. At the same time, there should be some signs of growth in concern for bettering the world. This could be manifested in various ways, from volunteer activities to supporting certain agencies or simply becoming more involved in government and politics. It could include more fervent prayer for the poor in addition to concrete actions to help them.

Summary

Authentic prayer grows in both personal and communal dimensions and roots us more deeply in the Catholic Church. The criteria

---

[19] Ibid., no. 18g.
[20] Ibid., no. 18h.

given for the evaluation of special charisms can be applied to the growth of any Christian in his life of prayer. They are criteria that a spiritual director should always keep in mind when helping a directee with his prayer life. If the fruits are not evident, there may be some things missing. A spiritual director should keep an eye on this as he lovingly receives the directee's vulnerably shared experiences. He may be able to ask a question or provide an intention for prayer, or encourage a particular reading or reflection to help a directee mature in his prayer life and its concrete expression in faith and charity. We consider now in more detail how our life in prayer takes the form of a journey with an ever-deepening spiral of growth in communion with God.

7

Passages in Prayer and the Spiritual Life

E ACH INDIVIDUAL'S RELATIONSHIP with God is personal and
unique. At the same time, because we share the same human
nature and we are affected by the same original sin, there are
commonalities in our spiritual development. The full treatment of
spiritual development can be found in more comprehensive and
systematic works of mystical and ascetical theology such as *The
Three Ages of the Interior Life* by Fr. Reginald Garrigou-Lagrange,
OP; *The Spiritual Life* by Fr. Adolphe Tanqueray, SS; *The Mystical
Evolution in the Development and Vitality of the Church* by Fr. John
Arintero, OP; or various others. More modern and less comprehensive works include *Spiritual Passages* by Fr. Benedict Groeschel,
CFR; *Fire Within* by Fr. Thomas Dubay, SM; or *The Fulfillment of
All Desire* by Ralph Martin, along with many more. These summary
treatments of the spiritual journey incorporate the teaching of
various mystical doctors, with St. Teresa of Ávila and St. John of
the Cross holding pride of place. These two doctors, in turn, build
on foundations laid by St. Thomas Aquinas and those who came
before him, including St. Augustine, and the various treasures of
ancient monastic spirituality.

We will not try to duplicate these great works, but will leave
it to the ongoing formation of spiritual directors to consult them
and gradually absorb them into the always-improving practice of
the art of their spiritual direction. At the same time, for the sake

of providing some simple guidance for cases that regularly arise, we provide some sketches here of the passage of the spiritual life that spiritual directors can be aware of as they accompany their directees.

From Purification to Union

The ultimate goal of human existence is union with God. This is a journey that begins with conception and is intended to progress throughout a person's lifespan, with the ultimate consummation in heaven when we are all one with God as the Father and Son are one in the Holy Spirit (cf. Jn 17). Because of our fallen humanity, the first step toward union must be a step of purification. This gives way to a clearer vision, or illumination, and frees us to give a more complete yes to God in a consummate union with Him.

The Three Ways

St. John of the Cross famously sketched out the three stages of the spiritual life, naming them the purgative, illuminative, and unitive stages. He was not the first to develop this presentation of the spiritual life, but his description is perhaps the best known. He also identified the purifications, which he called "nights," that accompany the passage from one stage to the next. He divided these purifications into two categories, *active* and *passive,* and identified principally two forms of night: the night of the senses (separating the purgative from the illuminative stage) and the night of the spirit (separating the illuminative from the unitive stage).

In her great work, *The Interior Castle*, St. Teresa of Ávila identified seven mansions that a person must pass through, with the seventh mansion corresponding to mystical marriage with God, the loving union to which He has invited us. The first three mansions correspond roughly to the purgative way, in St. John of the Cross' language; the next two mansions fall into the illuminative way; and the last two mansions, which are spiritual espousal and mystical marriage, respectively, fall into the unitive way.

Applying Mystical Theology in Spiritual Direction

In the teaching of these mystical doctors we can see that there are some general movements in the spiritual life that are important to be aware of. At the same time, there are unique ways that these movements are personalized in the life of each individual. The passing from one stage to the next is not like graduating from high school or college. The passage is much less distinct than that. Also, a spiritual director or directee is ill-advised if trying to analyze and definitively state which stage one is in. On the contrary, what is important is to learn about the process of purification and some of the particular qualities of purification so that the director can impart direction, hope, and courage to the directee, especially during a more intense period of purification and spiritual growth.

Although the three ways of the spiritual life are often thought of in terms of the whole of one's life, they can also be seen as applying to a part of one's life. Pope St. John Paul II built on the movement from purification to union and applied it to individual virtues.[1] For example, in developing the virtue of chastity, there must first be a negative (purifying) stage of avoiding sin against chastity. As a person persists in avoiding, he can grow in freedom and over time, he opens up to a deeper understanding (illumination) regarding the goodness of chaste living. "Thou shalt not" expands to include "Thou shalt." The final stage expands into a freedom to love in harmony (union) with the plan of God. Pope Francis taught about how the three ways interact with mercy and described an ever-deepening spiral of conversion and trust in God's merciful love: "Mercy helps us to see that the three ways of classical mysticism—the purgative, the illuminative and the unitive—are not successive stages that, once experienced, can

---

[1] Pope St. John Paul II, *Memory and Identity: Conversations at the Dawn of a Millennium* (New York: Rizzoli, 2005), 27–30.

then be put behind us. We never cease to be in need of renewed conversion, deeper contemplation and greater love. These three phases intertwine and recur."[2] It is important for a spiritual director to be aware of this general progression in order to encourage directees to continue on a path of purification, or, for those who are gaining some freedom, to encourage them to look for the insight that begins to come on the path to union with God. Furthermore, it is important to know that while some areas of life might be purified and more united with God, other areas might be lagging behind and should become a greater focus in the context of spiritual direction.

Some Insights from St. Ignatius

St. Ignatius of Loyola provided rules for discernment that help to turn these insights about the spiritual journey into advice for spiritual direction. We give only a sketch here and refer readers to the many works that cover these subjects. A pair of key concepts in the teaching of St. Ignatius of Loyola is *spiritual desolation* and *spiritual consolation*. (Spiritual desolation has some relationship with the kind of experience St. John of the Cross described as a night.) Spiritual desolation can last a few minutes or a few days or weeks. St. Ignatius recognized that it can occur for several reasons, including our own sinfulness or the work of the evil spirit. St. Ignatius provided practical guidelines (rules for discernment of spirits) for handling these periods of spiritual desolation. One important example can be found in Rule Five, which indicates that one should never change one's spiritual plan in times of spiritual desolation. Through this teaching, St. Ignatius helps spiritual directors guide their directees through the regular experiences of spiritual consolation and spiritual desolation, bringing them ever closer to union with God.

---

[2] Pope Francis, "Second Meditation: The Vessel of Mercy," in Spiritual Retreat Given on the Occasion of the Jubilee for Priests (June 2, 2016), https://w2.vatican.va/content/francesco/en/speeches/2016/june/documents/papa-francesco_20160602_giubileo-sacerdoti-seconda-meditazione.html.

Although we indicated that an analysis of the spiritual state of the directee (knowing whether he is in the purgative or illuminative way) can be confusing and is not always advisable, some determination of the progress of the directee is certainly necessary. For example, in the teaching of St. Ignatius, the guidance given by the spiritual director is modified based on the state of the directee. A person who is moving from mortal sin to mortal sin may experience interior pain (a kind of desolation) because God is trying to draw him away from a life of vice. On the other hand, when a person is moving from one good to another, he may experience interior pain (a kind of desolation) from the enemy trying to draw him away from a life of virtue. In the first case, the individual should repent and leave behind the life of sin. In the second case, the person should persevere in what he is doing. In other words, the same signal (interior pain) indicates two opposite courses of action depending on the context of the whole spiritual life of the directee.

The teaching of St. Ignatius also helps to clarify how to proceed when a person has certain interior words or images, based on whether the directee is in a state of consolation or desolation. In times of desolation, interior words or images are often tainted with lies from the enemy. They should not be followed. In times of consolation, interior words and images are often important lights that can continue to guide a person to truth even when the consolation has passed. In both cases, the words and images can be revelatory. In desolation, the words and images, with their lies, can point to wounds and weaknesses, and so they can become important points of reflection in spiritual direction. In times of consolation, the words and images can be received from God as a kind of prophetic gift, and they should be held onto. They can remain a beacon of light that continues to guide the path of the individual beyond the consolation.

There are many excellent books written on St. Ignatius' rules for discernment.[3] We will not try to reproduce those works here,

---

[3] The series of books by Fr. Timothy Gallagher stand out. See, for example, Timothy Gallagher, *The Discernment of Spirits: An Ignatian Guide for Everyday Living* (New York: The Crossroad Publishing Company, 2005).

but we will summarize some helpful points that St. Ignatius offers in the rules "proper for the first week" of the Spiritual Exercises. The spiritual director plays an important role in assisting an individual in navigating the vicissitudes of the spiritual life. He is a key figure for teaching the directee or reminding the directee of some basic approaches to significant movements (positive and negative) in the spiritual life.

CONSOLATION

St. Ignatius taught in Rule Three of the rules proper for the first week:

> I call it consolation when an interior movement is aroused in the soul, by which it is inflamed with love of its Creator and Lord, and as a consequence, can love no creature on the face of the earth for its own sake, but only in the Creator of them all. It is likewise consolation when one sheds tears that move to the love of God, whether it be because of sorrow for sins, or because of the sufferings of Christ our Lord, or for any other reason that is immediately directed to the praise and service of God. Finally, I call consolation every increase of faith, hope, and love, and all interior joy that invites and attracts to what is heavenly and to the salvation of one's soul by filling it with peace and quiet in its Creator and Lord.[4]

One key component of the spiritual life is knowing how to view consolation. This is a tangible grace and marks an important part of one's spiritual life. Consolations may be rare for some people or more frequent for others. Consolation is always significant and so it is important to take note of these experiences and to speak about them in spiritual direction. St. Ignatius identified some fruitful responses to consolation. The basic principle is that God's voice and presence is particularly explicit in times of con-

---

[4] St. Ignatius of Loyola, *Spiritual Exercises*, no. 316.

solation and so the experience and the accompanying thoughts should be savored and stored up in the mind and heart. At the same time, one must remember that it is God's initiative and God's work, and so is something to be grateful for, not something to be proud of. St. Ignatius encouraged humility during consolation by encouraging directees to remember how little they are capable of in times of desolation (Rule Eleven). This is an important counterbalance. It is not a matter of throwing a wet blanket on a beautiful experience, but in fact allows the beauty to shine more brightly by highlighting more clearly how actively God is at work in the experience.

It is also important to store up insights and make spiritual plans in times of consolation. Consolations come as a result of the closeness of God. As the prophet Isaiah advised, "Seek the Lord while he may be found, call upon him while he is near" (Is 55:6). St. Ignatius advised that one should plan for the next time of desolation in the current time of consolation (Rule Ten). Lastly, St. Ignatius guided his followers to remember the thoughts in times of consolation which come from God (Rule Three). These can be an ongoing guide and assist in perseverance when the times of desolation come (Rule Five) and these should be diligently shared with the spiritual director so that he, too, can help the directee remember them in times of desolation (Rule Thirteen).

DESOLATION

The majority of the rules for discernment from the first week of the spiritual exercises focus directly on the experience of desolation. Indeed, desolation is one of the most confusing and difficult parts of the spiritual life. It is always tempting to think that we are doing something wrong if we are experiencing desolation. It is also part of the nature of desolation that it is hard to think clearly or fight vigorously when we are feeling its weight. For this reason, desolation poses the greatest danger of derailing our spiritual journey and it requires the most care and guidance as we move forward. St. Ignatius offered several points of encouragement and clear direction in handling desolation.

First, he offered a description of desolation in Rule Four:

> I call desolation what is entirely the opposite of what is described in the third rule, as darkness of soul, turmoil of spirit, inclination to what is low and earthly, restlessness rising from many disturbances and temptations which lead to want of faith, want of hope, want of love. The soul is wholly slothful, tepid, sad, and separated, as it were, from its Creator and Lord. For just as consolation is the opposite of desolation, so the thoughts that spring from consolation are the opposite of those that spring from desolation.[5]

St. Ignatius was very practical in teaching on desolation and gave several approaches to understanding and responding to it. We will describe them briefly here and invite the reader to explore a greater depth by perusing other valuable works on the subject.

The first instruction St. Ignatius offered was to *persevere* through times of desolation (Rule Five). One should never change one's spiritual plans in times of spiritual desolation. It is a common occurrence that after starting out in the spiritual life with great fervor, praying the Divine Office, making a regular holy hour, or finding time for daily Mass for a week or a month or a year, it becomes dry and difficult and boring and one starts to wonder if it is still working or still the right direction to be pursuing. St. Ignatius offered clear and extremely important guidance: times of desolation are *not* the time to be changing course. Persevere until further light comes that can assist one in making a change that is inspired by the Lord. In other words, God does not tell us He wants us to change course by drying out our experience of spiritual practices. He guides us, rather, by positive lights. (There is a slight caveat to this teaching in the second week's rules, but that will be discernible not only through desolation but more importantly by detecting that there were bad fruits coming from what appeared to be a positive spiritual practice.)

---

[5]   Ibid., no. 317.

After first and foremost persevering, St. Ignatius also offered some *spiritual practices* that act directly against the desolation: namely, by prayer, meditation, much examination, and some penance (Rule Six). In regard to prayer and meditation, prayer can be considered as a simple, intercessory prayer, just asking for God's help. Meditation has to do with recalling certain points about God, praising Him for His attributes of goodness and mercy, His omnipresence, and intimate, constant care for our lives. Much examination indicates a thorough interior exploration to discern if the desolation might be pointing to some personal sinfulness that has pushed God away or some way that we are closing our hearts to a grace that He wants to give us. Lastly, penance can be as simple as extending a holy hour by a minute or two, looking for a small act of charity to undertake for a brother or sister, making a small sacrifice of a preference for food or drink, or turning off the television a few minutes early. Anything that goes against our preferences can help to push against desolation.

St. Ignatius counseled explicit acts of *faith* (Rule Seven) and *hope* (Rule Eight) to push against desolation. In these acts of faith and hope, a conscious trust in God's help develops as one's natural powers (feelings such as "great fervor," "abundant love," or "intense grace") fail (Rule Seven). This is strongly related to St. John of the Cross' understanding of purification—moving away from the natural powers and placing more of the weight of one's life on the power of God. Pope Benedict XVI also described this path of purification in *Spe salvi* as he contrasted natural, material security with the supernatural substance of faith: "This 'substance,' life's normal source of security, has been taken away from Christians in the course of persecution. They have stood firm, though, because they considered this material substance to be of little account. They could abandon it because they had found a better 'basis' for their existence—a basis that abides, that no one can take away. . . . Faith gives life a new basis, a new foundation on which we can stand."[6] Like persecution, desolation teaches us to shift our

---

[6] Pope Benedict XVI, *Spe salvi*, no. 8.

weight from the natural basis of material security to the supernatural substance of faith.

Another point counseled by St. Ignatius was *firm resistance* against desolation (Rule Twelve). St. Ignatius advises that we do not flirt with sin, including the doubt and despair that get stirred up by desolation, but rather that we firmly resist it. If we flirt with it, it can become a "fierce beast," but if we resist it firmly, it may quickly take flight.

As an example, a priest had been leading a group through the Life in the Spirit seminar and was preparing for the high point of the seminar, the Baptism in the Holy Spirit. It was his first time initiating the seminar and throughout the day, preparing for the Baptism in the Spirit, he was feeling anxious and insecure. The enemy played on his insecurities and some spiritual desolation set in. He began to wonder whether the Holy Spirit would really show up for the Baptism in the Spirit. He feared that no one would experience anything and his credibility would be ruined. These thoughts, which flowed from desolation, even led him to ponder whether he could cancel the Baptism in the Spirit or reschedule it. Recognizing the desolation, he made a firm decision to persevere and no longer entertained even the faint thought of canceling the seminar (faithfully following Rule Five). Furthermore, he resisted the desolation by turning to the Lord with acts of faith and hope, concretely affirming his trust in the Lord and his confidence that God wanted to bless the people in the seminar even more than he did. Although the desolation continued to linger, it did not gain strength and then it finally lifted as he prayed with the first person at the Baptism in the Spirit and saw what he believed to be God's hand at work. The fruits of the prayer time were further confirmed by the testimonies of the participants afterward.

St. Ignatius offered some additional insights on the *meaning* behind desolation (Rule Nine). The first point St. Ignatius offered, and the most common idea we tend to have, is that it is caused by our sinfulness (tepidity, sloth, or negligence). This is only one reason, though. Another is that God is building up our faith and hope (the remedies offered in Rules Seven and Eight), and a third is that God is reminding us that ultimately it is all His work. We are not the cause of consolation, He is. It is helpful to know that we can draw some insight from desolation. In addition to the insights about its cause in Rule Nine, St. Ignatius pointed out that desolation can point out the weaknesses in our souls (Rule Fourteen). This is extremely important because the points where the enemy attacks us are precisely the points where we need love and healing and precisely the best starting points for our prayer. By bringing forth the weakest points, where the devil is speaking lies and trying to hurt us and get us to give up, we can be strengthened by God's love. When we know we are loved in the weakest, ugliest points of our being, we truly know that we are loved unconditionally.

The last point of defense offered by St. Ignatius is *full disclosure* (Rule Thirteen). Everything should be revealed to the spiritual director, and this will be the greatest protection for the directee. The more that we keep in the dark, the more power the enemy has over us. In fact, along with Rule Five, this rule is the greatest safeguard for the directee. As long as the directee perseveres in going to spiritual direction (Rule Five) and reveals everything to the director (Rule Thirteen), the director can guide the directee through the rest of the rules as they apply to the particular situation.

Full disclosure in spiritual direction (Rule Thirteen) can lift desolation in two ways. One is that the directee himself recognizes the incoherence of his thinking as he tries to express it. Another is that the spiritual director is able to point it out to him. A businessman came to spiritual direction feeling the weight of ongoing desolation. He started sharing with his spiritual director the plans he was developing to cut down his prayer time and even his attendance at daily Mass so that he could expand his time at the gym. He gave his justifications about how he thought the exercise time would increase his energy levels and help him to better complete his work, and perhaps even enable him to feel better and pray better. As he spoke he began to acknowledge, out loud, that it sounded like he was making some rationalization. His spiritual director took the opportunity to ask him about his prayer time and about his participation at Mass and he admitted they were difficult and dry. His spiritual director explained Rule Five to him and advised him to persevere in his prayer routine. The director even encouraged him, in the spirit of doing a little penance (Rule Six) to stay in prayer the full time and even an extra minute or two. Finally, they discussed a way that he could get some exercise without compromising his prayer time. At the next meeting, the directee expressed his deep gratitude for the clear direction and was able to see the fruits of continuing in prayer.

In addition to the summary of the rules for discernment for the first week that we provide here, the reader might also appreciate the summary provided by Fr. Michael Gaitley, MIC, which he entitled "Rules for Little Souls."[7] Summarizing St. Ignatius' insights, he counseled three possible responses to consolation: "Eat it up!" "Humble yourself," and "Listen." Because consolation is from God and He is showering us with His love, we should receive as much as we can. At the same time, we must remember that the consolation is not our own doing, but it is a gift from God and so we must humble ourselves to receive it. Lastly, the words and direction that come to us during consolation come from God and so we should be sure to listen and remember carefully what He is telling us.

In response to desolation, summarizing the insights of St. Ignatius, Fr. Gaitley counseled, "Ask why," "Fight," and "Don't listen." Because the desolation sometimes comes because of our own sinfulness, or sometimes comes to test us, or sometimes comes to strengthen us, it is worth asking why we are going through the desolation, even though we do not always find an answer. The rules to persevere and to resist through prayer and penance can be summarized as "Fight." The final insight is that the enemy speaks during desolation and so we should not listen. Fr. Gaitley considers the rules at much greater length and his text is valuable for providing further understanding, but we provide the simple,

---

[7] Fr. Michael Gaitley, MIC, *Consoling the Heart of Jesus: A Do-It-Yourself Retreat* (Stockbridge, MA: Marian Press, 2010), 201–251.

three-point summaries in hopes that they can help the reader to remember the insights of St. Ignatius.

DISCERNING GOD'S WILL

A frequent concern in spiritual direction, and sometimes the reason that a person seeks it out at first, is discerning God's will in regard to a specific, significant decision. St. Ignatius provided some excellent guidance in regard to this type of discernment in the *Spiritual Exercises*.[8] In particular, he identified three modes of discernment. Fr. Timothy Gallagher provided an excellent, thorough treatment of this in his book, *Discerning the Will of God*.[9] We encourage the reader to consult that work for a deeper understanding, but the topic is important enough that we believe at least a summary of it should be found in a text on spiritual direction.

The first mode of discernment is when the answer is *beyond doubt* or *without hesitation*. "When God our Lord so moves and attracts the will that a devout soul without hesitation, or the possibility of hesitation, follows what has been manifested to it. St. Paul and St. Matthew acted thus in following Christ our Lord."[10] This is the kind of clarity in discernment that we all long for and sometimes we try to hold out until we have it. But certainty without a doubt does not always come, however, and the other two modes of discernment are needed. One young man experienced this while discerning his religious vocation. He was trying to decide between two religious orders. Although he was very attracted to one of them and it fit all of the criteria he felt were necessary for the way that he wanted to serve the Lord, when he visited, with an intention to seek entrance, he experienced deep unrest throughout the visit. Although he tried to push through, he could not find peace. When he used his imagination to envision himself in the habit of that religious order, he could only see himself in the habit of the

---

[8] St. Ignatius of Loyola, *Spiritual Exercises*, nos. 175–188.

[9] Fr. Timothy Gallagher, *Discerning the Will of God: The Ignatian Guide to Christian Decision Making* (New York: The Crossroad Publishing Company, 2009).

[10] St. Ignatius of Loyola, *Spiritual Exercises*, no. 175.

other order he was considering. When he tried to envision himself
with the men who were making their vows, he could again only
see himself in the other order. Finally he had the realization that
perhaps God wanted him to be in the other order and so he made
an act of surrender and said, "Lord, I want whatever you want for
me." In that moment, peace washed over him and everything was
resolved. That clarity moved him to go directly to the other order
and seek entrance. Even when he was met with some uncertainty
from the order, he had peace, persevered, and joined a few months
later. It is wonderful to have such clarity. In the case of this young
man, he did not know himself well enough to see why the religious order that God directed him to was the one that was best
suited for him. It would seem that God's stronger intervention
overruled the young man's preferences, although the Lord still
worked within his freedom, waiting for him to surrender before
making the matter so clear.

The second mode of discernment described by St. Ignatius
comes in following the experience of consolation and desolation,
"When much light and understanding are derived through experience of desolations and consolations and discernment of diverse
spirits."[11] A key insight in this case is that God often speaks in
times of consolation while the enemy speaks in times of desolation. As a result, by paying attention to the things that are coming
in times of consolation and desolation, the individual can get
some idea of how the Lord is calling. Unlike the first mode, the
second mode takes place over time. It gives motivation for the
practice of the daily Examen, in which an individual focuses primarily on the way that God is speaking through consolation and
desolation throughout a given day. Over time, one might see a
developing pattern by which God is guiding the individual in a
particular direction through repeated consolation and desolation.
For example, a young female missionary was devout and open to
God's will. She was not in an exclusive relationship and was open
to religious life. She sought some clarity on how to move forward

[11] Ibid., no. 176.

with her life. She wondered whether she should actively visit religious orders or focus more on dating and discerning marriage. In one of her first meetings with a new spiritual director, she asked this question and her spiritual director explained the three modes of discernment. In discussing the second mode, he asked her what comes to her when she feels close to the Lord, when she is at her best (he was asking about spiritual consolation, but since she was not familiar with Ignatian concepts, he paraphrased for her). She immediately replied, "Babies." Then he asked her what she thinks about when she is at her worst, when she feels far away from God and struggles to pray and even doubts what He is doing in her life or if He is doing anything. She replied, "I think that if I became a religious, maybe it would get better." From this, her spiritual director pointed out that the enemy's temptation in desolation and the Lord's encouragement in consolation appeared to be pointing to the same conclusion: that she should focus on the married vocation. This discernment is never fully complete until one's vocation is solidified through receiving a sacrament or making vows, but it was a strong enough guide to put her at rest and focus her attention on marriage.

The third mode of discernment takes up much more of St. Ignatius' text and it is the area that we most often find ourselves struggling through. St. Ignatius offered some practical guidance for how to navigate our way through this mode of discernment most effectively. In particular, St. Ignatius gave two ways and several points for each way. Again we will offer some summary points but the reader may want to go deeper by consulting another book, such as Fr. Gallagher's *Discerning the Will of God*.

A key point for the first way of the third mode of discernment is coming to a holy indifference: the willingness to accept either outcome is important for a true openness to God's will. Also, it is important to remember the purpose for which we are created (union with God) and that this decision is a means and not the end. A simple, but easily overlooked, point is praying a straightforward prayer for God's help. In the first way of the third mode, St. Ignatius counseled making a list of pros and cons. By looking at all the positive benefits of choice A and all the negative consequences of choice A, along with all the positive consequences of choice B and all the negative consequences of choice B, an individual can place everything in front of himself at the same time. This helps him to avoid the tunnel vision that can result from focusing on only one choice at a time. Likewise, a particular negative aspect may appear larger than it really is, but when it is on paper next to other pros and cons, it seems proportionately more reasonable. In listing all the consequences and looking at the possibilities, St. Ignatius intended to focus more on reason and less on emotional inclination in making a choice.[12] The final step is to make a choice internally and offer it to God, seeking His confirmation.

In the second way of the third mode, St. Ignatius offered some other practical ways to explore a question within ourselves. First, he counseled the individual to make sure that the love for the choice in question is connected with and causes an increase in love for God. Secondly, he encouraged the one discerning to separate himself from the choice and look at the question from the outside. That is, imagine if someone came to him and asked him the question that he was discerning. How would he guide that person? Thirdly, St. Ignatius recommended considering the question from the perspective of one's death bed. At the end of his life, which choice would he wish he had made. Lastly, from the perspective of standing before God in judgment, what decision does he wish he would have made.

These practical recommendations are good for a spiritual director to keep in mind in helping a directee to navigate the critical questions in life. These modes of discernment can apply to larger decisions, including one's vocation, changing jobs, making a significant move to a new location, starting a particular course of studies, or volunteering for a position of responsibility in a parish. One might want to utilize these steps of discernment when seeking to reach out to a family member who has been estranged for a long time or when putting a particular rule in

---

[12] Ibid., no. 182.

place to govern some family dynamics (a decision to pray a family Rosary three times per week, for example). One would probably not apply these modes of discernment to a more trivial decision, such as what to eat for dinner at a restaurant.

Aspects of Purification

As St. Ignatius identified, learning how to recognize and handle desolation is one of the greatest hurdles in the spiritual life. In this section, we spend some time describing aspects of purification so that the spiritual director can help to identify the purifications an individual might be experiencing and can better guide the directee through those times.

Purification can be understood best in terms of our ultimate goal. Because our ultimate goal is pure, loving union with God, we need to be purified of tendencies (thoughts, feelings, actions) that interfere with that union. The model for our union with God is the Trinity. In the Trinity, there are three Persons who are irreducibly unique, and yet whose union is so pure and absolute that they are truly *one* God. The bond of love that holds them together is stronger (more inseparable) than the force that holds together the most elementary particle of matter, and yet at the same time, each Person is radically free. The bond of love is not an obligation and involves no control of one Person over another, and yet the three Persons are perfectly one and absolutely inseparable. The Trinitarian union, which is the grounds of every other union, involves the fullest individuality and simultaneously the greatest freedom.

To enter into this kind of union requires radical trust that admits no suspicion, no self-protection, and no forms of control. To indicate how radical this trust must be, the expression "mystical death" is often used in discussing the spiritual life. We tend to avoid this in our spiritual life almost as much as we avoid physical death in our physical life. From our earliest moments we were forming patterns of control and self-protection. First identifying and then shedding those habits is a major work in our spiritual journey. The end result can be hard even to imagine. It may feel something like an endless freefall in which we have no control and yet we also never fear hitting the ground. It is something like an eternal dance in which we do not know the next step until the moment we need to take it. Pope Francis witnessed to this experience in his own spiritual development.

> It is true that this trust in the unseen can cause us to feel disoriented: it is like being plunged into the deep and not knowing what we will find. I myself have frequently experienced this. Yet there is no greater freedom than that of allowing oneself to be guided by the Holy Spirit, renouncing the attempt to plan and control everything to the last detail, and instead letting him enlighten, guide and direct us, leading us wherever he wills. The Holy Spirit knows well what is needed in every time and place. This is what it means to be mysteriously fruitful![13]

Active Purification

St. John of the Cross teaches about one aspect of purification that has an ongoing role in the spiritual life but is also the most primitive: *active* purification. Active purification is the purification we actively take on in various forms of self-denial such as fasting and other chosen penances. These practices are the substance of the ascetical life. Asceticism has been liable to many misunderstandings and confusion. Mortification, or "mystical death," is descriptive of the process that frees us from attachment and helps us give ourselves more generously to God. Although active purification is part of this process, the fact that we remain in control of it can also hinder it. By pacing ourselves in simple practices of asceticism and maintaining them with a desire for self-purification and also offering them as loving acts of intercessory prayer, these practices can become ways by which the Lord can further purify

---

[13] Pope Francis, *Evangelii gaudium*, no. 280.

us with passive purifications. For example, fasting on Fridays may be new and interesting at first, but it inevitably becomes irritating and difficult and on occasion will correspond with other events outside our control and we will be tempted to abandon the practice. Sometimes this may be prudent, but it may also be precisely the occasion when we are able to abandon ourselves to the Lord and genuinely trust in Him rather than merely in ourselves.

PRACTICAL GUIDANCE

Before giving some guidelines for active purification, it is necessary to provide a corrective for some distorted ideas that have entered into this realm. Although the language of "mystical death" is descriptive of what happens when a person entrusts himself radically to God and dies to every other form of security, this does not imply a destruction of our human nature. "Detachment is a necessity of our nature, but it does not mean the destruction of our nature. It is, rather, a restraining of nature so that its interference in the spiritual life can be kept to a reasonable minimum."[14] Indeed, our healthy psychology and natural drives assist us significantly in growing in holiness. The passions are necessary for the development of virtues. "None of this [purification and sanctification] is accomplished by the repression or elimination of human psychological faculties as such. No one ever arrived at the mountaintop by totally refusing to think, to desire, to feel, to reflect on the past, and to imagine the future."[15]

When discerning what forms of mortification will assist us in detachment, we must avoid the illusion that harder is always better or that self-punishment is the key to freeing us from our vices. These approaches can be a subtle mask for the vainglory that can come from pride or ambition, and can be an excuse to indulge a dangerous self-hatred.

In acts of self-denial, it is important to deny ourselves many things that are good, and certainly we should deny ourselves

---

[14] Dominic Hoffman, *The Life Within*, 31.
[15] Ibid., 30.

things that are evil. When we deny ourselves things that are good, we should always make of them an offering of love. Often the best way is not to abstain entirely from something but simply to have less of it. While doing so we can give God glory for the food we are eating and savor it in smaller portions. We can do the same with the enjoyment of anything else, including persons.

All acts of detachment and abstinence should be done joyfully. As Jesus advises in the Gospel, it is best to do this in a hidden way and to not even let our right hand know what our left hand is doing. In other words, active purification should be done in increasing self-forgetfulness, and one must be constantly vigilant to ensure it does not lead to self-preoccupation. This active purification can deepen love and fervor, and it prepares us for even deeper forms of purification which are passively experienced.

Passive Purification

The most powerful form of purification takes place when the individual's will is not involved in initiating or choosing a penance, but rather, only in whether to accept the purification as it comes. This passive purification is powerful and formative in opening up the freedom of the individual to respond generously and spontaneously to the will of God at each moment. Learning to give a heartfelt yes to trials and challenges is an ongoing development in the spiritual life. Trials and challenges are lived out daily and moment by moment. They come in the form of interruptions in our schedule, physical illness, minor and major failures, encounters with our weaknesses, confusion, desolation in our prayer, our own sins and the sins of others, and emotional suffering, to name a few examples. Although it can be hard to look forward to these painful experiences, they are precious pearls that mortify our will and teach us to embrace the divine will:

> The faithful soul rejoices in the upper part of the spirit to be crucified with Christ. But do not be worried by the resistance from the inferior part of the spirit. Resist the

evil suggestions of the enemy with a pure act of your will without, however, trying to force your head or your interior. In the time of these trials, it is the best thing to cast our will into the loving bosom of divine goodness.[16]

These passive purifications are an ongoing experience of dying. They give us a foretaste of the actual moment of death that will come for each of us. They give us practice and teach us how to die well—with peace and abandon. One of the marks of the heights of the spiritual life, called the "transforming union" in the language of St. John of the Cross, is a *peaceful death*. This does not necessarily indicate a painless or easy death, but ultimately a peaceful surrender in the last moment of our mortal life. By the one who is in a constant, living union with God's will, the moment of death is seen as simply one more opportunity for loving acceptance, like so many others that came before it.

We can see that there are two overlapping "lives" in us. These two lives are the mortal life that began at our physical conception in our mother's womb and the eternal life that began in our Christian conception in the Church's womb through the Sacrament of Baptism. Our mortal life will end at the moment of physical death, but the eternal life of Baptism grows in us and continues into eternity. In making the intentional transition from our mortal life to eternal life, there is an ongoing experience of dying and rising. St. Paul of the Cross, founder of the Congregation of the Passion, called the dying "mystical death." It involves the intentional letting go, more and more, of our mortal life. He called our growing entrance into eternal life "divine nativity," because Christ's life is born ever anew in us and we come to live more and more in Him until we can say with St. Paul, "It is no longer I who live, but Christ who lives in me" (Gal 2:20). St. Paul of the Cross, and the mystical tradition of spirituality in the Church in general, also called this mystical death "detachment."

---

[16] St. Paul of the Cross, *The Letters of Saint Paul of the Cross*, ed. Laurence Finn and Donald Webber, vol. 1 (Hyde Park, NY: New City Press, 2000), 392.

Passive purifications can take more extreme forms through accident, injury, and illness, but there is also a daily purification in each moment. Each moment is full of possibility, pregnant with God's presence, and yet we cannot remain in that moment. It is always giving way to the next moment, like a musical score that delivers each note one at a time as it passes into non-existence and gives way to the next note. The spiritual life demands that we develop a trust in God's musical score so that we can take in each note, one at a time, without clinging to the notes that have passed, nor missing the note that is present, all the while listening to the sound between the notes and living in anxious anticipation of notes to come.

We experience the purification of passing moments most poignantly when preciousness is closest to us. As sweet as that preciousness is, it does not fulfill all of our desire. Not only that, but we cannot hold on to it as it passes away like sand between our fingers. As our purification develops, however, we learn to embrace and appreciate even the smallest moments of preciousness, discovering the truth about God found in the epitaph on St. Ignatius' tomb: "Not to be controlled by the greatest but to be found in the least, that is divine."[17]

Assisting a Directee Experiencing Purification

A spiritual director plays a very important role in helping a directee to move through the process of purification. In particular, the spiritual director can provide recognition and explanation of what is happening, encouragement and reassurance that this is a good direction, and guidance on how to pray with and accept the purification.

IDENTIFYING THE DARK NIGHT
We spoke above about discursive, meditative prayer, noting that it is the starting point of prayer and also that it gradually moves one

---

[17] "*Non coerceri maximo, contineri minimo divinum es.*"

toward greater silence. In this silence is born the grace of infused contemplation. To understand this better, it is worth referring back to the earlier description given in the chapter on interiority which describes the soul in terms of an inner and outer circle.[18] The outer circle involves the spiritual senses, such as the imagination and memory, as well as the reason that is able to draw conclusions deductively. The inner circle consists of an intuitive knowing in the intellect and also the ability to make a simple, prolonged act of love in the will. Knowledge and love, experienced in the outer circle, are naturally limiting because they are more defined and delimited by images and words. It is like trying to grasp truth and grasp God within closed hands. Knowledge and love in the inner circle are more expansive. They are able to touch truth and enter a communion with God with open hands that remain unlimited.

Transitioning from one form of prayer (loving and knowing God) to the other is a purifying experience that St. John of the Cross calls the passive night of the senses. He provides three criteria by which one can discern that this purification is taking place:

> The first is that since these souls do not get satisfaction or consolation from the things of God, they do not get any from creatures either. . . .
>
> The second sign for the discernment of this purgation is that the memory ordinarily turns to God solicitously and with painful care, and the soul thinks it is not serving God but turning back, because it is aware of this distaste for the things of God. Hence it is obvious that this aversion and dryness is not the fruit of laxity and tepidity, for lukewarm people do not care much for the things of God nor are they inwardly solicitous about them. . . .
>
> The third sign for the discernment of this purgation of the senses is the powerlessness, in spite of one's efforts, to meditate and make use of the imagination, the interior sense, as was one's previous custom. At this time God does

---

[18] Cf. Chapter 2 of this book.

not communicate himself through the senses as he did before, by means of the discursive analysis and synthesis of ideas, but begins to communicate himself through pure spirit by an act of simple contemplation in which there is no discursive succession of thought. The exterior and interior senses of the lower part of the soul cannot attain to this contemplation. As a result the imaginative power and phantasy can no longer rest in any consideration or find support in it.[19]

We can tell, especially in the third sign, the way that the active use of the outer circle of our soul is being frustrated, and we can only find satisfaction in the use of the inner circle. The satisfaction that comes through the inner circle, however, is unfamiliar and feels dry because of its subtler taste. The lack of concrete words and images, feelings, and other sensory stimulation experienced in the outer circle is uncomfortable to us and we have not yet developed a taste for the knowledge and love of God that we receive in the inner circle, in what St. John of the Cross calls "infused contemplation."

For example, a seminarian named John, who was very faithful and growing in prayer, found himself drifting away from his normal spiritual practices late in the school year because they had become more dry. Upon further investigation, his spiritual director helped him to discern that the three signs were met in this case. The first sign: He was experiencing a malaise in other areas of his life as well, including his studies and relationships. Everything had lost some of the flavor that it had before. He had not substituted worldly pleasures for these spiritual practices, because the worldly pleasures had lost their savor as well. The second sign: John felt that he was not serving God adequately in his responsibilities as a seminarian nor in his studies, but God was continually

---

[19] St. John of the Cross, *The Dark Night*, bk. I, chap. 9, nos. 2, 3, 8, in *The Collected Works of St. John of the Cross*, trans. Kieran Kavanaugh and Otilio Rodriguez (Washington, DC: ICS Publications, 1991), 377–378, 380.

on his mind and his desire to pray more was strong. The third sign: John had found much fruit, earlier in the year, through an Ignatian-style *lectio divina*, in which he used his imagination to place himself in biblical scenes. He was struggling to do that during this passive night of the senses.

The spiritual director can be profoundly helpful in these cases because he can discern what is happening and encourage the directee to stay the course and not get discouraged. The transition from solely discursive prayer to an addition of infused contemplation can be an awkward transition. The spiritual director can reassure the directee that he is not crazy and he is not falling backward, but his prayer is good and fruitful and he has to get used to this new movement in his spiritual life. He can also be aware of others who might be going through this purgative transition and thus able to help them as well.

RECOGNIZING AND UNDERSTANDING PURIFICATION

One of the most difficult things for us psychologically is not understanding what is happening to us. Medical patients experience notable relief in simply being diagnosed with an illness, even if it is untreatable or treatments for it have a low rate of success. It is a relief to know that there is a logic to what is taking place and that someone has experienced it before us. Furthermore, when we can see the value and meaning in our suffering, it helps us accept painful experiences, even agonizing experiences. This is a very valuable service that the spiritual director can provide.

The spiritual director performs a great service simply by acknowledging that there is a purification taking place in the directee. For the directee it is new territory, and the unknown tends to frighten us. The opportunity to share the unknown in spiritual direction and the undisturbed or even enthusiastic response of the spiritual director can be a great support to the directee. This starts with giving the experience a name such as purification, dark night, desert, mystical death, and so forth.

The support from the spiritual director continues with an explanation of how this process leads to freedom and holiness.

A directee often fears that the process only leads to diminution or destruction, because that is what it feels like in the moment. It is scary and disorienting when we feel the loss of those physical, psychological, and spiritual supports we depend on, such as comfortable feelings, bodily health, successful ventures, or lights in prayer. The spiritual director does well to explain that this is helping the directee to let go of his security in his own control and to place more trust in God alone. This is part of the normal process of growing in holiness.

Talking through this in spiritual direction is not going to change the directee's experience, but now he has a name for his experience and a path forward. This is a great improvement. When the dryness in prayer or the experience of failure, the cloudiness of his mind or the heavy feelings return, he can now identify them on his own: "Ah! This is purification." He can also take consolation in connecting the experience with a positive path forward, trusting, for example, in the words of Jesus in the Scripture, "Truly, truly, I say to you, unless a grain of wheat falls into the earth and dies, it remains alone; but if it dies, it bears much fruit" (Jn 12:24).

A woman who was very faithful and growing in the spiritual life experienced many trials in her relationships in community. There were conflicts with other women who had been close friends; there were feelings of failure and pointlessness in her work; her family was more distant than usual. She was feeling the fearful pain of the loss of these supports. Naturally, her spiritual director talked with her about the difficult relationships in hopes of finding some resolution and also talked with her about her work, in hopes of helping her see that there was some good fruit and that the difficulties were not merely due to behaviors that she could correct. Additionally, however, the spiritual director pointed out that she was carrying her cross with Jesus and that these experiences were purifying her of the natural supports in her life and helping her cling more closely to Christ. This acknowledgment of the purification taking place gave her additional strength and purpose in embracing her cross and persevering through the painful difficulties.

ENCOURAGEMENT AND REASSURANCE IN PURIFICATION

The spiritual director may sympathetically respond to the sufferings of the directee and spontaneously feel the urge to fix them or heal them. The inability to ease the suffering of the directee or to find some remedy for what is happening may be a source of struggle for the spiritual director. A director may have a desire to get more involved with the situation and provide concrete assistance. When the directee is being purified by the Lord, however, the best thing a spiritual director can do is provide encouragement and reassurance. Although it may seem repetitive or redundant, the encouragement to persevere through the trial, the reassurance that the Lord is near, and the confident projection that this is leading in a good direction can provide tremendous support to a person who is suffering. Of course, expressions of sympathy and concern are also helpful and should not be omitted. These provide the human support and encouragement to persevere and trust in the purifying love of the Lord.

When one is in the midst of suffering, it can be hard to see the forest for the trees. This is where a spiritual director can provide reassurance from his higher-level view of observation. Simply acknowledging that the directee is carrying a cross, sharing in the sufferings of Christ, or being courageous and strong in bearing his cross can be very helpful. The spiritual director knows the directee's history in such a way that he can point out the faithfulness and strength of the directee in bearing so much purification. Sometimes recounting what has happened and then recognizing, in a positive way, how the directee has responded to difficult experiences, can be a boost of strength to help the directee keep moving forward.

The spiritual director is in the role of a spiritual father or mother for an individual. Our parents played a very important role in our lives when we experienced new and difficult experiences. Their confidence in us, the firmness of their support, and their lack of fear in our regard was transferred to us and gave us courage, peace, and confidence to tackle the problems at hand. The spiritual director can fulfill this role for the directee as well by communicating confidence in the directee's ability to grow through a particular situation. The spiritual director can also enthusiastically acknowledge how the directee is handling the difficulties and express confidence that he is going to make it out to the other side and be holier because of the experience. At times, such support can feel insufficient, especially in the midst of great suffering, but it can be profoundly strengthening for the directee to feel that someone, especially his spiritual father or mother, believes in him.

It is important that this supportive work be sincere, authentic, and tailor-made to suit the directee. The spiritual director must steer clear of canned responses or cliché motivational speeches. The spiritual director can personalize the encouragement to the directee, calling on specific examples of patient endurance or faithfulness in the directee's life and can acknowledge some of the particular fruits of purification that have already emerged. The spiritual director can also recall experiences of perseverance from the directee's past to give reasons for his confidence that the directee will also pass through this trial and be better for it.

The directee often forgets earlier darkness or trials. When the director reminds the directee of earlier difficulties—how dark they were, and how things have worked out—the directee may remember with a smile the earlier reassurances and how they were fulfilled. This can be fortifying for him and help him to endure in the present circumstance.

Praying with and Accepting Purification

A third area where the spiritual director can support a directee in times of purifying trials is through offering ways to pray in the pain. This is related to our earlier reflections on helping directees to place their lives in the context of Sacred Scripture. St. Paul of the Cross was an expert in helping his directees to connect their experience with Jesus' Passion:

> I will try with all my strength to follow the footsteps of Jesus. If I am afflicted, abandoned, desolate, I will keep him

company in the Garden. If I am despised and injured, I will keep him company in the Praetorium. If I am depressed and afflicted in the agonies of suffering, I will keep him company faithfully on the Mount, and in a generous spirit I will keep him company on the Cross with the lance in my heart. Oh, how sweet it is to die![20]

A spiritual director can personalize the Gospel through the inspiration of the Holy Spirit by offering images or the example of saints. When the directee is experiencing a particularly difficult time of prayer that he describes as "dryness," the spiritual director can speak to him about the stark beauty of the desert: "Although the flowers are few and far between, they are profoundly beautiful. Be on the lookout for those profoundly beautiful flowers that may emerge suddenly and momentarily in your prayer or in your relationships or in your work. Don't pass them by too quickly, but take in their beauty." The process of purification is, after all, also a process of sensitization, and as the Lord sensitizes us, we are able to savor even the subtlest graces and signs of His presence.

Another struggle in purification is the simple step of accepting it. Sometimes that step seems superfluous because one really has no choice. Think of a mother who must raise a severely disabled child, a man with cancer, a priest with a difficult parish assignment, or a consecrated religious woman with a strained relationship in community. These are not situations that are granted by our choice, and yet the choice to accept the situation is still very important. As long as an individual holds on to an inner resistance, an inner denial, or an inner bitterness, the purification is not able to transform the soul as it is supposed to. It is like driving a car with the emergency brake on. Analogously, the brake tends to wear away over time, so it is much better simply to release the brake. The spiritual director can help a directee see that he is

---

[20] St. Paul of the Cross, "Treatise on Mystical Death," in *St. Paul of the Cross: A Source/Workbook for Paulacrucian Studies*, ed. Jude Mead (New Rochelle, NY: Don Bosco Publications, 1983).

resisting and help him to take that step of acceptance and even to utter the prayer of Mary, "Behold, I am the handmaid of the Lord; let it be to me according to your word" (Lk 1:38).

There was a religious sister who had a number of health problems. She had grown tremendously in learning to pray through her suffering and she had taken the appropriate steps to get the best possible medical treatment. She was still agitated and irritated and feeling unproductive, however. Her sufferings repeatedly interfered with her regular work and ministry. Her spiritual director sympathized with her suffering and encouraged her to think about the Lord's love for her, but it made little impact. She knew all that. Finally, her spiritual director recognized what was missing. She was handling everything—she was carrying her cross—but she was still fighting it. Her spiritual director said to her, "Only one thing is missing. Your will. You are bearing this, but are you willing to choose it?" This word broke through and she realized that not only must she not reject her cross, but she needed to embrace it, to choose it. The spiritual director's words became a regular mental reminder to her when she found herself resisting.

Moreover, when Jesus told us to take up our cross He said we were to follow *Him*, not to keep our eyes on our cross or on ourselves. More and more we must take our attention and focus away from ourselves and place it upon Christ. This allows the greatest and deepest purification. We then stop paying attention to ourselves or our prayer and instead focus on the Lord and what He is doing in our prayer. St. Elizabeth of the Trinity wrote that she did not really need to do anything during prayer, so enraptured was she by Him who did everything: "I have only to love Him, to let myself be loved."[21]

As these things happen, transformation is taking place—a transformation into the likeness of Christ. We are passing through purification into illumination and union, but we hardly notice because our heart is set on *Him*.

---

[21] St. Elizabeth of the Trinity, *Elizabeth of the Trinity: The Complete Works*, vol. 1 (Washington, DC: ICS, 1995), 177.

8

Psychological Models and Healing

G RACE BUILDS ON and perfects nature. For this reason, some understanding of psychology will be very helpful for spiritual direction. An academic understanding of psychology is not a necessary prerequisite for beginning spiritual direction, but it is an area of study that can assist the ongoing formation of the spiritual director. It is always important to emphasize that a spiritual director is *not* a substitute for a psychologist, and there are pathologies that should be treated in a professional and dedicated way that is outside the realm of spiritual direction. A spiritual director can work quite well together with a psychologist, but should not try to substitute for a professional unless he has the proper credentials. We do not propose to give a treatise on psychology in this book, but simply to offer insights and explain how they work within spiritual direction.

One benefit of psychological models is that they help one to develop *working theories* when listening to a spiritual directee. This is possible because certain behaviors and attitudes tend to go together, and certain patterns of development tend to repeat across many persons. Without knowing the person's whole life story, a little bit of knowledge, combined with a psychological model, can inform good guesses about some other ways that a person feels, thinks, or behaves. These "guesses" should always be considered as such and not hardened into facts until they can be checked out with the directee.

The application of psychological models to develop working theories is not systematic or programmatic but rather falls under the *art* of spiritual direction. These insights from psychology are intended as tools for the spiritual director to apply as he feels guided by the Holy Spirit. We provide these images and insights into the psycho-spiritual anatomy of human persons in hopes that spiritual directors might have a better grasp on how to recognize and speak to the wounds, weaknesses, and strengths we all have in our humanity. At the end of the chapter we also consider some ways that prayer along with the process of spiritual direction can facilitate psychological and spiritual healing for the directee.

Some Helpful Insights from Psychology

The field of psychology has gathered a great deal of data from extensive interactions with a wide variety of people over the last several decades. From this data, combined with certain worldviews, psychologists have drawn many conclusions, developed models, and offered insights about the psychological development of the human person. Depending on the assumptions about the human person hidden in the worldview of the psychologist, the conclusions will be more or less trustworthy. There are many problems in popular psychology, but there are also many beneficial discoveries and theories that are worth learning and using in spiritual direction. A basic dimension of those discoveries is the formative impact that fundamental relationships have on us. These areas will certainly come up in spiritual direction and the more that the spiritual director can get a handle on the psychological patterns that are playing out, the more helpful he will be in drawing that directee closer to God.

Biologically speaking, everyone has a father and mother. The reality of today's broken families, however, is that many people grow up in single-parent households. Children are very sensitive to the effects of abuse, neglect, and deprivation. A child raised in a single-parent household is deprived of something. We are impacted, as children, by whether we have both fatherly and motherly influences.

There are distinct ways that a mother interacts with a child, starting with the unique relationship of carrying that child in her womb. A mother who then nurses her child at her own breast carries out, many times a day, the most intimate interaction of bonding and providing, from her own body, something essential for that child's survival. A mother ideally has the majority of daily contact with a newborn child.

A father has the second most intimate early contact with a child. A father normally develops a relationship with a child through the mother's relationship. It is the mother who introduces a baby to the baby's father. A father, generally, provides strength and stability for a child and for a family. A mother, generally, provides sensitivity and tenderness, nurturing the daily needs of children in the family. Women are particularly well suited, due to their usually more sensitive natures, for the majority of care in early childhood, while fathers are better suited for a larger portion of the care and formation as children get older.

The way that a child was raised can affect his psychological formation, and that impacts spiritual direction. Knowing whether a person was raised in a single-parent household, or raised in day care, or raised primarily by a grandparent can impact some of the ways that person is responding to stressors and can give insight into ways he might need God to complete areas in which his formation is lacking.

The personality of parents can also affect children significantly. The normal dynamics of parenting involve a father helping a son or daughter to distance, in a healthy way, from the mother whose strong attachment to the child is an important part of forming initial stability in that child. Consequently, a father or mother with a stronger or weaker personality can have a particular impact. A mother who is strong and detached can teach a child to be more independent. A mother who is anxious and clingy, or who has mood disorders, will have a different impact on the child. It can be helpful to understand how a person fit or did not fit well into the relationship with each parent, and how those dynamics show up in the directee.

Of course, children also have their own personalities. Although personalities and temperaments will form as children grow, they can be quite apparent from the earliest days of a child's life. Some are more nervous, some are more precocious. Various things will cause traits to develop based on the child's relationship with his parents. A smothering mother and an absent father will have a particular effect on a child. Not all children in the family will be affected to the same degree or in the same way by that dynamic, but all will be affected.

The earliest human relational formation is with a mother in a relationship of strong dependence, starting from the mother's womb. The father is introduced as a third person into that relationship and it is, ordinarily, the first triangle that a child must deal with. The father "breaks up" the relationship with the mother and child, and introduces a separation in a particular way. There are also important processes of identification that happen between fathers and sons in that separation from the mother. Daughters identify with mothers in a different way, but the father still plays a role in separating mothers and daughters, thus enabling a daughter to accept that identification with the mother more freely. These dynamics are all affected by a mother or a father who is insecure or a marital relationship that is weak and unable to sustain the roles of mother and father for the sake of the children.

If one parent is distant or absent, this process of separation and identification might still happen but without the security, affirmation, and closeness that is needed. If parents are critical and never satisfied, or say harsh or damaging things, a child might deal with this rejection by trying harder or by giving up. Both of these responses can lead to the formation of patterns that continue to emerge later in life and come up in spiritual direction. Children may also rebel or feel guilty and ashamed. Two children from the same family may respond differently to the same parents, and parents also grow so that they may be better or worse parents for later children than for earlier children. In any event, no parent is perfect, and the strengths and limitations of the parents affect the children in various ways.

Some of the consequences of these parental dynamics appear in spiritual direction. A person may struggle with having a man as a boss or a woman as a boss. A person might struggle with calling God Father. A person whose mother was always critical, cold, and unable to deal with weakness may have a hard time identifying with the more passive or tender qualities of the Blessed Virgin Mary. On the other hand, a person is sometimes able to identify the longing for tenderness and understanding and develop a relationship with Mary precisely because his mother was so difficult or demanding.

Personality develops as real people in one's life become a part of one's psyche: whether they are affirming, rejecting, never satisfied, scolding, and so forth. Analogous to psychotherapy but in a distinct way, spiritual direction focuses on relationships and particularly how those relationships affect one's relationship with God. We tend to project our parental relationships onto God. One person can find in God the unconditional love he received from his mother, while another has a hard time believing in unconditional love, even from God, because he has never known it in his life.

Ambivalence can develop for many reasons. A child tends to want a mother to be strong, but then he also wants to be strong and free himself. A child may feel protected by a mother's strength but also feel restricted by it. This can lead to ambivalence. Ambivalence may also stem from a father who did not allow his sensitive child to be sensitive, for example. After being told clearly that "Boys don't cry," a boy who is sensitive may not know how to reconcile his sensitivity with the masculine, insensitive identity that has been bestowed on him by his father. This can lead to ambivalence about his own feelings and the way he is made. Such ambivalence may be resolved in spiritual direction simply through the consistent, balanced strength of the spiritual director himself as he accompanies a directee through various situations. Concomitantly, a spiritual director may be able to help a directee see the ambivalence and its origins so that he might take it to prayer and rediscover in God the ultimate Fatherhood that he needs.

In addition to the individual influence of mother and father, we also deal with our parents as a unit. A child has to figure out how he fits into his mother's relationship with his father. He comes to understand that his mother and father have their own relationship that he does not share in. What does it mean to be excluded from their relationship? This dynamic gives rise to the Oedipal complex, as described in Freudian psychology. While it is extreme to say that boys want to kill their fathers and marry their mothers, there is a certain dynamic that plays out here that can bring insight into how a personality has developed with the feelings one has toward father and mother, feelings which get stirred up by other paternal and maternal influences in his life.

There are wounds that develop from sibling relationships as well. Harmful comparisons may have been made by parents ("You're not like your brother"). We generally underestimate the sensitivity of children and how much of an imprint such words can leave on them. The competitions that develop between brothers and sisters affect self-understanding, including identity and destiny. A boy who could never keep up with his brothers or a girl who was not as popular as her sister can begin to incorporate these shortcomings into their identity. They see themselves as less than other people. They may also incorporate this into their destiny, only hoping ever to be second best. In this area, prayer can be a powerful remedy, as we discuss later.

A person's *experience* of family life also has a major impact on that person's *perception* of family life. Some children decide early on that family life is miserable, by definition, and they cannot wait to get out. This may be a motivation for celibacy, but it would not be a sound motivation. Restoring a proper image of family life through meditation on the Holy Family of Nazareth, for example, can be a remedy for this struggle.

The way that religion is presented in the family makes a significant impact on a person's religious beliefs. Is religion only for the weak and vulnerable, or for the powerful, or for the tender?

How is God presented? So many people have an idea of God that is very different from how He has presented Himself in Christ. Many people see God as a domineering, demanding, angry figure. In reality, that understanding is like the curtain concealing the Wizard of Oz, and through spiritual direction a person can come to discover the true God that is hidden behind the curtain. When a directee says he sees God as a heartless bully, the spiritual director can explore that and see where the roots of that image come from. Then he can work with the directee to renounce the lies and replace the distorted image of God with the image that Christ has revealed to us.

Our psychology lays a foundation for our spirituality because we can only interact with God from our own humanity. As human beings, we are made for and formed by relationships. The most fundamental relationships are the ones that have been there from our earliest moments of existence, starting in the womb. All of these relationships form the way that we think, feel, and interact with other people and the way we interact with God. A spiritual director will benefit from exploring these fundamental relationships with questions such as "What has been the most important relationship in your life?" "Who is the person you are closest to? Describe them." "How is your relationship with God?" "Who has influenced your idea of God? How?" "What will it be like to be a mother? A wife? Who is your model mother and wife?" "What qualities are you lacking? Describe the strengths you feel you are lacking. What strengths do you have?"

The experiences of love in our lives provide the vocabulary that we use to interact with and talk about God. Our feelings and experiences of human love provide the template for our interaction with God. If our life has been loveless or our experience of love has been very limited, that may significantly impact our ability to relate with God. We can explore human loves with questions like, "How have you been loved?" "Who loves you?" "Who do you love?" "Have you ever fallen in love?"

The people who have hurt us provide a certain template for our sensitivities toward God. We have a way of replaying old wounds in our encounters with others and in our encounters with God. We can explore these areas of a person's heart with questions like, "Who has hurt you the most? What was that like? How did you deal with it?"

Over time, as a spiritual director meets with a wide variety of people, he naturally develops insight into the generalities of human psychology. Further study of temperaments, personality theories, and psychological models can help a spiritual director recognize repeating patterns and gain further insight into his directees.

Models for Understanding Woundedness

The human person is made in the image of God who is love. Consequently, the human person, too, is meant to become love. This simple insight has generated many images of heaven and it can guide the work of healing that the spiritual director is privileged to participate in. Heaven and purgatory are not really places but are beyond space and time. Yet, we inevitably use the language of place or space to describe them. In his encyclical on hope, *Spe salvi*, Pope Benedict XVI described the eternal life of heaven. "It would be like plunging into the ocean of infinite love, a moment in which time—the before and after—no longer exists. We can only attempt to grasp the idea that such a moment is life in the full sense, a plunging ever anew into the vastness of being, in which we are simply overwhelmed with joy."[1] In her writing on purgatory, St. Catherine of Genoa used the image of the fire of love as purifying and replacing all the areas of sin in our lives.[2] Purgatory is the "place" (really a state of being) where all of the empty "spaces" in us are filled with love.

---

[1] Pope Benedict XVI, *Spe salvi*, no. 12.
[2] Catherine of Genoa, *Purgation and Purgatory: The Spiritual Dialogue* (New York: Paulist Press, 1979), 73–74.

From this starting point, we can gain some insight into what is happening in the human person when we are wounded by our sins or by the sins of others. These wounds leave a kind of hole in us, an empty place where there should be love. Instead of love, that hole becomes a place where certain lies and false interpretations of reality can find root. These holes can also become places where evil spirits can gain influence, get a foothold, or even establish a stronghold. To use another analogy, these spiritual wounds can become more easily infected by evil spirits. A spiritual director benefits greatly from understanding the dynamics of these spiritual wounds.

There are psychological ramifications and spiritual ramifications to these wounds. Just like the body compensates for physical wounds (e.g. limping in order to avoid putting too much weight on an injured leg), our psychology reorganizes itself around spiritual wounds to diminish pain and help us function better. Furthermore, these spiritual wounds become a target of the enemy of our human nature (as St. Ignatius calls the devil), but also are an opening and the primary point of access for receiving God's healing grace.

Healing Prayer

In an Easter Vigil homily, Pope Francis used two images to describe the transforming power of the Gospel. He encouraged us to let the light of the Resurrection shine on our problems and he also encouraged us to "evangelize" our problems:

> We see and will continue to see problems both within and without. They will always be there. But tonight it is important to shed the light of the Risen Lord upon our problems, and in a certain sense, to "evangelize" them. To evangelize our problems. Let us not allow darkness and fear to distract us and control us; we must cry out to them:

the Lord "is not here, but has risen!" He is our greatest joy;
he is always at our side and will never let us down.[3]

This is a beautiful description of healing prayer. The power
of the Resurrection and the truth of the Gospel can be applied
to the specific areas of our lives to bring about healing. Healing
prayer, as we discuss it here, is a specifically Christian application
of God's grace to areas of our lives that have been wounded by
life experiences. There are many ways to go about this, but the
fundamental truth is rooted in the power of the Resurrection to
bring new life to areas of death, and the power of the Gospel to
bring truth to areas in which our lives have been distorted and
diminished by lies.

The goal of healing prayer is to receive divine love in the
exiled parts of our interior life. The consequence of doing this is
that we experience a little more of heaven, because in heaven we
will be immersed in an infinite ocean of love and completely filled
with love. At the same time, we will see some patterns of behavior
start to diminish. Our defenses, which have been trying to help
us by preventing our wounded parts from experiencing pain, will
be able to reintegrate into our psyche in more productive ways.
Our exiled parts, which have been held back from further development by carrying burdens and being hidden away, will become
free and joyful as they experience love. God will have access to
more of our interior, and our union with Him will grow stronger
and deeper.

This process can be very powerful, but one should not expect
it to be instantaneous. Furthermore, even after we free an exiled
part so that it is no longer a hidden source of pain but has rather
been brought out in freedom, it is often important to continue
receiving love in that part of us. The littler, poorer parts of us are so
attractive to the Lord that when we open those parts of ourselves,

[3] Pope Francis, Homily for the Mass of the Easter Vigil in the Holy Night (March 26, 2016), https://w2.vatican.va/content/francesco/en/homilies/2016/docu-ments/papa-francesco_20160326_omelia-veglia-pasquale.html.

we often discover the blessing Jesus promised in the Beatitudes, "Blessed are the poor in spirit, for theirs is the kingdom of heaven" (Mt 5:3). We can return regularly to these poor and little parts of us and continue receiving love from God. These are pathways into our interior that can allow us to receive more and more grace.

The Role of the Spiritual Director in Healing Prayer

We have places of pain and darkness where parts of us have been exiled, and various layers of defenses have formed to keep us from falling into those places. There are places in us that terrify us—places where we have simply given up. We are afraid they will terrify others as well so we work hard to keep them hidden behind various defense mechanisms, such as perfectionism, anger, denial, flight, workaholism, or fear.

These defense mechanisms can make the spiritual director's role challenging because they will keep him from seeing or touching the darkness. The tremendous trust that is necessary for healing will only develop through consistent and unconditional love. It is worth reiterating that divine love and mercy must always lead the process of interior exploration. The spiritual director has the privilege and challenge of being that face and voice of divine mercy encouraging the directee to explore painful places. The director is also called to be a safe haven in which the directee can speak about those painful and dark places without fear of condemnation.

The good news is that Christ, in His descent into hell, has the power to descend into all our personal hells as well, and His mercy can always reach there. He only needs our permission. Those dark places that seem to be only leaky buckets, leaking out all of God's grace, are in fact "vessels of mercy." At first, in their weak or sinful state, they are unable to carry much grace, but they can be transformed by the Lord's mercy and forgiveness to become new wineskins:

[T]he "vessel of mercy." This is not something complicated. Let me simply say that the vessel of mercy is our
sin. Our sin is usually like a sieve, or a leaky bucket, from
which grace quickly drains. . . .

Let us take a closer look at this mercy of God that is
always "greater" than our consciousness of our sinfulness.
The Lord never tires of forgiving us; indeed, he renews
the wineskins in which we receive that forgiveness. He
uses a new wineskin for the new wine of his mercy, not
one that is patched or old. That wineskin is mercy itself:
his own mercy, which we experience and then show in
helping others. A heart that has known mercy is not old
and patched, but new and re-created. . . .

That heart, created anew, is a good vessel; it is no
longer battered and leaky.[4]

One of the privileged and powerful roles of the spiritual
director can be to bring the Father's mercy into those dark places
by being a safe place for the directee to open them up and share
them. The spiritual director has the power to impart the Father's
blessing and pour the Father's mercy into those personal, exiled
places of pain and darkness. While never losing a quality of poverty
and the memory of pain, a person can learn to face and touch and
even remain in the dark places, so long as he can also allow the
Father's mercy to enter there with him. In this way, these places
can become repositories of grace and deep recesses of prayer and
communion with God.

In the vision in which she learned her mission, St. Teresa of
Calcutta felt called to bring the light of Christ into the holes
where the poorest of the poor lie hungry, hurting, neglected,
abandoned, and dying. She wanted to reach those in deepest darkness and bring them love and hope, even if only briefly. When
given the choice between helping a person who was beyond hope
of medical assistance and about to die, and another person who

---

[4] Pope Francis, "Second Meditation: The Vessel of Mercy."

could be physically saved, she chose to minister first to the one who was dying, because of her urgent desire to bring a ray of light to that one's deepest darkness before he died.

This is a depth that spiritual direction must reach to be most effective. In order to help others to let God's mercy into that place in themselves, the spiritual director must learn to let God's mercy into that place within himself as well. St. Teresa of Calcutta not only went into the holes of the poorest of the poor, but she shared their dereliction and was also brought into the depth of her own darkness and misery and learned throughout her whole life to live there in the obscurity of faith and hope.[5] Every spiritual director must likewise be in touch with his own interior darkness in order to enter and bring the light of Christ into the interior darkness of others.

It requires a great deal of trust for a directee to explore and invite the spiritual director into these dark areas of the interior life. Our wounds are profoundly personal and thus also profoundly vulnerable. People will even cling to their suffering, because they have formed an identity around it and it can feel like all they have. Suffering becomes a kind of defense that prevents one from facing the deeper pain or fear of meaninglessness or loneliness that threatens him.

When a person has the courage to let in the Father's mercy by sharing these dark interior places with a spiritual director, it can be such an incredible experience that he may start to fear losing the director. Once, when a director commented that the directee seemed to be doing better and getting well, the directee looked concerned and said, "Why would I want to get better? Then I wouldn't be able to see you twice a week anymore!"

HEALING COMES IN THE SHARING
The spiritual director becomes a powerful source of healing simply in his willingness to accompany his directee down into

---

[5] To read more on this, consult Fr. Brian Kolodiejchuk, *Mother Teresa: Come be my light: the Private Writings of the Saint of Calcutta* (Waterville, ME: Wheeler Pub., 2008).

those areas of pain and darkness. The spiritual director's vulnerable, attentive listening becomes sacramental in the experience of the directee, helping him know that God Himself is willing to enter and indeed has already entered into those painful, dark places. Furthermore, the spiritual director's firm grasp on the love of God and strong hope in His power help truth and light to shine into those dark places. As the directee gives access to the interior recesses of the heart, where lies and pain have a way of nesting under the influence of the enemy, the spiritual director is in a powerful position to speak God's love in those places—to "evangelize" them.

Healing prayer enters into these places to call upon the power of God's mercy to heal them and to chase out all sin and evil. Yet this is only possible by first being open to receiving and truly understanding the pain and darkness, the depths of misery and despair that can find root in the human heart. Pope Francis heralded the greatness of St. Gregory of Narek in this regard:

> I would like to appeal to one concrete example, a great herald of divine mercy, one to whom I wished to draw greater attention by making him a Doctor of the Universal Church: Saint Gregory of Narek, word and voice of Armenia. It is hard to find his equal in the ability to plumb the depths of misery lodged in the human heart. Yet he always balanced human weakness with God's mercy, lifting up a heartfelt and tearful prayer of trust in the Lord who is "giver of gifts, root of goodness . . . voice of consolation, news of comfort, joyful impulse . . . unparalleled compassion, inexhaustible mercy . . . the kiss of salvation" (*Book of Lamentations*, 3, 1). He was certain that "the light of God's mercy is never clouded by the shadow of indignation" (ibid., 16, 1). Gregory of Narek is a master of life, for he teaches us that the most important thing is to recognize that we are *in need of mercy*. Despite our own failings and the injuries done to us, we must not become self-centred but open our hearts in sincerity and trust to the Lord, to

"the God who is ever near, loving and good" (ibid., 17, 2), "filled with love for mankind . . . a fire consuming the chaff of sin" (ibid., 16, 2).[6]

As Pope Francis expressed, the power of healing prayer comes from mercy, but we must learn to "plumb the depths of misery lodged in the human heart" while carrying the lamp of divine mercy to bring the power of healing love. It is important for us always to balance human weakness with the mercy of God. Another example of this from St. Gregory of Narek is the following text in which he acknowledges the feeling of "eternal despair" and the temptation to beat ourselves up with doubts. He then courageously takes up a prayer for mercy, offering it even with just the "slightest hope."

Although I have let myself fall
into seemingly eternal despair,
beating myself with the rod of doubt,
let me now dare with the slightest hope
to call upon the Holy Trinity to help me, a sinner.[7]

Obviously, God has the power to communicate grace, mercy, and healing even before undergoing a process of understanding and without being able to explain exactly what happened to facilitate the healing. There is a place for prayers of healing such as those offered at prayer services or healing Masses. A simple blessing can do so much. There are stories of miraculous healing that have come even just from touching the fringe of a humeral veil that is holding the Blessed Sacrament. For the sake of this book, however, we are focusing on those experiences of healing that clearly need and involve the power of God's grace, but also build

---

[6] Pope Francis, Homily at Holy Mass in Vartanants Square, Armenia (June 25, 2016), https://w2.vatican.va/content/francesco/en/homilies/2016/documents/papa-francesco_20160625_omelia-armenia-gyumri.html.

[7] St. Gregory of Narek, *Book of Lamentations*, prayer 12, http://www.stgregory-ofnarek.am/book.php.

on the natural dimensions of human psychology and the empathetic, pneumatic participation of the spiritual director.

GUIDING DIRECTEES TO PRAY FOR HEALING

At the end of a spiritual direction meeting, it is important for the director to consider where things stand, and it can be a provident opportunity to encourage a directee to take some of the insights and pray with them on his own. Some things can be resolved within a spiritual direction meeting, but things will often be resolved when the directee can take them to prayer on his own. The spiritual director plays an important role in sending the directee off with hope, courage, and confidence, and even some concrete direction on how to pray through the wounds or how to open up to healing graces from the Lord.

The vulnerability of deep sharing in spiritual direction may open up some ugly places. It is important to strengthen the directee in believing that he is not an ugly person just because there are some ugly places in his heart or in his past. The director can reinforce that these are places where the love and mercy of Jesus abide. By remembering some key points in the directee's sharing, the director can return to these points in summary fashion and point out where the temptation came in, where the negativity comes in, and where things have gone off track. At the same time, he can reinforce that the directee is not defined by his mistakes or by his weaknesses or temptations: "You're really not a negative person. I actually think you're a very good person. I know you told me those horrible things you did—you beat your dog, you yelled at your wife—but I know you did that because you were beaten so much. Wouldn't it be nice to move past that? Could you pray to forgive your father?"

Especially after many years of pain and failure, a directee might need some persistent encouragement. A directee that has been sorely tried will often suffer from doubts and try to test the spiritual director's claims about hope and goodness. Sometimes he is not even willing to try to forgive, and a spiritual director could persist, "Could you pray for the grace to be able to forgive him?"

The spiritual director can then follow up in the next session and ask if the directee prayed for his father. If that prayer stirred up a lot of anger, for example, it is a great opportunity to take the directee through that, asking, "How was the anger different this time?"

Perhaps there was a positive step and the director is met with the happy statement, "Well, I was actually able to forgive my father and pray for him." This should be strongly affirmed, "That's fantastic! Look how far you're coming! I know you went through terrible anger, but you needed to come through it to be purified and to be ready to get beyond this."

If the prayer stirred up more pain, the director can still affirm, "God was right in the pain with you. When you pray, open up that pain and let the Lord show you how He sees it, where He is in that pain." If the directee is willing to take some instructions on how to pray through these experiences, this can be a golden opportunity to deepen his prayer, strengthen his relationship with God, help him form some patterns of relating with God for healing, and actually bring about the healing. The spiritual director can be very explicit in guiding that prayer and then see how the directee works through that in between sessions. Sometimes the spiritual director will have to accompany explicit directions with some faith statements. In response to a directee's doubts, the director might reply, "I am telling you this based on my own experience and on the teachings of our faith. I know God and I know how He works and how He loves you."

It can be exciting to speak about the ways God can and wants to heal a person, but the director must be careful not to get out ahead of the directee so that the directee can hold on to the insights and personalize them. Otherwise the person can get discouraged. Even in that case, they can be prompted to talk through it and find the Lord's grace at work in the experience. However, it is better to keep the connection, meeting the individual at the level of faith or freedom he presently enjoys, and try to lead him further. There is no system or formula for this kind of guidance, but the spiritual director should be convinced that the Holy Spirit wants this healing and formation in prayer more than both the director and the directee combined. God will provide the words and guidance through the spiritual director—or even in spite of him at times. The spiritual director is not simply a guru with all the answers; he will often feel his own poverty as he gropes for words and images to guide the directee. This is a good experience to keep him humble. Both director and directee should be humbly open and listening to the Holy Spirit.

Praying with Directees

Healing comes through talking with a spiritual directee, when the directee can experience God through the mediation of the spiritual director. Directees also experience healing by taking the truths from the time of spiritual direction back into their own prayer. But there is also a time when the spiritual director may decide to address God directly in a meeting with a spiritual directee. Prayer in spiritual direction can take several forms.

One form that prayer could take, in the context of spiritual direction, is praying at the beginning or ending of the meeting for the directee. Pope Francis commented on the power of such prayer in the context of evangelization and how a prayer can summarize and bless what has been shared.

> If it seems prudent and if the circumstances are right, this fraternal and missionary encounter could end with a brief prayer related to the concerns which the person may have expressed. In this way they will have an experience of being listened to and understood; they will know that their particular situation has been placed before God, and that God's word really speaks to their lives.[8]

These words may be spoken in the context of concluding a session of spiritual direction or, if the director is a priest, in the celebration of the Sacrament of Reconciliation. In the spirit of

---

[8]   Pope Francis, *Evangelii gaudium*, no. 128.

prophecy, as an extraordinary gift of the Holy Spirit that has been warmly embraced by the charismatic renewal, this prayer may also take on a note of spiritual insight or encouragement (see 1 Cor 14:3–5, 31). Prophecy here is not the gift of having oracular knowledge of the future so much as it is receiving more explicit signs of how the Spirit is working in the individual. The spiritual director, especially at the end of a session, is in a particularly privileged place to be open to what God is doing in the life of the directee. By creating the space for prayer and turning to God directly, the spiritual director may find that he can speak some words or present an image or images that he believes come from God for the sake of the directee.

In one case, after a time of spiritual direction in which a directee was struggling with her weakness and the wounds and fears of her past, the spiritual director began to pray with her and received the image of a horse's mouth. Uncertain what that was representing, he continued to pray for clarity and received the words from a psalm, "Be not like a horse or a mule, without understanding, which must be curbed with bit and bridle" (Ps 32:9). He realized then, that in his image, there was no bridle or bit in the horse's mouth. He was still not entirely certain what the image meant, but he described the image in faith. He said that the horse symbolized the directee and Jesus wanted to ride that horse without bridle and bit. Namely, the rider would be so closely in touch with the horse, without any intermediate interference that He would be attuned to the movement of the horse herself and she would be like an extension of Him. The spiritual director knew that the directee had a love for horses, but he did not know if the image made sense completely. He certainly did not realize that this was actually an image that had long been a fascination in her heart since she had once seen a man ride a horse in such a way. She understood the image perfectly and it stirred much hope in her heart. It strengthened her to continue her journey, knowing that after all the struggling and wrestling she was doing, that beautiful image of her closeness with Jesus would be the final result.

This beautiful example of how powerfully the Holy Spirit

can work in spiritual direction should not dismay or discourage
the spiritual director who has no recollection of receiving such
images during prayer and who finds his verbal interventions seem
to sound all too much like his own thoughts rather than divine
inspiration. Some individuals have special gifts (*charismata*) by
which they visualize or receive words which they can convey with
some confidence to the directee. The spiritual director has more
justification for confidence if he remains poor, more convinced
of God's desire to assist the directee through him than of his own
powers. It is a very good practice for the spiritual director to allow
himself to remain attentive to divine inspiration by allowing his
imagination to float and being prayerful and attentive while he
listens to the directee. Most of what floats through his mind should
not be shared with the directee, but it may attune the director to
himself and his own responses and personal issues. Sometimes, by
God's grace, he will feel something enter into his mind that gives
him insight into the directee. If the image or thought persists or
"insists," he must weigh it before the Lord to see if he should bring
it up. The more he recognizes the working of God rather than
himself, the more likely he is to be on track. The more gifted a
spiritual director is, the more careful he must be not to become
an oracle, not to try to be a mind reader, nor to give in to the
tendency to tell directees what to do or how to live their lives.

Another benefit of praying with a spiritual directee is making
sure that the spiritual direction remains focused on God. As mentioned earlier, God can do many powerful things in us without
our understanding what is happening, in whole or in part. Simply
to turn to the power of God in the midst of spiritual direction
can be an important and meaningful act of faith that may be of
great help to the directee, and it may bear fruit that astonishes
both parties. The spiritual director should be praying throughout
the meeting anyway, and verbalizing that prayer may be especially
helpful on some occasions. Such humble faith is all the more necessary, though, in praying for highly vulnerable people, including
those who are badly wounded, possibly seriously abused, and who
are seeking healing.

Exorcism and Spiritual Direction

There are some important parallels between exorcism and spiritual direction. Spiritual directees can be tempted, oppressed, or even possessed by demons. It helps to call the demons out, name them, and look at them together in the safety of spiritual direction. Ultimately, the devil is just a big bully. He loves to intimidate. The more he can bully us and get us to forget about God's love and victorious power, the more power he gains over us. In contemporary movies about demons and demonic possession, it is strange that God is always absent, and the devil always invincibly prevails in the end over the religious people who are usually presented as frightened and powerless. It is actually a rather sobering symptom of satanic power in our world that the entertainment industry presents things in this way. In reality, the devil simply tries to convince people that he himself is not real. Then he tries to convince us that God is not real. He has a way of stirring us up in hysteria and then he becomes a gravitational center in our lives as we spin around him in the agitation he is causing. When we play into this dynamic, we play directly into his hands.

One well-developed model of deliverance prayer, called Unbound,[9] encourages the one who feels bound or oppressed to name and renounce the demons and lies that hold him back. It helps to see and name our demons for what they are—demons of fear, spirits of depression, anxiety, shame, and so on. Unbound is also balanced in recognizing that it is important to see the ways that one has cooperated with the demons through personal sin and unforgiveness. At the same time, the culmination of the Unbound ministry is the Father's blessing, reminding us that the ultimate goal of healing prayer is attaining the freedom to know God as Father and to know our identity as His beloved children who are made to be saints.

---

[9] Neal Lozano, *Unbound: A Practical Guide to Deliverance from Evil Spirits* (Grand Rapids, MI: Chosen Books, 2003); Neal Lozano and Matthew Lozano, *Unbound Ministry Guidebook: Helping Others Find Freedom in Christ* (Clinton Corners, NY: Jubilee Studio, 2011).

The spiritual director must be careful not to feed the problem. He wants to take these aspects of the directee seriously and expose these areas so that he can help with the underlying problems, but he should be careful not to add his own hysteria to the directee's. We already have a King, and He has already won the battle. When people treat demons with too much awe, we give them power. When we act like the demons might win, then we let them set the agenda. Spiritual direction brings light into dark places in the heart and reassures the directee that sooner or later, Christ is always victorious if we let Him be.

The directee's best option is to be vulnerable and let the spiritual director look into those dark places with him. Something powerful happens when another person looks into taboo places in the heart where no one is allowed to go. Doing this has a way of exposing the "old man" hiding behind the screen and using a megaphone to try to exert power over us, like the Wizard of Oz. Ultimately, the devil is only a pathetic old man hiding behind the screen acting like he has unlimited power. Influenced by that lie, people can let depression, fear, weakness, and anxiety bully them. Sometimes these lies can be unmasked by pushing into them with questions like, "Tell me about your anxiety. What is the worst thing that could happen?" When the person gives a reason, it is often extreme and the spiritual director can probe further, "Do you really think that is going to happen?" Even when they paint the worst-case scenario, these things appear ridiculous when they are brought into the light, or they appear less severe than when they existed only in the fearful heart of the directee. The devil knows how to make a lot of noise, but he cannot deliver on his threats. He is like a yapping little dog that is already safely tied up.

In serious and extremely rare cases, when a directee has willingly invited the devil into his life through spells, satanic activity, Ouija boards, séances, or similar activities—so much that he has integrated the devil into his personality—a genuine exorcism may be called for. Exorcism is a ritual ministry of the Catholic Church that is provided only through the authority of the bishop delegated to specifically designated priests. Exorcism, as an official prayer of the Church, puts the power of the Church in the service of a person who is trying to be freed from possession by a demon. These cases are extremely rare and most spiritual directors will never encounter a single one. If there is reason to believe that an individual is genuinely possessed, however, the spiritual director should seek the assistance of the diocesan office for exorcism. This would include cases when the spiritual directee could not say the name of Jesus or could not receive the sacraments, or when he is burned by holy water or cannot stand to be in the presence of holy images, like crucifixes or an image of our Lady. The symptoms are quite extreme and the cause may sometimes be mysterious, though it can often be traced to some specific occult activity.

Apart from these extreme situations, opening up the dark places in us and sharing them in spiritual direction can do so much good for us. We spontaneously have a way of unmasking the illusions and exposing the emptiness of the devil's lies and threats. Likewise, we have a way of seeing the good that God is doing in us. We can often forget about these things or consider them insignificant if they are not shared. A spiritual director can help a directee see that he is growing. For this reason, continuity in spiritual direction with the same spiritual director can be a great benefit. A long-term spiritual director knows the whole story and can point out the growth that has taken place. This disarms the devil's lies that the directee is hopeless and can never change. Sometimes a person will describe his prayer as dry, but the spiritual director can bring up some things that he has shared previously, reminding the directee of what is taking place in his soul. This can lead the directee to focus on the power of God and not be swallowed up by his temptations or doubts.

All of this takes place in the depths of ourselves. Healing prayer can reach the depths of the directee with God's love and the power of His grace. These depths are the most important places in us and they permeate every other place. This is what Pope St. John Paul II described as original solitude, as we discussed in the first chapter. To be human is to be conceived into relationship with God. When the depths are distorted by broken human relationships, burdened with lies, agitated by evil spirits, and buried beneath protectors, all of our relationships are affected. When God's grace can rearrange, unburden, transform, and heal those areas, however, all our relationships are positively affected and we experience the freedom of salvation in Christ.

Other Models of Healing Prayer

As already mentioned, spiritual direction is distinct from psychological counseling and a spiritual director need not be learned in psychological theory. Because, however, spiritual direction and psychology overlap in their common focus on the interior life of the directee, a spiritual director can be greatly aided by the insights and models of modern psychology. Furthermore, armed with the power of prayer, a spiritual director can be a robust instrument of psychological and spiritual healing for a directee. In this chapter we have only touched on some basic starting points in the application of psychology and healing prayer to spiritual direction, but a spiritual director will certainly benefit from further study in these areas. There are many positive developments in modern psychology and several structured approaches to healing prayer. All of them are approximations of the unique and complex reality of the human soul and so they have their own advantages and limitations. In an effort to provide spiritual directors with some pointers for further study we now mention a few models that we have found helpful.

One helpful model that was developed out of the area of trauma therapy is called Internal Family Systems[10] and it provides many insights and techniques for bringing love and healing to exiled parts of our interior life. Another model that has been fruitfully applied for healing and interior freedom is Unbound.[11] Unbound

---

[10] Jay Earley, with a Foreword by Richard C. Schwartz, *Self-Therapy: A Step-By-Step Guide to Creating Wholeness and Healing Your Inner Child Using IFS, A New, Cutting-Edge Psychotherapy* (Larkspur, CA: Pattern System Books, 2009).

[11] Neal Lozano, *Unbound: A Practical Guide to Deliverance from Evil Spirits* (Grand Rapids, MI: Chosen Books, 2003); Neal Lozano and Matthew Lozano, *Unbound*

identifies five keys: repentance and faith, forgiveness, renuncia-tion, authority, and the Father's blessing. These keys are applied to oneself as prayers that facilitate spiritual freedom. A spiritual director can serve as a guide for praying through Unbound. Other models such as Theophostic prayer and healing of memories also seek to bring the healing grace of God to the wounded parts of our souls. While some models, such as Internal Family Systems, developed from a purely psychological realm and others, such as Unbound and Theophostic prayer, developed from an entirely spiritual realm, we believe that these approaches are steadily coming closer together and converging in the center with great promise for how they can be applied for the purpose of sharing the freedom that is rightly ours in Christ.

Ministry Guidebook: Helping Others to Find Freedom in Christ (Clinton Corners, NY: Jubilee Studio, 2011).

9

The Spiritual Director

WE HAVE REFLECTED at length throughout this book on the process and experience of spiritual direction, primarily focusing our attention on the spiritual directee. We step back in this chapter to focus on the spiritual director. We look at the qualities, both natural and supernatural, that make for a good spiritual director. These qualities may already be substantially in place and may also grow over time, especially with some particular effort and prayer on the part of the spiritual director. We also recognize that spiritual direction can be personally challenging and cause various feelings and thoughts to come up in the spiritual director. The spiritual director must learn to deal with his own internal state and also bring some of his experience and his struggles to his own spiritual director.

In short, the bare necessities for being a spiritual director are that one has a spiritual life and that one is in his own process of spiritual direction. In the first half of this chapter, we consider some of the qualities of the spiritual life that can be developed to improve spiritual direction. In the second half of this chapter, we reflect on some experiences a spiritual director may have in spiritual direction of which he should try to be aware. These are experiences that he can or sometimes should also bring to his own spiritual director.

Important Qualities for Spiritual Direction

We see the necessity for certain natural and supernatural endowments in a spiritual director. At a natural level, he should be humble, prudent, and have a mature disinterestedness. He should be a patient and empathetic listener, learned in spiritual theology, and he should be receiving spiritual direction himself. At the supernatural level, he should have a zeal for souls, a spiritual-mindedness, trust in divine providence, and personal experience of the spiritual life and prayer. The teaching of St. Paul of the Cross on spiritual direction provides a good summary of the qualities needed in a spiritual director: "Paul expected the Spiritual Director to have learning, prayer and experience, holiness and prudence."[1]

Learning and Experience

St. Teresa of Ávila emphasized the importance of learning in regard to the spiritual life asking that the Superiors allow that the Carmelite nuns, "besides speaking with the ordinary confessors . . . might sometimes speak and discuss their souls with learned persons, especially if the confessors, however good, may not be learned. Learning is a great help in shedding light upon every matter. It will be possible to find both learning and goodness in some persons."[2]

Pope Francis likewise highlighted the importance of having formation in spirituality. In addition to the value of having an awareness of the psychological sciences, it is most important to have knowledge of the spiritual life, even drawing from ancient and monastic sources:

---

[1] Silvan Rouse, *Reflections on Spiritual Direction in St. Paul of the Cross*, Studies in Passionist History and Spirituality, vol. 12, ed. Norbert M. Dorsey, CP (Rome, Italy: Passionist General Curia, 1982), 17.

[2] St. Teresa of Ávila, *The Way of Perfection*, in *The Collected Works of St. Teresa of Ávila*, vol. 2, trans. Kieran Kavanaugh and Otilio Rodriguez (Washington, DC: ICS Publications, 2001), 159.

The superiors have the responsibility of looking, in the community, in the congregation, in the province, for those who have this charism, to give this mission and form them, help them with this. . . . Today you cannot go only with good will: today the world is very complex and human science also helps us, without falling into psychologism, but it helps us to see the path. Form them with readings of the greats, of the great men and women spiritual directors, especially of monasticism. I don't know if you have had contact with the works of early monasticism: how much wisdom and spiritual direction there was there! It is important to form them with this.[3]

When Pope St. John XXIII addressed seminary spiritual directors, he likewise spoke to the importance of learning, especially from magisterial sources and recommendations. He said that the spiritual director "must study the psychology of students for the priesthood; he must live with his eyes open to the world around him; he must learn from life. But he must learn from books too: from study, from the experiences of his confreres and from the progress made in the pedagogical sciences, and especially from those texts and authors recommended by the Congregation of Seminaries."[4]

St. John of the Cross emphasized the importance of personal experience for guiding directees in the intermediate and sublime stages of contemplation, writing: "Besides being learned and discreet a director should have experience. Although the foundation for guiding a soul to spirit is knowledge and discretion, directors will not succeed in leading the soul onward in it when God bestows it, nor will they even understand it if they have no experience of what true and pure spirit is."[5]

---

[3] Pope Francis, Address to Consecrated Men and Women.
[4] Pope St. John XXIII, Address to Seminary Spiritual Directors.
[5] St. John of the Cross, *The Living Flame of Love*, in *The Collected Works of St. John of the Cross*, stanza 3, no. 30.

While experience of the spiritual life is essential, it is not always necessary to be more advanced than one's directee, nor even to be traveling precisely the same path. Because the spiritual direction relationship is not an apprenticeship, the spiritual director only needs to be transparent, to truly know and love the directee, and continue to reflect God back to the directee. This can be done by one who does not experience God in the same way as a directee (perhaps through extraordinary phenomena), or one who has a different charism in the spiritual life (as happens when a priest directs a contemplative religious, for example), or when one directs a person much more advanced in the spiritual life. Spiritual direction is not a matter of giving clever advice, but rather a matter of receiving the directee with love and living out the spiritual direction relationship in a way that the Lord is truly, explicitly present.

Learning and experience go hand in hand and the saints vacillate over which is more important. In one case, St. Paul of the Cross emphasized experience over and above learning, when he wrote, "Besides being very learned, he should also be a man of deep contemplation, while without experience, the very deep and marvelous deeds which God works in the soul are not understood."[6] In another context, St. Paul of the Cross emphasized learning, "If you cannot find a man with all these qualities, then at least let him be learned."[7] Without making a final decision about which is more important, we can certainly say that it is important for spiritual directors to continue growing in *both* their learning *and* their personal experience of the spiritual life.

Humble, Prudent, Disinterested, Zealous for Souls

Humility, prudence, disinterestedness, and zeal for the sanctification of souls are all qualities identified by Fr. Jordan Aumann,

---

[6] St. Paul of the Cross, quoted in Silvan Rouse, *Reflections on Spiritual Direction in St. Paul of the Cross*, 18.

[7] Ibid., 19.

OP, in his *Spiritual Theology*.[8] These are some fundamental human, moral qualities that spiritual directors must have. Humility is the *sine qua non* of the Christian life and is especially important for spiritual directors. Because of the esteem that people have for spiritual directors, pride is always knocking at their door. Since the spiritual director is in a position of representing God and also exercising judgment and discernment about the movements of God in the lives of his directees, he may easily start to feel superior to his directees. A Christian who is truly advanced in the spiritual life, however, should rather be well acquainted with his weakness and be very humbled to be in a position to serve others through spiritual direction.

A regular part of spiritual direction involves guiding directees in choosing the good. A spiritual director should have a well-developed virtue of prudence to be able to identify the good in various situations and help a directee to see and take hold of that good. Prudence also has a component of common sense to it. A spiritual director should have a healthy dose of humanity and some good, old-fashioned common sense.

Spiritual direction develops intense relationships and a spiritual director naturally becomes interested in the lives of his directees. At the same time, he needs the freedom to listen to the Holy Spirit and offer the best guidance. He needs the openness to see the spiritual directee as he is, rather than as a projection of his own ideas onto the directee. He needs to foster freedom in the directee, and for this reason he has to be able to let go and let the directee develop in his own time through his own relationship with the Holy Spirit. A spiritual director will have a healthy love and attachment for directees, but must not develop any disordered attachments.

A spiritual director is in the position of directing others to holiness. He makes many sacrifices in offering his time and attention to the directees who approach him for direction. If he does

---

[8] Jordan Aumann, OP, *Spiritual Theology* (Huntington, IN: Our Sunday Visitor, 1980).

not have a supernatural motivation and does not truly desire for men and women to be holy, spiritual direction can fade into mere conversation or disappear into nothing. For the spiritual director to keep the conversation focused on the Lord and the good of the soul who is seeking guidance, he must have a zeal for the sanctification of souls. This can also be a source of suffering for the spiritual director as he experiences the conflict between his desire for everyone to grow in holiness and the limits of his own ability, time, and energy to guide them. In every case the suffering can only be resolved through surrender to God's will, but in some cases that surrender may also lead to additional creative outlets in apostolic ministry. A spiritual director may find ways to communicate his knowledge of God and the spiritual life to a larger audience through preaching, retreats, books, social media, or other forms of mass media.

Spiritual-Mindedness and Psychological-Mindedness

At the natural level, a spiritual director must have an interest in people and have a heart that cares for people. This interest and caring must be especially directed toward a person's spiritual life, not just for the externals. The interest in externals should always move toward the deeper meaning of the exterior life and the impact that various exterior qualities and events have on the interior life. We could call this a *spiritual-mindedness*. (The traditional word for this is *pneumatikos*.) This spiritual-mindedness is developed and directed first of all toward one's own life, seeking to integrate one's exterior life with one's interior life by prayer and faith. Being in spiritual direction makes one more spiritually-minded.

While it is necessary for a spiritual director to be spiritually-minded, it also helps to be *psychologically-minded*. This means that without reducing everything to the spiritual, one is able to see the natural processes at work, including aspects of temperament, personality, and psychological makeup. This does not require one to understand all of psychology or even to have a degree in psychology, but to be aware of some dynamics of natural, psychological processes in human experience, thought, and behavior. While a good spiritual director will be aware of the limitations of psychology, without any knowledge of psychology there is a danger of over-spiritualizing. Grace builds on nature; it does not replace it. A spiritual director should be able to appreciate the supernatural work of grace perfecting, purifying, and elevating the natural potential of the human being he is directing. It is important to know one's limits in psychological knowledge, but a little psychological-mindedness goes a long way.

Empathetic Listening

A good spiritual director must be able to sit and listen, staying with a person even through long periods of time when a directee is highly resistant to opening up or being vulnerable. A spiritual director needs a lot of patience and compassion to accompany a person dealing with depression or anxiety, and while that directee may need additional, professional help, the spiritual director continues to meet with them at the same time.

Sometimes spiritual direction is exciting, especially when a directee is growing rapidly, receiving a lot of grace for conversion and setting out in a new direction. On the other hand, people are not always very interesting, and they can get stuck and be tedious to listen to. In fact, this tediousness can cause a person to be isolated so that his spiritual director is the only one who listens to him. This can be a particularly difficult dynamic in spiritual direction—a spiritual director may end up being an oasis in a very lonely life.

Furthermore, it is important for a spiritual director to be able to empathize with a person, to put himself in another person's place. In our time, there is an increasing number of people with a limited capacity for empathy while the number of narcissistic people is growing rapidly. A spiritual director who is highly narcissistic will be very problematic. To the contrary, a spiritual director needs to have the interior freedom and maturity that generally come through suffering and self-denial. With empathy, a spiritual director listens to the heart: "For spiritual direction, you must examine what has happened in the heart; such as the movement of the spirit, whether I have been desolate, if I have been consoled, if I am tired, why I am sad: these are the things to speak about with a spiritual director."[9]

Trust in Divine Providence

Another factor in being a good spiritual director is trust in divine providence. One concrete manifestation of this is in being able to be generous with one's time. Spiritual direction takes a lot of time and reaches only a small number of people. Not everyone can sit and listen for hours at a time. The rewards are often hidden and intangible, making it more a way of life than merely a job. A spiritual director does not usually count up hours and charge fees, but rather must learn to see that there is a movement of the Holy Spirit in a person's life and that becomes the motivation for him to keep going deeper with the directee. As Jesus said, "You received without pay, give without pay" (Mt 10:8). Spiritual direction begins when a person comes for some spiritual help, wants to go to Confession, needs to talk, or starts coming regularly because they can see that meeting with a spiritual director is helpful. There is an element here that is not part of the practice of the secular professional. That element is divine providence.[10] A spiritual director must have a lot of trust in divine providence. He needs to be able to discern and to believe that God has brought directees to him and that God knows what He is doing. God

---

[9] Pope Francis, Address to Consecrated Men and Women of the Diocese of Rome.

[10] See Jean-Pierre de Caussade, *Abandonment to Divine Providence* (Garden City, NY: Image Books, 1975); Jean-Baptiste Saint-Jure and St. Claude de la Colombière, *Trustful Surrender to Divine Providence* (Rockford, IL: Tan Books and Publications, 1983); Wilfrid Stinissen, *Into Your Hands, Father: Abandoning Ourselves to the God Who Loves Us*, trans. Clare Marie (San Francisco: Ignatius Press, 2011); and St. Alphonsus Liguori, *Uniformity with God's Will* (Rockford, IL: Tan Books, 2009).

provides the people and their needs, and He provides the grace and time we need to help them. A spiritual director may not feel like he has time to meet with another person but time is a gift to begin with—it belongs first to God who freely entrusts it to us. If one is worried about time, he will always be running out of it, while the one who offers the little he has will find that God has a wonderful way of multiplying his time.

At the same time, a spiritual director must be prudent, which requires him to carefully and prayerfully discern his availability. He may have to tell a directee he cannot meet with him more than once a month. He may not be able to be on call in the same way as other professionals are. At the same time, a spiritual director needs to develop a profound trust in divine providence. God leads people to a particular spiritual director and God will provide the gifts, including the time to lovingly, prayerfully guide that person. If the spiritual director puts the pressure on himself as if it all depends on him, he will quickly be overwhelmed.

A parish priest may not feel he has the time necessary to do much, or any, spiritual direction. On the other hand, Dom Chautard, in his classic work *The Soul of the Apostolate*, puts out the challenge: "It would be an omission, and sometimes a grave omission, in a priest, bound by his duty as teacher and surgeon of souls, if he were to deprive them of this great supplement to Confession, this indispensable source of energy for the spiritual life, which is spiritual direction."[11] Furthermore, he concludes his reflections on spiritual direction by relativizing the other activities of a parish priest that are intended to reach a great number of the faithful in favor of forming more intensely the more fervent souls in his parish:

> The more zealous priests become in perfecting themselves in the art of spiritual direction, and in devoting themselves to it, the more will they realize how unnecessary are certain exterior means which might, it is true, have some

---

[11] Chautard, *The Soul of the Apostolate*, 169.

use to begin with, in establishing contact with the faithful, and drawing them in, grouping them, arousing their interest, holding on to them, and keeping them under the influence of the Church. But the Church, faithful to her true end, will never be fully satisfied until souls are intimately incorporated into Jesus Christ.[12]

A good spiritual director will have to be prudent in determining his physical limitations and establishing boundaries. These need to be adjusted according to one's vocation to priesthood, religious life, marriage, consecrated virginity, and so forth. All have their own unique demands. A spiritual director does no one any favors if he cannot make a priority out of his own responsibilities and spiritual life so that he can most effectively help others. Within the realm of these very real limitations, however, an ongoing openness to divine providence continues to be necessary. When one is praying and trusting in God, it is amazing how things always work out. God has a way of providing exactly enough, like the jar of oil and flour that never ran out but continued to provide bread for the widow of Zarephath and Elijah the prophet (see 1 Kgs 17:8–16).

State in Life

The collection of characteristics listed in the first part of this chapter will more readily describe those who are able to devote themselves to the spiritual life. The vows of poverty, chastity, and obedience provide an opportunity for separation from some of the more burdensome and time-consuming parts of life in such a way that facilitate a greater sensitivity of heart for the matters of the spirit. Spiritual-mindedness, great trust in divine providence, extensive experience in receiving spiritual direction, experience in prayer and in the movements of the spiritual life, adequate time for meeting with directees, and substantial knowledge of the

---

[12] Ibid., 182–183.

spiritual life are all going to be found more readily in priests and consecrated men and women. Of course, humility and empathetic listening are qualities that are found more broadly than in those special vocations. With this in mind, we can see that priests and consecrated men and women are more likely to be good candidates for giving spiritual direction, but some uniquely prepared lay men and women surely also have the capacity to be good spiritual directors. "There are to be found also well formed lay people—both men and women—who offer this service of counsel along the journey of holiness."[13]

Self-Awareness

In a time when a great number of jobs are being automated and replaced by highly advanced computer systems, spiritual direction is not a job that can be replaced by automatons. This is a result of the human qualities of the one-on-one interaction that are irreplaceable in effective spiritual direction. These human qualities are also inherently messy; or, as Pope Francis described it, "wonderfully complicated."[14] As described in Chapter 3, as the directee opens his interior life and becomes vulnerable, the spiritual director also becomes vulnerable in a different way. He opens his heart to the directee in a way that allows him to empathize and share in the experience of the directee. The spiritual director is wasting his time if he is handling a directee in a purely automatic way, like a computer algorithm would do. At the same time, the complexity or messiness requires the spiritual director to be self-aware and also to be in supervision or spiritual direction himself.

Supervision is essential for a spiritual director to continue growing and to prevent him from going astray. Supervision is a word often used in the professional, secular world, but the same concept can be found in the world of ancient monasticism. The

[13] Congregation for the Clergy, *The Priest, Minister of Divine Mercy*, no. 65.
[14] Pope Francis, *Evangelii gaudium*, no. 270.

ancient monastic tradition witnessed the importance of a spiritual
father or mother continuing to have his or her own spiritual director. One never reaches the point of graduation as if he could learn
the sum total of all wisdom and thus no longer need guidance.
To the contrary, additional wisdom is appropriated as a spiritual
director continues to engage in a process of vulnerability through
his own spiritual direction.

As a consequence of the mutual vulnerability that occurs in
spiritual direction, the spiritual director is necessarily affected by
giving spiritual direction. Even though he is careful not to make
spiritual direction about himself and so does not ordinarily share
vulnerably about himself, just the process of prayerful, empathetic
listening, which we have called *vulnerable attentiveness*, opens the
spiritual director's heart in a very intimate way. This can lead to
feelings of affection for the directee that the spiritual director
needs to be aware of and handle properly. At the same time, as the
spiritual director becomes vulnerable in listening to the directee,
he will inevitably get emotionally involved in the life of the
directee such that he cares when the directee is hurting himself or
resisting guidance or reacting against the director. In this case, the
spiritual director may need to be careful about feelings of anger
or irritation that rise up in his heart. The spiritual director may
also become the object of the directee's discontentment and the
directee may make some accusations against the spiritual director or blame the spiritual director for not helping more or not
helping in a particular way. This can lead to hurt and resentment
for the spiritual director. All of these scenarios, and many more,
can easily develop in the course of spiritual direction.

Our Lord gives the example of being emotionally involved in
the lives of those He serves. He wept over Jerusalem and longed
to gather her to Himself (Lk 19:41–42). He burned with longing
as He desired to set the earth on fire (Lk 12:49). He wept over
the death of His friend Lazarus (Jn 11:35). He was moved by the
widow of Nain who had lost her son (Lk 7:13). He does not simply
act or react out of emotion: He is self-aware and carefully chan-
nels or expresses the emotional energy at work within Himself

for the sake of His beloved children. This is what the spiritual director must also learn to do. He will burn with zeal, ache for the freedom of his children, weep at their pain, and be moved by their tragedies. In all this, his emotions are not a hindrance but a help, so long as he is aware of them and always properly directs them to the service of his directees, properly praying about them and talking through this with his own spiritual director.

Feelings of Pride or Vanity

A spiritual director will be moved by his experience of spiritual direction. The most important thing is to ensure that his emotions do not cause him to become centered on himself. Emotions are powerful and can become self-referential. It is natural for us to be aware of what is going on within us and to wonder what others think about us. There is the temptation for the self-awareness to become self-absorption, however. The feeling of being loved can become especially intoxicating and can move us into a self-exalting feedback loop that interrupts the flow of service to the directee and becomes vanity, leading one to solicit attention, affirmation, and love from the directee. To prevent this, we must always keep Christ rather than ourselves at the center of our world, and others in the center with Him. In his homily for the Jubilee for Priests, Pope Francis exhorted priests to be spiritual fathers, saying, "Like every good Christian, and as an example for every Christian, [the priest] constantly goes out of himself: he is not centered on himself, he is only centered in Jesus. The epicentre of his heart is outside of himself. He is not drawn by his own 'I', but by the 'Thou' of God and by the 'we' of other men and women."[15]

A good spiritual director can be in high demand and can be very loved. This is beautiful, but there is a danger here if the spiritual director does not remain centered on Christ, grounded

---

[15] Pope Francis, Homily for Mass on the Occasion of the Jubilee for Priests (June 3, 2016), http://w2.vatican.va/content/francesco/en/homilies/2016/documents/papa-francesco_20160603_omelia-giubileo-sacerdoti.html.

in humility, and rooted in prayer. He should enjoy the feelings of being loved and take care not to become addicted to them, but instead to transform those feelings into humble thanksgiving. With his sin always before him (Ps 51:3), the spiritual director can best remember that it is truly Christ who is at work through his ministry of spiritual direction. It is an awesome experience to meet with many spiritual directees, to hear confessions, and to see profound breakthroughs in individuals' lives. It is important, however, for the spiritual director to remain humble and vulnerable. In vulnerable attentiveness, the spiritual director goes out of himself, empties himself, and places Christ and others in the center of spiritual direction. This is the most important safeguard against self-adulation or self-preoccupation. It is the gift of the fear of the Lord, of a holy reverence, that enables the spiritual director to remain humbly in awe of God's work through such a weak and sinful vessel. This is a gift that the spiritual director should pray for and foster.

Along with this, a spiritual director must be careful that he does not form a following that becomes cultic. He can promote a kind of gnosticism, acting as if he and his directees have an inside track on holiness, truth, or divine revelation. This can turn into an exclusive, self-centered elitism that closes out other people and really places the spiritual director in the center rather than God. It should be a red flag if the spiritual director discovers he is regularly getting irritated at directees that do not respond to his commands. Commands in spiritual direction should be rare. Spiritual direction requires space for the directee to feel profoundly free. A spiritual director who is becoming overly directive and issuing many commands is in danger of forming a cultic following that can even lead to abuse. There are times when directees need to be addressed firmly and times that strong directives can be helpful when a directee is stuck in a self-destructive behavior. This should be the exception rather than the rule, however.

Rather than issuing directives and having a feeling of being in control, it is proper for the spiritual director to feel a profound poverty as He witnesses God's miracles and receives lavish appreciation from his spiritual children. This poverty is felt again and again in the midst of spiritual direction as the spiritual director feels empty of wisdom and devoid of words. The challenge of helping each soul is an overwhelming and impossible task, and the spiritual director should never allow himself to indulge in pride, as if he were the master of this practice. Rather, he should allow the feelings of helplessness to be present even as he boldly trusts in the work of the Holy Spirit within him and the desire of Christ to love the soul in front of him. If he does not feel this poverty, he should pray for it. It is a necessary protection against pride. At the same time, the spiritual director should not become lost in self-pity or become self-absorbed by focusing on his unworthiness. Rather, by holding in tension the dignity of his ministry and the shame of his unworthiness, both are enhanced and together will best help him move forward in the path of holiness.

The poverty of the spiritual director requires the emptying of himself—of his own ideas and his own rhetoric, making space for the Holy Spirit. The void can feel uncomfortable until he learns to trust that the Lord is faithful. "Open your mouth wide, and I will fill it" (Ps 81:10). As the spiritual director opens his mouth to speak, trusting in the Holy Spirit, the words come. The spiritual director is not infallible, but he will be regularly delighted at what happens and he may even learn quite a bit from the words that come out of his mouth. This shows that those words do not originate merely from himself. As he relates with his directee in this way, he should also watch carefully to see the response of the directee.

As we have already emphasized, it is important that the spiritual director does not become a kind of oracle, simply spouting all the answers to life's questions. This is a sign that he is merely full of his own ideas. It is true that human beings have many similarities, and scenarios can tend to repeat themselves, but a spiritual director should always hold himself back before simply regurgitating old responses. Each person is unique and the Lord wants to love each one uniquely, even if one has struggles or experiences similar to another one. In this light, a spiritual director empties himself in each meeting, embraces the Cross, is mindful of the presence of Jesus, and allows himself to be filled with the Holy Spirit. This will make him feel poor and empty, but it will enable a radical availability to divine wisdom.

Likewise, before making proclamations, a spiritual director must be very careful about his own motives and not imposing his own will. It can become intoxicating to start proclaiming God's will for a directee. A spiritual director who wants to make every young man into a priest or send every young woman into a convent needs to be aware of that temptation and employ a healthy self-doubt before making such suggestions. Wisdom and counsel are gifts of the Holy Spirit, and the spiritual director should pray for those before, during, and after spiritual direction.

Because this process requires so much emptiness and availability, the spiritual director must be very careful and aware of the interference that inevitably arises out of our fragile human nature. Attraction, a desire to please, anger, frustration, irritation, boredom, fears, and anxiety can all interrupt the spiritual director's vulnerable attentiveness in the course of spiritual direction. These emotions are not to be feared nor hated, nor will they necessarily spoil spiritual direction, so long as they are carefully managed. By having a simple awareness and holding out these feelings to the Lord like a poor child holding out a broken toy to his father, the spiritual director can remain both vulnerable and open to the directee at the same time.

Feelings of Attraction

It is not uncommon for spiritual directors to feel affection for or become attracted to their directees. Of course, all interactions in spiritual direction must be absolutely chaste. It is easy, however, for a spiritual director to be charmed by a directee. Sexual energies are an essential part of every human being and every human interaction, and they can be very active in spiritual direction. It is important for the spiritual director to be aware of that and honest about it. Various kinds of emotional energies can be stirred up by good spiritual direction.

This can also be the case for the directee, of course. A directee who is being especially vulnerable in spiritual direction might be experiencing more vulnerability than he ever has before and even comment, "How can you be this vulnerable and not feel all kinds of things?" A spiritual director can allow a directee to discuss any feelings that are uncomfortable or which are causing difficulties or discomfort, and then calmly reassure him, "It is perfectly normal to feel things, but we are not going to act on them." Establishing firm boundaries is tremendously helpful while giving the directee the freedom and permission to feel. When there is no ambiguity about where the spiritual direction relationship is heading (i.e., not becoming a different relationship, but remaining in the roles of director and directee), both director and directee can have a safety that allows them to feel the emotions that might come up without fear of things getting out of control.

It is helpful even just to presume that sexual energies are present in spiritual direction. This is true between people of the same sex as well as of people of the opposite sex. It is true of people of different ages. To say there is sexual energy does not mean that there is sexual attraction or that there are conscious erotic feelings. Sometimes the sexual energy takes the shape of competitiveness, of jealousy, or even of repugnance. It may be implicit and not obviously felt, but the powerful energy that comes from such trusting relationships naturally develops strong, healthy bonds that are important for spiritual direction.

A spiritual director who is engaged and attentive, listening prayerfully, empathetically, and vulnerably will naturally notice and be drawn to the little mannerisms and unique qualities of directees. The unique ways that an individual expresses himself or behaves when he is sharing vulnerably—facial expressions, gestures, and words—can all become very charming to a spiritual director who allows a unique love for each directee to develop in his heart. Everyone has something charming about him. It might be the way that he approaches direction, organizes his thoughts, or laughs when he is uncomfortable. It might be the way he softens his voice when he talks about his wife, turns his feet inward, or tucks his leg under him. An astute spiritual director will start to connect those behaviors with the topics or level of vulnerability in the sharing. It goes without saying that sometimes the mannerisms of the director or directee can also be irritating to the other party. The director might begin to feel like the directee is doing something deliberately to irritate him. Sometimes it can become necessary even to point out certain behaviors and to talk about them during spiritual direction. Usually it is enough simply to learn to tolerate them and to dismiss any tendency to interpret them in ways beyond their actual meaning. This again is all part of the experience of poverty and humility.

This is also where a spiritual director must be careful to monitor his own feelings. Those little charming qualities of the directee are very vulnerable. Comments made about them by the spiritual director can be interpreted in a way that makes the directee feel affirmed or might heighten the self-consciousness and sensitivity of the directee. When they are signs of vulnerability, and when they are appropriately expressed, these observations can be taken as signs that the spiritual director truly understands the directee. It can be a sign of affirmation and love, that he or she is understood or uniquely appreciated and cherished. This is a powerful way of soliciting personal love and attention, and for this very reason it can be perceived as being seductive. This is the kind of thing that lovers do and so it is not normally an appropriate grammar of interaction for spiritual direction.

Primarily, these qualities should be silently loved and appreciated by the director and only infrequently, if ever, recognized or affirmed out loud. When the director makes loving comments, he should be very clear about his true intentions and very careful that his heart is pure and that he is not flirting with his directee. It is always sinful to use another human being, and this obviously includes using a spiritual directee to get an emotional charge by pushing the right buttons.

Feelings of Anger

It is easy for the spiritual director to get angry in spiritual direction. Many things can precipitate this. The spiritual director may be overworked and feel exhausted and unappreciated. Sometimes the director may feel directly attacked and become defensive. At other times the spiritual director gets angry on behalf of the directee. A directee who has experienced injustice or even abuse may stir up ire in a spiritual director's heart. The spiritual director may feel a fatherly (or motherly) protection for the person and even have a desire to intervene in a particular situation.

On some occasions it can be therapeutic for the spiritual director to express these feelings. By sharing the feelings that are rising up in his heart, the spiritual director can help the directee to feel loved and protected, giving him an experience of God's love and protection. When there is injustice, the cry, "Does anybody care?" can rise up from our hearts, and the fact that the spiritual director is moved by the injustice can be very consoling, even when no further action is taken. Normally it is inappropriate for the spiritual director to get involved in affairs outside of spiritual direction. Exceptions could include interventions that are necessary to prevent the directee from harming himself or someone else. Moreover, outside of the confessional seal, a spiritual director may be a mandated reporter of any sexual abuse of minors. However, it is inappropriate for the spiritual director to vent his anger for his own sake. If the directee does not seem to need the empathetic resonance of the spiritual director, the director should handle his anger another way without making it an issue for the directee.

As with any of these examples of emotional response from the spiritual director, it is good for him to take note and work through these experiences in his own spiritual direction. The anger may have been caused by the directee triggering something in the director's own experience of past trauma. By acknowledging the anger in himself, the spiritual director will be in the best position to determine how to handle it. He may want to share it with the directee, as described earlier, or he may lovingly set it aside to deal with it later, on his own.

One spiritual director was angered by a directee because she complained whenever he was late. Because he did not process his feelings, one day he finally let his anger show. Instead of ignoring his anger, he should have acknowledged to himself that he was becoming resentful that she was taking him to task for being late and taking his generosity for granted. After his abreaction, he apologized for his anger, and the ensuing discussion gave her a chance to express why being on time was so important to her and how it made her feel when he was late. This led to a deeper discussion of her insecurities that bore good fruit in her life. When feelings are handled appropriately, they can be a blessing for both director and directee.

Feeling Defensive

The spiritual director can sometimes become the target of the directee's discontentment and the directee can make accusations against him. This may be direct or indirect. An example of an indirect attack occurs, for example, when the spiritual director is a priest and the directee attacks the priesthood. It may also occur when the directee attacks someone close to the director, or something else that is precious to the director.

Acting out of defensiveness is never a good approach in spiritual direction. It is very important for the spiritual director to be aware of his defensiveness and at least try not to act out of it. Optimally he is able to hear out the directee, and he should also explore the question of whether the attack appears to be deliberate on the part of the directee. Sometimes a directee will speak about a group or a person, not knowing that he is indirectly attacking the spiritual director. Sometimes he will even talk directly about the spiritual director, not knowing that he is touching a nerve. For example, a directee might share honestly about how he handled his irritation when the spiritual director missed the last appointment. A directee that is more sensitive might be explicit in reassuring the director that he is not attacking him, but another directee might presume that the director knows this.

In any event, a spiritual director must be careful about feelings of defensiveness that arise in the context of spiritual direction. It might be important to clarify a situation or even apologize, but the spiritual director should try to anticipate the effect this will have on the directee as much as possible before doing so. Sometimes it is important to apologize or explain on behalf of a brother priest, a religious sister, or a fellow counselor. If the spiritual director is not absolutely sure that this is necessary, he can simply preface his comments with a caveat, such as, "I am not sure if you need to hear this, but I feel it would help for me to explain . . ." Likewise, the spiritual director can express his own defensiveness, saying, "Perhaps I am being defensive about this, but maybe it will help if I explain to you the way I see the situation . . ."

Sometimes a directee will blame a spiritual director for something or will call the competence of the spiritual director into question. Here again it is better to focus on the directee as much as possible. A willingness to accept blame and apologize can also be very helpful. Every spiritual director is flawed and makes mistakes. It can be better to admit our weaknesses and accept blame than to fight. Here again self-awareness is very important. We must learn to be aware of any excessive desire to be right, any fear of failure, or any other weaknesses that would put us in a defensive posture at the expense of the directee. On the contrary, if it is possible to bring out the directee's feelings and focus on the pain or feelings of betrayal or fears that are bringing out his complaints, this can be a helpful way to turn the situation to the good and make it profitable for the directee. Comments such as, "I can tell that I really hurt you. That was not my intention, but I am very sorry about that. Can you tell me more about what you are feeling?" can be helpful. Somewhat later, after the directee has been able to work through his feelings as much as possible, they can perhaps be integrated by asking, "Did you bring that to Jesus in prayer? He experienced betrayal from his closest friends and He really understands what betrayal is."

In the event that the directee is questioning his spiritual director's competence, it is good to affirm that this is an important issue of which to be aware and to resolve. It is valuable to bring out doubts and concerns and to talk through them. The spiritual director should resist, as much as possible, any impulse he feels to provide credentials or prove his worth. In particular, he should clarify what the concern is before defending his competence as a spiritual director. He may end up defending himself based on criteria that are of no consequence to the directee. For example, the spiritual director may list the training courses he has participated in or the years he has been doing spiritual direction, but the directee's concern has more to do with the fact that he is uncomfortable sharing with a celibate man some details about struggles with intimacy in his marriage. It is important to draw out where the concern is coming from and use the situation to the directee's advantage by helping with those fears which are often bigger than the concerns about the spiritual director per se.

Feeling Inadequate or Overwhelmed

A spiritual director may find himself feeling inadequate or overwhelmed in spiritual direction. A certain amount of this is part of being poor enough to let the Lord be very present in the spiritual direction sessions, as discussed above. However, there are situations when the spiritual director may feel completely overwhelmed or even paralyzed. Some directees need professional help. A person who has suffered significant abuse or a person who is having a psychotic episode that is manifesting in spiritual terms may be best served by a professional psychologist or psychiatrist. Another person may just be having a particularly difficult period in his life and be very emotional. The amount of emotion that comes out in a spiritual direction meeting may be surprising and may overwhelm the spiritual director.

In these cases, prayer is indispensable. The spiritual director is always going to be stretched and these are opportunities when he can place his trust prayerfully in the hands of the Father. God has arranged every spiritual direction meeting and the spiritual director must trust that God will provide for it. Prayer, surrender, and trust can strengthen the spiritual director to help him get through a difficult meeting. After the meeting, it is important for the spiritual director to process what has taken place. He can do this in both prayer and his own spiritual direction. If the directee has issues that are ongoing, such as abuse or psychosis, it may be necessary to consult a psychologist or to refer the directee to someone for additional help.

Feeling Afraid

A spiritual director may experience some feelings of anxiety in the context of giving spiritual direction. To a certain degree, the feeling of anxiety caused by knowledge of one's inadequacy is a prerequisite for being a truly Spirit-filled director who does not interfere with but facilitates God's work. If the anxiety is more crippling and prevents the director from thinking clearly, he will certainly do well to bring this up with his own spiritual director. He may also be able to find some strength in prayer. Perfect love casts out fear, and allowing the love of God to reach his anxiety can bring strength and cast out fear in the context of spiritual direction.

In very rare situations the spiritual director may be afraid for his or her own safety when alone with the directee. In such an instance the reasons for this fear need to be clarified, substantiated, and resolved or else the direction cannot proceed. The same is true if the directee is experiencing enormous fear that does not abate over time. In less serious cases, the direction might be able to proceed with another director.

Incredulity

Periodically one will have a spiritual directee who presents extraordinary situations. In those cases, it is important for the spiritual director to maintain a healthy skepticism in order to discern the authenticity of such phenomena. It is wise to let the directee present everything. By making the spiritual direction atmosphere as welcoming and trusting as possible, it helps the directee to share all that he believes is taking place. At the same time, the spiritual director can mentally bracket out the unbelievable with the reservation that it may all be true or none of it may be true. As evidence mounts while the spiritual director follows the points of discernment presented earlier in Chapter 6 on Guidance in Prayer, he may come to the point that he can believe everything and welcome that bracketed material into a place of belief in his heart. During the process of discernment, as St. John of Ávila advised, the spiritual director should be gentle and not critical or mean-spirited, allowing the directee to share as freely as possible. Of course, the spiritual director may come to a point of judging the directee's sharing as knowingly or unknowingly untrue. That could be due to a psychological disorder or, in the worst case, intentional deception. In any event, a spiritual director's healthy incredulity will be a help to a spiritual directee in coming to a discovery of truth. In fact, a directee who is genuinely having an extraordinary experience will often sympathize with the director's incredulity, because the directee himself is struggling to believe what is taking place. Whatever the case, the spiritual director needs to be aware of his incredulity and be careful to choose intentionally whether to let that show and to try to control how it affects his charity in handling the directee. The spiritual director may find it necessary to state explicitly that he is having some difficulty believing what is being shared, and he could give reasons why. In so doing, it might turn out that there was a misunderstanding that could be easily cleared up.

Boredom

Spiritual direction is not supposed to be entertaining, but some meetings in particular and some people in general are less engaging than others. The spiritual director could hurt a directee who is trying hard to open his heart, and so it is very important not to show signs of boredom, as far as possible. A spiritual director might also be tired and sometimes yawns can be hard to stifle. If the directee seems disturbed by that behavior, then the spiritual director can reassure him. It may simply be that the director has had a long day. The act of reassuring can also stir greater charity in the heart of the director and perhaps also stir him awake. These can be very natural and human experiences. A simple response to the experience of boredom is for the spiritual director to look again with eyes of faith and see the image of God sitting in front of him. He can recalibrate his ear to listen to the Holy Spirit and ask what God is trying to share through the directee's narrative.

The spiritual director should also ask himself, when fighting boredom or weariness, if he is resisting something that the directee is sharing. Is there something that he does not want to hear? Has he developed a negative attitude about the directee and in his mind labeled the directee as boring? Is he disturbed or threatened by certain behaviors of the directee—perhaps excessive talking, excessive emotion, or excessive detail on things that are not very deep? The directee might be sharing something that could trigger the director, for example, about his mother or about a particular shared acquaintance or about a particular experience, and the director is resisting the emotions or memories that might arise, and so he is keeping himself emotionally distant from what is being shared.

Ongoing Formation

One of the most important traits in a good spiritual director is a substantial experience of being in spiritual direction and the ongoing experience of spiritual direction. This will be one of his most important venues for ongoing formation as well. A person will gain the most important experience by learning to open up his own soul before a spiritual director. As he learns the contours of the spiritual life, he can humbly start to share those with others, but he needs to explore them first in himself with the help of a faithful and wise guide.

One's experience of giving spiritual direction will naturally affect one's own spiritual life and thus it will become a natural topic of discussion when one receives spiritual direction. God is profoundly present and often tangibly experienced in spiritual direction, and that naturally has a significant impact on the spiritual director. He will want to discuss this with his own spiritual director. As discussed earlier, spiritual direction may also stir up fears, desires, joys, hopes, attractions, frustrations, and so on. These are important areas to process with one's own spiritual director or other trusted spiritual directors. The mystery of grace that is opened up in spiritual direction has a way of spreading itself in every direction, including to the directee and the director, but also to the director's own spiritual director and the directee's close friends and family. Like a ripple of water, grace moves out in every direction.

For the sake of ongoing formation, it is important for a spiritual director to continue seeking insight beyond his own spiritual direction through books, workshops, conversations, and consultations. By sharing scenarios from spiritual direction (with due discretion, proper anonymization, and absolute confidentiality), a spiritual director can gain insight from another experienced director on particular issues. This may be especially important, even necessary, in areas he has not had to handle previously, such as particular psychological disorders or particularly extreme forms of satanic activity, extraordinary phenomena, more unusual forms of holiness, or unique vocations.

In addition to seeking guidance on particular situations, it is helpful to talk with other spiritual directors for the sake of remembering the general principles, importance, and goals of spiritual direction. It is always possible to lose sight of the forest for the trees. We hope this book provides a template for the balanced presentation of general principles together with particular cases. The heart of spiritual direction, of course, is the soul of the individual and his relationship with God.

Conclusion

> It is not easy to accompany. It isn't easy to find a confessor, a spiritual father. It's not easy to find a man with rectitude of intentions; in order that this spiritual direction, this confession not be a nice chat among friends but without depth [or a chat with] rigid men, who do not really understand where the problem may be, because they do not understand [the spiritual] life.[1]

As POPE FRANCIS EXPRESSED, there is a dearth of good spiritual directors. This is partly because there are men and women with a capacity for spiritual direction who are not responding to this calling or who lack formation. We hope this book will help to provide some of the needed formation to encourage men and women to take up the "art of arts" as spiritual directors. At the same time, spiritual direction requires certain qualities that not everyone has: "The Holy Spirit gives to certain of the faithful the gifts of wisdom, faith and discernment for the sake of this common good which is prayer (*spiritual direction*). Men and women so endowed are true servants of the living tradition of prayer" (CCC 2690).

As we have noted, many books have been written about spiritual direction and the spiritual life. We hope that this book

---

[1] Pope Francis, Address to Consecrated Men and Women of the Diocese of Rome.

may encourage more people to delve into the mysteries of intimacy with God. We repeat, in conclusion, that the most essential quality of the spiritual director is that he himself is seeking that intimacy with all his heart. We believe that the spiritual direction of individual souls is an essential part of the New Evangelization and truly a movement of God's grace through this twenty-first century.

Appendix: Saints for Spiritual Directors

S PIRITUAL DIRECTION IS AN ART that has been mastered by many saints throughout history. There are men and women, clerical, religious, and lay saints who carried out a ministry of spiritual direction in various forms. The form of the regular confessor is most common in recent history. Naturally, we have little in the way of direct accounts from this form of spiritual direction except that which is reported by the penitent. This was the case with St. Faustina's spiritual direction with Blessed Michael Sopocko. There are also spiritual directors that offered direction in the form of correspondence. In these cases, we tend to have the letters of spiritual direction that were collected by the directee, but we can only intuit the letters sent by directee to director. A one-sided correspondence is lacking a great deal in modeling the kind of spiritual direction presented in this book, but we can draw some insights about what is important to the spiritual director and we can sometimes read how the spiritual director lovingly received, echoed back, and responded to the directee's expressed concerns.

In holding up these saintly spiritual directors, we hope to draw some insights from them. But we do so also in the hopes of simply providing patrons and intercessors for today's spiritual directors. This is by no means an extensive list, but rather a small sampling of great spiritual directors in the Church's history. Knowing that there are friends in the communion of saints who carried out the same ministry and bore the same crosses that we do—and that doing these things made them holy—can be a great source of strength. In the following accounts, we hope above all to inspire the formation of friendships with these fellow members of the Body of Christ.

St. Vincent Pallotti

Pope St. John XXIII, in his address to seminary spiritual directors, lifted up the example of Vincent Pallotti, whom he later canonized. Ten years after his ordination, St. Vincent Pallotti was assigned as a seminary spiritual director and confessor. He worked hard, was universally available, and was universally appreciated by the seminarians for his kindness, clarity, and sound direction. At the same time, he carried in his heart the desire to spread the Gospel far and wide and to touch the souls of all. This led him eventually to found the Pallotine Fathers and also the lay movement Catholic Action. Pope St. John XXIII summarized this Saint in the following words: "All of the activity of this outstanding priest was directed toward the sanctification of the clergy and, as he left in writing, to the defense and conservation of the faith, and to the spread of charity among Catholics. His intention was that through the spread of faith and charity in the whole world, there would soon be but one flock and one shepherd."[2]

St. Joseph Cafasso

St. Joseph Cafasso was held up as an example by Pope Benedict XVI during the Year of the Priest. We do not have direct records of his spiritual direction, but we have many testimonies from others, including saints whom he directed, such as St. John Bosco. St. John Bosco witnessed to the power of this saint who was able to do much good with few words, "A single word from him—a look,

---

[2] Pope St. John XXIII, Address to Seminary Spiritual Directors.

a smile, his very presence—sufficed to dispel melancholy, drive away temptation and produce holy resolution in the soul."[3] St. Joseph Cafasso knew the importance of listening and was able to be present and offer a gaze of love.

When he did teach or counsel, his teaching did not consist of pious platitudes offered from abstract theological heights, but rather consisted of true responses to the needs of human hearts. He knew how to share the Father's mercy one-on-one. As Pope Benedict XVI summarized it:

> He was . . . a wise spiritual counsellor to many who became Saints and founders of religious institutes. His teaching was never abstract, nor based exclusively on the books that were used in that period. Rather, it was born from the living experience of God's mercy and the profound knowledge of the human soul that he acquired in the long hours he spent in the confessional and in spiritual direction: his was a real school of priestly life.[4]

As mentioned earlier, the fundamental requirement for giving spiritual direction is to have a spiritual life and the principal way to grow in spiritual direction is to grow in holiness. As Pope Benedict XVI explained it: "His secret was simple: to be a man of God; to do in small daily actions 'what can result in the greater glory of God and the advantage of souls'. He loved the Lord without reserve, he was enlivened by a firmly-rooted faith, supported by profound and prolonged prayer and exercised in sincere charity to all."[5]

The ministry of St. Joseph Cafasso was truly one of transforming mercy and he exemplified so many of the principles that we have sought to teach in this work. The result was that he helped

---

[3] Quoted in Ann Ball, "Saint Joseph Cafasso," in *Modern Saints: Their Lives and Faces Book 2* (Rockford, IL: TAN Books and Publishers, 1991).

[4] Pope Benedict XVI, Audience of June 30, 2010.

[5] Ibid.

to form saints and religious founders who themselves transformed the face of the Church. This is precisely what we pointed out in the Introduction to this work through the words of St. John XXIII, "Do you not think that the Church would have many more saints if generous souls, especially priests and religious, received more serious direction?"[6] St. Joseph Cafasso exemplified this conviction of Pope St. John XXIII. He carried out this ministry of forming saints not by forming copies of himself but simply by caring for each soul with prayer, love, and personal attention, patiently listening to the way the Holy Spirit was at work in that individual's life. As Pope Benedict XVI described it:

> He was versed in moral theology but was likewise familiar with the situation and hearts of people, of whose good he took charge as the good pastor that he was. Those who had the grace to be close to him were transformed into as many good pastors and sound confessors. . . . How many priests were trained by him at the "Convitto", and then accompanied by him spiritually! Among them as I have said emerges St. John Bosco who had him as his spiritual director for a good 25 years, from 1835 to 1860: first as a seminarian, then as a priest and lastly as a Founder. In all the fundamental decisions of his life St. John Bosco had St. Joseph Cafasso to advise him, but in a very specific way: Cafasso never sought to form Don Bosco as a disciple "in his own image and likeness", and Don Bosco did not copy Cafasso; he imitated Cafasso's human and priestly virtues, certainly and described him as "a model of priestly life" but according to his own personal disposition and his own specific vocation; a sign of the wisdom of the spiritual teacher and of the intelligence of the disciple: the former did not impose himself on the latter but respected his personality and helped him to interpret God's will for him.[7]

[6] Pope St. John XXIII, Address to Spiritual Directors.
[7] Benedict XVI, Audience of June 30, 2010.

St. Paul of the Cross

The spiritual direction of St. Paul of the Cross was focused on the Cross. His life corroborated his own teaching. "You may observe the sureness which the doctrine of this wise Director carries with it. He always puts the foundation of the faith in the depth of humility and self-emptying." St. Paul of the Cross said about himself, "The direction of souls has been entrusted to me, and some of these persons are marvelously gifted by God and graced with very deep prayer. . . . Oh! great God, who would have ever thought that this most vile sinner would walk through these ways?"[8] St. Paul of the Cross was a man who lived humility and taught humility. Without false humility, but truly knowing his own weakness, he accepted spiritual directees out of obedience to God. "Yet Paul directed men and women in the ways of the Spirit for 54 years with a sureness and ease which ranks him among the great spiritual masters of the Christian tradition."[9]

St. Paul of the Cross made many contributions to the art of spiritual direction, but one area that he speaks about clearly, firmly, and repeatedly is related to the Cross and the presence of God's will in secondary causality:

> The soul is fortunate who, espoused to God's Will, cherishes the Bridegroom in naked suffering within and without—resting on the heart of the Father and feeding on the Divine manna of God's Will in spirit and in truth—tasting and delighting that it be fulfilled in every event, bitter though it be. Paul is pointing out that the highest degree of union with God's Will takes place when it becomes one's very food—as in the example of Christ.[10]

---

[8] St. Paul of the Cross, quoted in Silvan Rouse, *Reflections on Spiritual Direction in St. Paul of the Cross*, 10.

[9] Ibid.

[10] Ibid., 38.

In a related way, St. Paul of the Cross wrote frequently of human nothingness and the All of God: "Remain in your dreadful nothingness, but let your nothingness disappear immediately into the *infinite all*, which is God. Immerse yourself there and remain there, always a true adorer of the Most High in spirit and in truth."[11] Paul sees nothingness always in reference to attention to God, the Infinite All.

These teachings of St. Paul of the Cross culminate in his teaching on mystical death and divine nativity. "For Paul, mystical death eliminates everything which is contrary to God's Plan. It means death to what is not authentic. Paul expressed this purifying reality in a variety of ways in his letters of direction, e.g., as mortification, sacrifice, poverty, detachment, stripping, nakedness, renunciation, solitude, desert, silence, forgetfulness of self, etc."[12] The Death takes place in three phases: detachment from the external world, detachment from self, detachment from God's gifts.

The Spiritual Journey includes both mystical death and simultaneously a divine nativity. "Death to self is never definitive in this life and the new life is never perfectly possessed. Therefore a constant rebirth to Divine Life is necessary. Divine rebirth is repeated on ever-deepening levels in proportion to the deepening action of grace and man's increasingly unconditional surrender to the Spirit."[13] In this way, the directee experiences a detachment from the things of this world and a greater attachment to the things of heaven. He has to learn to open his hands and let go of this world's securities in order to receive from God the graces of a new life, a new vision, a new heart.

St. Peter Faber

St. Ignatius of Loyola gave us a great wealth of teaching in his spiritual exercises, but it was St. Peter Faber, according to St. Igna-

---

[11] Ibid., 39.

[12] Ibid., 42.

[13] Ibid., 44.

tius, who had first place in giving the exercises. St. Peter Faber provides an exemplary model of spiritual direction in the universality of his reach. He was a man who could speak with both prince and pauper, as well as Catholics and Protestants at the very time of the Reformation. Pope Benedict XVI described him as a "modest, sensitive man with a profound inner life. He was endowed with the gift of making friends with people from every walk of life."[14]

At the same time, St. Peter Faber was exemplary for spiritual directors in his restless desire to do great things in spreading the Gospel. Spiritual direction can never become merely a refuge to keep the spiritual director hidden away in a safe place. To the contrary, spiritual direction must also be accompanied by interior experience, and St. Peter's "familiarity with God led him to understand that interior experience and apostolic life always go together."[15] A spiritual director must be restless for the transformation of souls and the spread of the Gospel throughout the world even if his ministry brings him into contact only with a limited number of people.

Bl. Michael Sopocko

Bl. Michael Sopocko was one of the spiritual directors of St. Faustina. In her *Diary*, she offered many insights about spiritual direction and wonderful, personal testimonies about its importance in her own life. She "prayed ardently" for the "great grace" of a spiritual director.[16] And the Lord provided Fr. Michael Sopocko, whom He confirmed for her through two interior confirmations: "One day I saw him in our chapel between the altar

---

[14] Pope Benedict XVI, Address to the Fathers and Brothers of the Society of Jesus (April 22, 2006), https://w2.vatican.va/content/benedict-xvi/en/speeches/2006/april/documents/hf_ben-xvi_spe_20060422_gesuiti.html.

[15] Pope Francis, Homily for Holy Mass on the Liturgical Memorial of the Most Holy Name of Jesus (January 3, 2014), https://w2.vatican.va/content/francesco/en/homilies/2014/documents/papa-francesco_20140103_omelia-santissimo-nome-gesu.html.

[16] St. Faustina, *Diary*, no. 34.

and the confessional and suddenly heard a voice in my soul say, *This is the visible help for you on earth. He will help you carry out My will on earth.*[17] She thanked God for him many times, as she wrote in her *Diary*, "because I know very well how much harm I myself experienced when I did not have this help. It is so easy to go astray when one has no guide!"[18]

St. Faustina did not speak extensively about the personal qualities of Bl. Michael Sopocko, but she noted his trustworthiness, his fidelity, and also the way that God tested him through great suffering. "Once as I was talking with my spiritual director, I had an interior vision—quicker than lightning—of his soul in great suffering, in such agony that God touches very few souls with such fire. . . . When will this happen? I do not know. How long will it last? I do not know. But God has promised a great grace especially to you and to all those . . . *who will proclaim My great mercy*."[19] Suffering took on a special quality for Bl. Michael Sopocko, but it is a part of the life of every priest who chooses to direct the souls of others. There is the suffering of disappointment when directees choose their own will over God's will and the suffering of not being understood by one's peers after spending hours in spiritual direction and not being able to share any of it. There is the suffering of special works like the revelation of Divine Mercy that Bl. Michael was drawn into with St. Faustina, or the revelation of the Sacred Heart that St. Claude de la Colombière shared with his directee St. Margaret Mary Alocoque.

Bl. Michael Sopocko also modeled Divine Mercy in his preaching: "I heard a sermon given by my confessor [Fr. Sopocko]. This sermon about Divine Mercy was the first of the things that Jesus had asked for so very long ago. When he began to speak about the great mercy of the Lord, the image came alive . . ."[20] He modeled faithfulness, patience, humility, dedication, personal

---

[17] Ibid., no. 53.

[18] Ibid., no. 61.

[19] Ibid., no. 378.

[20] Ibid., no. 417.

sacrifice, and hard work: "Seeing Father Sopocko's sacrifice and efforts for this work, I admired his patience and humility. This all cost a great deal, not only in terms of toil and various troubles, but also of money; and Father Sopocko was taking care of all the expenses."[21] She lauded his faithfulness on other occasions as well: "I see Father Sopocko, how his mind is busily occupied and working in God's cause in order to present the wishes of God to the officials of the Church. As a result of his efforts, a new light will shine in the Church of God for the consolation of souls. . . . I have never before come upon such great faithfulness to God as distinguishes this soul."[22] She also remarked on how he reflected in prayer on matters of direction, "Once, I saw Father Sopocko praying as he was reflecting on these matters. Then I saw how a ring of light appeared suddenly above his head. Although distance separates us, I often see him, especially as he works at his desk, despite his fatigue."[23]

At the same time, Bl. Michael Sopocko was exemplary in being close to the Child Jesus. Spiritual direction can lead to temptations of pride, as one can feel important in falsely conceiving that they are godlike masters of the lives of others. Bl. Michael Sopocko was little enough to evoke the presence of the Child Jesus and even to disappear in His heart, as St. Faustina described,

> Once when my confessor [Father Sopocko] was saying Mass, I saw, as usual, the Child Jesus on the altar, from the time of the Offertory. However, a moment before the Elevation, the priest vanished from my sight, and Jesus alone remained. When the moment of the Elevation approached, Jesus took the Host and the chalice in His little hands and raised them together, looking up to heaven, and a moment later I again saw my confessor. I asked the Child Jesus where the priest had been during the time I had not seen

---

21 Ibid., no. 422.
22 Ibid., no. 1390.
23 Ibid., no. 762.

him. Jesus answered, *In My Heart*. But I could not understand anything more of these words of Jesus.[24]

She added later, "I was greatly surprised that the Infant Jesus
loves him so much."[25]

She offered a conclusive description of her spiritual director as
having a heart like the Heart of Jesus. This is what every spiritual
director should strive for and the fruit of this loving union with
the Heart of Jesus will be a great comfort to the souls entrusted to
that spiritual director, "*He is a priest after My own Heart; his efforts
are pleasing to Me. . . . Through him I spread comfort to suffering and
careworn souls.*"[26]

St. Francis de Sales

St. Francis de Sales is a great model for spiritual directors, particularly in the aspect of his deep love for humanity. He was a true
lover of the human heart and was capable of developing a profound communion with his directees. Pope Benedict XVI testified
to these qualities in his catechesis on St. Francis de Sales:

> In reading his book on the love of God and especially
> his many letters of spiritual direction and friendship one
> clearly perceives that St. Francis was well acquainted with
> the human heart. He wrote to St. Jane de Chantal: ". . .
> this is the rule of our obedience, which I write for you in
> capital letters: do all through love, nothing through con-
> straint; love obedience more than you fear disobedience. I
> leave you the spirit of freedom, not that which excludes
> obedience, which is the freedom of the world, but that
> liberty that excludes violence, anxiety and scruples."[27]

---

[24] Ibid., no. 442.

[25] Ibid., no. 562.

[26] Ibid., no. 1256.

[27] Pope Benedict XVI, Audience of March 2, 2011, http://w2.vatican.va/content/
benedict-xvi/en/audiences/2011/documents/hf_ben-xvi_aud_20110302.html.

Pope Benedict XVI also gave him credit for laying the spiritual foundations of saints that came centuries later:

> It is not for nothing that we rediscover traces precisely of this teacher at the origin of many contemporary paths of pedagogy and spirituality; without him neither St. John Bosco nor the heroic 'Little Way' of St. Thérèse of Lisieux would have come into being. . . . St. Francis de Sales is an exemplary witness of Christian humanism; with his familiar style, with words which at times have a poetic touch, he reminds us that human beings have planted in their innermost depths the longing for God and that in him alone can they find true joy and the most complete fulfilment.[28]

St. Francis de Sales continues to provide spiritual direction through his classic, book-length guide, *Introduction to the Devout Life*, that was written for one of his directees. That text remains a good guide for both directors and directees on a wide variety of issues.

---

[28] Ibid.